REAL ESTATE
The Money
Angle

A Realistic Guide to
Real Estate Investment

John P. Wiedemer
University of Houston

REAL ESTATE
The Money
Angle

A Realistic Guide to
Real Estate Investment

 Reston Publishing Company, Inc.
A Prentice-Hall Company
Reston, Virginia

Library of Congress Cataloging in Publication Data

Wiedemer, John P.
　　Real estate, the money angle.

　　Includes index.
　　1. Real estate investment.　I.　Title.
HD1382.5.W54　1983　　　332.63′24　　　82–20529
ISBN 0–8359–6540–6

Editorial/production supervision and
interior design by Camelia Townsend

© 1983 by Reston Publishing Company, Inc.
A Prentice-Hall Company
Reston, Virginia 22090

10　9　8　7　6　5　4　3　2　1

PRINTED IN THE UNITED STATES OF AMERICA

Contents

Preface

So many books covering real estate and its investment potential either oversimplify the problems involved or become too engrossed with technical details, statistics, or with government agencies and their many regulations. That is why this book, first and foremost, offers the potential investor, professional real estate agent, student, or reader a selective review of the practical steps involved in acquiring real property. It points out problems, suggests solutions, and sorts out potential gains from the various investments. It provides examples, charts, and innovative ideas. Answers to elementary questions are offered along with solutions to more complex problems, such as present worth and internal rate of return analysis methods. Using a step-by-step procedure, information is provided on new variations in financing methods and on the analysis of financial statements. The substantial savings that may be gained from the 1981 Tax Act are also discussed.

As a further aid to the reader, a review of real estate legal terminology plus the pros and cons of different types of business organizations is presented. The principal classes of real property investments are considered separately with a focus on potential problems and probable rewards for each.

The material is divided into eight separate sections for easy reference. Each section can be read on its own as a self-contained unit. The first two sections, "Overview of the Real Estate Market" and "Dealing for Profit," are directed primarily towards the real estate novice. Later sections are aimed at the more advanced reader and practitioner, as well as the novice developing a need for more in-depth information.

The underlying theme of this book centers on money and how real estate can be financed. With high interest rates and volatile money markets, careful financing becomes even more important. So each of the eight sections has a money angle to it. Topics include how to structure a deal with available financing, where the money comes from today, and ways of minimizing the tax bite. The emphasis on money is also reflected in the discussions of legal questions concerning borrowing money, the importance of accurate financial statement analysis, plus the advantages and disadvantages of each of the major classes of real property investment.

To conclude, it is the author's belief that there is no easy path to a real estate fortune. But with adequate knowledge and sound preparation, investment in real property can be exciting, gratifying, and financially rewarding. The available opportunities are more apparent to those actively engaged in the business than to the spectators. *Real Estate: The Money Angle* is dedicated to giving the reader a head start on the basic knowledge and fundamental information needed for success in this field. The hard work to make the dream come true follows.

John P. Wiedemer

ONE

Overview of the Real Estate Market

1

Real Estate as an Investment

What does real estate offer the small or moderate investor in the decade of the 80s? Isn't it true that the escalating inflation of the 70s has tapered off and that there are greater immediate cash returns to be found in other investments such as money market funds? For the present, the answer has to be yes. However, a basic truth should be kept in mind: real estate represents a stable and lasting value that has proven security year after year.

Remember, with only one exception, four of the five greatest fortunes of this country were based on land and its resources: Mellon from oil and aluminum, Morgan from iron ore and steel, Rockefeller from oil, and DuPont from chemical resources. Only Ford is based on manufacturing. Many other large but less publicized fortunes have derived from land, especially those founded on timbering operations, farming, mining, and, of course, the development of land for housing, working space, storage room, transportation facilities, and recreational use.

Real estate is a field that offers opportunity to anyone with imagination and even a limited amount of cash—financing is most always available for well-thought-out projects. Most important, it is not necessary to start *big*. As a matter-of-fact, the idea that only big investors can succeed may well be the single most inhibiting factor of all. The small investor, willing to add his or her own labor and imagination to a project, can prosper at an astounding rate. New doors continually open to those who demonstrate (not just talk about it) a willingness to work and an ability to produce successful projects, small or large. The potential for success in a real estate investment is increased because income can often be sheltered from taxes and a degree of leveraging obtained through borrowed money. The new investor is well advised to start small—buy one rental property—then make it succeed. Both lenders and sellers of commercial properties look for that "track record"—Does this buyer know how to make it work? Once over that hump, growth can be continual.

The pattern to follow is not new, it is time-proven:

1. Save enough money to buy the equity in a small rental property—a house, a small store, a small apartment.
2. Improve the property, preferably through your own labor or that of a trusted contractor.
3. As the property is upgraded, the rental structure can be improved.
4. Because the rental income can be increased, the value rises separately from that induced by inflation alone.

Remember that the increase in property value must exceed that from inflation. Otherwise one finds later that all the gain is eaten up by the loss in the dollar's purchasing power. *It is the increase in value resulting from your own expertise and labor that produces the real gain—and that can be achieved whether or not inflation persists.*

Do you see now why real estate values are not so dependent on inflation for profit? The real gain comes from the value produced by upgrading the property and the resulting increase in rental income.

While the formula for success is simple, there are, of course, some caveats:

1. It helps immensely to know the basics of buying and selling real estate in your local area. Not every deal is workable.
2. Income property, such as a house purchased for rental, can be priced too high to allow rental payments to meet the out-of-pocket costs. Also, there is the possibility that the house will not be rented 100% of the time. Make sure that your own other income is not overburdened.
3. Maintenance and upgrading of an income property are essential steps in achieving a profitable resale, but great care must be taken that the repairman does not end up with all the profit.
4. While there are good examples of speculative gains in property sales in less than a year of ownership, most property investment achieves its greatest returns after a fairly long holding period.

5. Real estate is not liquid; that is, it is not readily converted to cash. In a forced sale, the real value is most often lost.
6. The management of real property normally requires a considerable amount of time on the part of the investor. Large companies can afford to pay for well-qualified management personnel, but small operations usually depend on the owner-investor.

THE PROFIT IN REAL ESTATE

An investment in real estate offers a broader range of returns than may be found in other forms of investment. If you will consider three types of returns, the advantage in real estate becomes more apparent. These are as follows:

1. Income from operations
2. Appreciation in property value
3. Value gained from property improvement

Let's compare these returns with some other investments. In a money market fund, the "income from operations" is, of course, the interest paid by the fund for the use of your money. There is no appreciation of the principal itself. In general, the purchasing power of the dollar is decreasing, so a reduction in the value of the principal is inherent in this investment or any other which only pays interest on a cash deposit. You as an investor have no opportunity to "upgrade" your investment and thus increase its return. Allowing interest earned to remain on deposit can increase the return through compounding, but this amounts to a reinvestment of your earnings and is not a measure of appreciation. You are at the mercy of the money market managers plus the vagaries of the financial markets. If your concern tends towards collectibles—something tangible such as paintings, art objects, stamps, or gold—you find no regular income, only a hoped for appreciation in value. Also, there is the cost of safekeeping these assets.

An investment in common stocks has shown a mediocre to poor return. Dividends have been low, averaging in the 5 percent to 7 percent range for high-quality stocks, and the growth in value has not always kept pace with inflation. There have been some exceptions, but the average has not been good. Bonds have been a poor show. Investors have backed away from the long-term 25- and 30-year issues and have demanded very high interest rates on 10-year bonds. Even so, the value of bonds has dropped as interest rates have continued to rise. They offer an investor little opportunity to alter the down-slide.

Real estate need not be a dormant investment. Except in those areas where rent control laws and land use constraints have upset marketplace competition, you are not so much at the mercy of other people to create value. You can exercise your own control if you are willing to spend some time on upgrading plans. It is this extra effort that can make all the difference. If an investment is made in, say, a small rental property and the investor sits back to just "watch it grow," chances are, nothing much will happen. If careful plans are made to upgrade the property and then the plans are implemented, an increase in income is most likely to result.

REAL ESTATE HAS TAX ADVANTAGES

Later chapters will discuss in much greater detail the specific tax advantages accruing to real estate income. Primarily, they center on the owner's right to recover the cost of an investment over a limited span of years, through deductions from taxable income. (The older concept of *depreciation* was replaced in 1981 with the new *Accelerated Cost Recovery System*—ACRS.) A number of investments offer tax advantages, so real estate is not unique. An investment in mining, timber, or oil and gas offers depletion allowances that are deductible against taxable income. The new tax laws offer substantial tax advantages to corporations that lease machinery and equipment to others. For real estate investors, the new laws have created mandatory *recovery periods*, generally 15 years for new or used buildings, that allow larger initial deductions and are expected to reduce the area of controversy with IRS regulations.

A special section of the new tax act permits increased deductions for rehabilitation of older buildings. Most real estate operations require the use of machinery, furniture, or other equipment that can qualify for major deductions of its cost as an expense in the year of acquisition.

The new tax laws were designed to encourage investment in productive assets that help create more jobs. Real estate has been favored with many new tax advantages.

PRIDE OF OWNERSHIP

A special advantage that can be found in a real estate investment is the personal satisfaction that comes with its ownership. Other investments, particularly collectibles, may also provide this additional incentive for

ownership, but few are as easy for others to see and admire. There are in-
dications that real estate has become the "prestige asset" of the 80s!

PERSONAL QUESTIONS

Investment means putting one's money to work for profit. Real estate,
unlike some other forms of investment, generally means an investment of
your time as well. The amount of time involved depends very much on
the type of property that you find of most interest and your ability to find
people capable of handling management and maintenance needs. Without proper controls, an investment in income property can become a bad
experience.

Time Commitment

There are a number of ways to handle the time requirements of real
estate. One is to team up with a person who is capable and willing to
spend the necessary time overseeing the investment. If your funds are
limited, you might seek a person with greater resources to help you provide the necessary capital.

   Another method of reducing the time demands is to join an investment syndicate that is headed by an experienced (and honest) practitioner. There are also realty funds that provide many of the tax advantages of direct real estate investment. They are handled (tax-wise) like a
partnership with gains and losses passed through to the individual unit
owners. The Real Estate Investment Trusts are slowly returning to the
real estate market after some disastrous experiences in the 1974–1975
market crunch. But all of these larger groups remove the direct management (and time required) from the investor to sometimes very remote individuals.

Other Income

One of the personal considerations that should be examined before making a real estate investment is the impact on your other income. If your
income is such that tax deductions are of little value, one advantage of
real estate investment is reduced. If your other income is such that additional cash each year is needed, care must be taken to pursue only investments that do produce a *spendable* cash flow. These are not always
easy to find in real property for many investors enter the market for the
appreciation gain and push prices upward to uneconomic levels.

Estate Questions

Real estate presents problems at death unlike those that can result from other forms of investment. First, it is not easily liquidated if cash is needed to settle estate commitments. Second, estate and trust administrators often are not familiar with the management of real property; many are more qualified to administer cash and securities than other assets. Third, passing title to land can involve cumbersome, and expensive, legal procedures after death. This is particularly true if the real estate is held in other than the state of residence. However, many of these problems can be minimized through careful estate planning with competent legal counsel.

Family Considerations

While most investments can well be considered a family matter, real estate is probably more so. It is an asset of record (recorded in state or county records), and potential heirs to a family estate have a concern for its future. As an asset demanding time to manage and maintain, family members become the obvious partners or associates in the enterprise. As an investor, is your own situation such that additional advantages can be gained for the entire family? Can real estate investment provide experience and training for sons and daughters? Are the family members really interested in participating in the endeavor? These kinds of considerations cannot be easily measured in dollars but can be important for future success.

CONCLUSION

This brief overview of real estate investment provides an introduction for the newcomer to the business. Further information follows on how land achieves value.

2

The Value of Land

Land can be seen, touched, and enjoyed. It gives fulfillment to a deep-seated human urge to own something tangible. And most important for the investor, it can appreciate in value while producing a reasonable income.

The productivity of land can be realized in many ways. Underground resources can be quarried, mined, or drilled. The productivity of the soil provides grains, fibers, and timber that can be harvested. The surface can be developed to support man's complex living requirements, working environment, and recreational needs. Even the air rights above the land have some value. While all investment in land-related productivity may be broadly classified as "real estate investment," the focus here is on the development of land for homes, work places, and recreational areas. For this purpose, the value of land is dependent on its accessibility and its use by people. The formula is simple: the more people, the more valuable the land.

There are five major influences which attract people to live in certain areas. These are:

1. *Job Opportunities.* So what is it that brings people into any area? Of course, there are many reasons—a construction project, a mineral discovery, newly irrigated land, accessible recreational sites—but paramount is the availability of work opportunities. The origins of all urban

areas stem from work-related situations. Cities grew up around locations where, for example, a river could be easily crossed, where an ocean going vessel could be loaded, and in later periods of development, where trains provided service. People settled in areas where they could find work. And that basic pattern has not changed. Now, however, the distances from living areas to places of employment are greater because of the mobility offered by cars and expressways.

2. Transportation Networks.   People are also attracted to specific areas because of the transportation network. In earlier times it was the railroads and their urban arm, the commuter lines. Since World War II the federal government has pumped billions into a vast expressway system, both freeways and tollroads, which has shaped or reshaped many cities as well as the countryside. People now work and live near expressways as they formerly followed railroad lines. Energy restrictions are slowly altering the transportation patterns, but it will be many years before a major new trend develops. Mass transit systems have not yet significantly altered existing transportation patterns. Also, efforts to develop new methods of powering smaller cars will not affect present patterns.

3. Living Environment.   The third, the least important, influence on where people choose to settle is the living environment. While the desire, or dream, of better housing is almost universal, a more attractive homesite is not by itself the most important factor in any decision to relocate. A means of support, which usually involves getting back and forth to work, takes precedence. However, there are some areas of the country that have benefited from simply becoming desirable places to live. These are mostly resort centers and retirement communities that attract people who can spend money that has been earned elsewhere.

From a consideration of these three factors—availability of jobs and work opportunities, transportation networks, and living conditions—comes the answer to that all-important question for the real estate investor. The vital question, of course, is whether or not the investment property is located in an area that has the greatest likelihood of increasing in value. And that means an increase in value *greater* than the persistent inflation. An investment that grows in value at the same rate as inflation provides no real gain to the holder. So it is necessary to find an area with good prospects of growth in population.

Historically, land values in many areas of the country have undergone boom and bust cycles like many other investment forms. The reasons are derived from both long-range and short-range economic pressures. The short range is speculative. The long range are those that influence the movement of population. Always there are pressures that influence the direction in which population moves. How these pressures will affect the local area in which land acquisition is being considered is crucial.

Two additional factors affect the value of land. These are zoning requirements and the physical characteristics of the land itself.

4. Zoning Requirements.   As urban areas developed in the nineteenth century, the need for better control of growth became more apparent. It was difficult to plan streets and utility systems without some idea of what usage might be made of the land within a city's limits. However, it was not until 1916, when New York City passed the first zoning ordinance, that communities began to regulate their growth. Obviously, land zoned for higher density residential or commercial use would indicate a higher value per square foot than that zoned for single-family residential. Whether the zoning or the location of the land creates the actual value is a debated subject. However, there is little question that zoning exercises a powerful influence on the value of land. The development of zoning laws and their impact on land is more fully discussed in Chapter 22, "Restrictions on Property Rights."

5. Physical Characteristics.   It is difficult to place a plus or minus value on the physical characteristics of land which is to be used for residential development. A home builder developing a suburban tract would most likely prefer absolutely flat, unobstructed land. In this view, even land with a beautiful growth of trees presents a negative: it costs the developer money to remove the trees. Other builders with greater imagination will prefer land with some obstacles to building, such as hills, ravines, rocks, or trees, and develop the land into a more attractive homesite. Some of the most beautiful haciendas in Mexico City are built atop an outcrop of black volcanic rock! Thus, it might be said that land value for this purpose rests to some degree with the ability of the developer.

The physical characteristics of commercial land are more important. Since accessibility is of greater importance to a shopping center or office building than, say, to a single-family residence, the land must be suitable for that purpose. As the value of a particular commercial location increases, there is a point at which the cost of preparing the land for usage can be justified. For example, a thoroughfare that cuts around the side of a hill offers difficult frontage on both sides: one drops away, the other forms a sharp bluff. In such a case, the value of the land may increase because of the growing traffic volume, and it may be economically feasible to cut away the bluff on one side or to fill the drop-off on the other side, thus creating good commercial land. Modern earth-moving equipment can alter the face of the land rather rapidly.

Industrial land may have a special need for such physical characteristics as access to water for shipping or for processing, proximity to a particular raw material, and many others. However, most industrial usage requires land with minimal physical obstructions which will permit the construction of large buildings and facilitate easy movement throughout the plant site. In such an application, the cost of leveling an industrial site would add to the land cost and would thus reduce the primary value of the land itself.

POPULATION GROWTH PATTERNS

The best source of general trends in population growth is found in the U.S. census figures. For many years, census reports have shown a movement of population from the North and Northeast into the Sunbelt states. So does this mean that the better opportunities lie to the south? Perhaps; but it also means that more prospective investors are exploring the South. And the competition can make those areas less rewarding.

The fact is that there are good real estate investments in just about every area of the country, but it takes some "digging" to find them. The person who can *perceive* a trend a little before others and then be able to *act*, has a better chance of success. No productive long-term investment is easy to come by, and real estate offers more complexities than most other investment forms. Big investors with substantial cash resources, of course, have some advantages in being able to attract proposals and to analyze consequences. But the same complexities that inhibit some provide a fertile field for the individual with imagination, with knowledge, and the ability to act quietly and quickly. The possibilities are so diverse that there truly is an opportunity for everyone.

Following are some observations on the growth patterns that are occurring throughout the country. Keep in mind that for this purpose, the definition of *growth* is not related to an increase in population generally, but to its movement to different areas. And that does not mean *new* areas only. One of the major forces that is altering land use patterns is the shift from an energy surplus economy to one of reduced supply. It means movement of population to locations closer to the job markets. It means movement to smaller towns. It means a shift in recreational patterns and a growth in those facilities closer to population centers or with adequate mass transportation available. Changing business requirements are placing greater emphasis on education and the capabilities of technical specialists. These observations are generalities; for the successful real estate investor, the concepts must be directly related to a local situation. Anything that affects whether or not people are attracted to a given area directly affects the value of the land thereabouts.

WHAT TO PAY FOR LAND

Are there any formulas or rules to establish practical values for land? Not really—so much depends on the local market, the supply and demand for suitable land. However, there are some guidelines that can be followed. It is important to consider, for example, how the land can be used.

As people are attracted to a given area, the land becomes more useful and, thus, more valuable. There is a demand for more buildings—to live in, to work in, to play in, and to store goods in. Land in a growth area increases in value in relation to its location, which in turn dictates its use. For our purposes, land usage may be broadly categorized as (1) single-family residential, (2) multifamily residential, (3) commercial, and (4) industrial. The value base for each category is considered next.

Single-family Residential

The largest portion of land used for development goes to build single-family houses. This usage provides a guide to the price local builders are willing to pay for a building lot. The range can be wide but look to the most active builders and the new subdivisions in the local area. An old rule of thumb still followed in most areas is that the price of a single lot is approximately the value of an acre of undeveloped land.

There are several other factors which can be considered when trying to estimate land values. First, a modern single-family subdivision meeting local standards (and usually Federal Housing Administration requirements under their ASP–9 form) will have a housing density of approximately 3.5 to 4.3 building lots per acre of land. This density allows for curb and gutter streets and utility easements. A small lot in this category would be 60′ × 110′ and a large one, 80′ × 120′. Thus, one acre of undeveloped land converts to an average of four single-family building lots. As land values and costs of construction have escalated, the trend toward smaller housing units is reflected in lot size. Where building codes have permitted, developers are working towards a reduction in the amount of land allocated to streets and utilities. More pathways and central parking areas are being designed. A further reduction in lot size is being achieved with *zero lot line* buildings; that is, patio homes and townhomes joined by common walls. The townhouse generally follows the pattern of the older row house found in many eastern cities, but now includes modern variations in exterior design and materials to avoid a monotonous appearance. Patio homes are a *cluster* type of housing, where three or four units use common or closely spaced back walls, patio or courtyard-style front areas, and country lane streets. Density of both types of housing can be increased to at least six or seven units per acre, thereby spreading the higher cost of developed land.

Second, the value of a building lot usually is related to the value of the finished house. That is, neighborhoods or subdivisions tend to follow a similar ratio of land value in relation to finished property value. Where land is fairly plentiful, the land value may represent as little as 15 percent of the finished property value. For example, a $70,000 house may be located on a lot that is worth $10,500: the building represents a value of $59,500. Where the availability of land is restricted, as it is by water barriers in San Francisco, the value of the land may represent well over half the value of the finished house.

Third, the cost of developing an unimproved tract of land into a finished building lot has escalated substantially and continues to increase. Up through the 1960s, the cost component of a developed building lot was about 25 percent of its selling value. Then it was one of the more profitable forms of real estate activity. The 1970s changed this pattern as regulations multiplied and requirements to protect the environment escalated. Large developments call for environmental impact statements which are reviewed by various interested agencies. Public hearings must also be held. Even full compliance results in long time delays to make sure all interested parties have been allowed proper input. The result has its benefits and its higher costs. Today, the cost component of a finished building lot is moving past 50% of the sales price, and many small developers have withdrawn from the business. Only the large builders and development companies have the money to hold on through the two to three years it takes to convert raw land into usable lots.

The physical characteristics of land for development have a direct bearing on the cost. Flat, easily accessible land can be developed at much lower cost than hilly or mountainous land. As a result, developers tend to move into the more easily accessible areas where costs are lower.

Multi-family Residential (Apartment)

Land suitable for an apartment commands a higher price per acre than land suitable only for single-family housing. How much higher? Consider the use density. The number of living units per acre of land for an apartment starts at about 18 to 20 per acre for a one- or two-story garden-type apartment. A three-story design can accommodate 32 to 40 units per acre. High-rise apartment buildings can achieve a much higher density. The axiom is: the higher the land cost, the greater the number of apartment units needed.

Because of the substantial variation in density, there are few solid guidelines to follow. One comparison might be made with single-family housing lots: if single-family usage supports 4 units per acre and multifamily supports 28 units per acre, the ratio is one to seven. Thus, with other components equal, an acre of land to be used as an apartment project could be worth seven times more than that used for single-family housing. Another method of achieving a comparison of land costs comes from an apartment builder's own allocation of costs. This also varies considerably, but one average figure is that the land cost per unit should not exceed 20 percent of the finished cost of the unit. Thus, if an apartment unit totals out at $30,000 complete, the land cost should not be more than $6,000 per apartment unit. If the density of units is planned at 26 per acre, the land cost should not exceed $156,000 per acre (26 × $6,000). These cost figures must be related to the local market as they, of course, are reflected in the apartment rental structure. And this must be competitive if good occupancy is to be maintained. Land suitable for apartment usage is seldom undeveloped land, and the totals suggested include the costs of streets and utility systems needed to service the apartment project.

Commercial Land

Commercial land is that which is suitable for stores, service facilities, and office buildings. For commercial land, the need for accessibility by the general public places a premium on frontages along major thoroughfares and freeways. In fact, commercial land is often valued by the *front foot*—a linear footage measurement.

There are few, if any, guidelines for estimating the value of commercial land. One common measure is the traffic count; that is, How many cars per hour pass a given point? This is an essential measurement for the location of a gasoline station, and it carries considerable weight with shopping center developers. In downtown areas, a *people count* can serve a similar purpose.

In the development of a shopping center, some merchants, such as Sears, Roebuck, for example, are able to place some value on their ability to attract traffic. In this manner, the merchant is able to bargain down the price of a tract of land or press for a lower cost lease. The value that their presence adds to the shopping center is worth the difference to the developer.

Industrial Land

Land used for a manufacturing plant, a refinery, or other process industry must usually satisfy more specialized needs than that used for people-oriented residential and commercial purposes. Good industrial land must provide access to extensive support facilities, including adequate transportation, power, materials, manpower, service areas, and suppliers. Of increasing importance is the fact that industrial land must be so located that its usage will not violate local environmental standards.

The value of land for industrial use follows no pattern. It depends on how well a particular tract of land fits the purchaser's requirements. And probably more so than with the other categories of land, the financial strength of the purchaser can create an increase in the value.

CONCLUSION

The small investor may not be able to undertake multifamily or large commercial projects at the outset. Yet an understanding of the broad range of land values will provide a proper perspective when judgment is called for.

TWO

Dealing for Profit

3

What to Look For

WHAT SIZE PROPERTY?

The amount of an investment depends on the cash resources of the investor and his or her ability to sustain the investment in periods of low occupancy. Real estate has been particularly attractive to some investors because it permits them to control a much larger asset through the use of other people's money. This is called *leveraging.* The popular idea that real estate has such good leverage value that all the money needed can be borrowed is pretty much a myth for the entry-level investor. Down the road, perhaps, but to start with, don't count on it. Consider the doctor explaining to the patient that this is the first time he or she has ever actually removed an appendix. Lenders have a similar concern over a newcomer to a business investment.

One of the greatest misconceptions is that you have to start big. Hardly anything else starts big. Study those people in your own area who have made successful real estate investments: with the exception of those who inherited land, almost all have started with small properties. Success comes from growth, and growth comes from success. The big property owners have usually spent many years developing their investments, acquiring ever larger properties, culling out the least successful, and spending many hours over the upgrading and improvement of what they have.

The type of investment is not necessarily controlled by size. There

19

are many small rental houses, small apartment properties, small store buildings, small office buildings, and warehouse units. Because there are more housing units in the country, it is much easier to find a suitable house that can be converted to rental property than it is to find potentially good rentals from among the smaller categories of investments. But any good investment property requires some searching. The best deals are not likely to be the most advertised.

How much cash is needed? Generally speaking, 20 percent of the purchase price. With the escalation of property values and the increased difficulty of obtaining suitable financing, the demand for larger down payments is growing. (In later chapters there is more information on the many new ways that financing may be arranged to reduce the cash requirement.) If the investment is in residential property, there are some interesting government programs that can be of great help. After a good "track record" has been established, the investor will find many more doors open for financing packages. Remember, however, that borrowed money is not the single answer to success in real estate. It is a very important ladder in the climb to success, but if debt is not properly structured, it can bring total collapse. Borrowed money is becoming increasingly expensive, and the days of the fixed interest mortgage loan are giving way to variable rates. That assurance of a fixed mortgage payment which helped investors of the past is going to be harder to find.

WHO SELLS THEIR PROPERTIES?

If real estate is such a good deal, why does anyone want to sell it? There are, of course, many reasons. And knowing who the owners are in your local area can be very helpful.

Real estate, like many other things, has its "the best deal was yesterday" syndrome. How many times have you heard the complaint, "Oh, if I had only known you were selling it, I could have paid you more." Or, more likely, "I just sold that yesterday at a bargain price." The trick is to keep abreast of the local market situation through real estate brokers, mortgage loan offices, and all other available contacts.

Investment Strategy

People choose to sell their real estate for any number of reasons. For example, they grow tired of the various problems involved with an operating income property and decide to alter their investment to a more passive form. Sellers in this category are the most likely prospects for a seller-financed sale. Interested in a reasonable return on their money, they may consider their own property a logical security for the financing.

Another example is an investor who desires to sell a not-so-good property and use the cash to acquire a larger, hopefully more profitable, property. This seller is more interested in obtaining as much cash as possible from the sale and perhaps a complete refinancing of the existing debt to relieve liability.

Relocations

One of the biggest reasons a person sells property, and this is primarily houses, is because of a job change or a move to another city. Several of the large real estate brokerage concerns have become national in scope through the handling of relocations generated by large companies. Because companies often grant financial support to facilitate the employee's transfer, this may not be the best way to find a bargain. The large real estate firms usually have a service that arranges to purchase the employee's house if it is not sold within a limited time period. The price is set by an appraisal, and the discount plus sales commission is paid by the employer. The large real estate firms are under little pressure to sell cheap, and they have the resources to hold on for awhile.

However, there are many property owners who seek better employment and must move—bearing all costs. A quick sale, even at a sharp discount in price, can be beneficial to such a person. The alternative may be higher cost temporary housing in the new location because of an inability to purchase a home from lack of down payment cash.

Distress Sales

Some property owners in periods of recession find themselves overextended in their obligations and must liquidate a portion of their investments. Favorable prices can often be arranged under such circumstances, but the cash requirement for purchase is generally high. Depending on the circumstances, "distress" properties may result from unrelated financial problems; that is, the property itself might be in excellent shape and can be refinanced on favorable terms. Or, the problem may be with the property itself; it may have been mismanaged or not properly maintained. In such a case, refinancing is not easy nor is the seller's bargaining position very strong.

Involuntary Disposition

Should a property owner declare, or be forced into, bankruptcy, his or her property is placed under the jurisdiction of a bankruptcy court. Depending on the court's determination, the property may be sold through negotiation or by public auction. Sometimes advantageous deals can be found when the court must convert assets to cash in a limited time period. Similar favorable deals may be found when property becomes subject to foreclosure by a creditor.

Executor and Administrator Sales

When property has passed to the estate of a deceased party, the executor, or later, the administrator of the estate may want to dispose of any real estate quickly. There is usually a need for cash to settle estate obligations and for distribution to the beneficiaries of the estate. Even when cash is not needed to settle affairs, estate administrators, particularly if the administrator is a bank, are reluctant to accept responsibility for operating an income property. In many cases administrators simply do not have the qualifications for property management. Also, a division of the estate assets is not as satisfactory when real estate is involved. Estates are most efficiently handled by administrators when the holdings are in the form of securities which can be more easily traded as the market may require. While the estate may require payment for property in cash, the price is usually negotiable within the limits of an independent appraisal, and assistance in financing may be offered through the contacts of the administrator.

Repossessions

Some of the better deals to acquire property can be made in cases where a lender has had to foreclose and now has title to the property. Most lenders are really not interested in property management and in many cases are under some pressure to convert the repossessed asset to a more acceptable form. The "more acceptable form" of asset for the lender is not necessarily cash, although that would be nice. Regulated lenders are examined periodically and are expected to keep their assets in a form that sustains the solvency of the institution. This generally means interest-bearing investments, not necessarily those most likely to increase in value. So the lender is often interested in selling the foreclosed property at its cost of acquisition and carrying favorable financing as well. The catch here is that lenders are not willing to risk such property to the hands of an unproven operator. Only one with a solid record of operating experience is able to make the favorable deal.

DECIDING WHAT TO BUY

Real estate is essentially a long-term form of investment. It is complex to acquire and requires sometimes cumbersome legal procedures. Therefore, a decision to buy should not be hurried but made only after careful deliberation of all information that can be obtained on the subject.

The basic steps that should be followed in reaching a decision start with the determination of the type and size property that is desired. Are you more interested in rental houses, apartment properties, small store buildings, shopping centers, small office buildings or large ones? Then there are all sizes of warehouse properties, mobile home parks, recreational facilities, and business properties such as motels, restaurant buildings, and fast food franchise outlets. Do you have some ability for construction and are you able to develop improved or unimproved land for rental purposes or for resale? Or, perhaps the decision as to type of property desired can await a review of what is available on the market.

The next steps:

1. Accumulate all the information you can find on what properties are being offered for sale. And keep this information window open. The best deals are not the ones made last year or five years ago; the market you are seeking is the one yet to come. And the good deals are here today—only it may be another ten years before most of us learn where they were! An important point to remember is that at any one time there may be no good investment properties available. But keep looking as the market is constantly changing.

2. Personally inspect and evaluate the available properties. Eliminate the obvious misfits.

3. Those properties that appear acceptable upon initial evaluation deserve greater study. Since this takes time and can cost some money, only the most likely prospects are worth it. This step involves analysis of financial statements, a review of any alternative financing methods, and an estimate of the returns that can be anticipated.

4. Small properties, those of less than $200,000, require less time to evaluate than large ones. If there is some complexity in the analysis, an additional step should be taken to hold the property in a manner that allows adequate evaluation. The method may be an option, an earnest money contract, or possibly a sales agreement with suffi-

cient reservations, or outs, to allow a withdrawal without obligation should the property not measure up. At this point it might be wise to consider the use of a qualified attorney. Whenever an agreement is undertaken, legal counsel should be considered; whenever title to property is being transferred, legal counsel is necessary.

SOME CAVEATS

Not every property is the "gold mine" it may be represented to be. How does one tell the difference between good and not so good, or just plain terrible? It is easy to fall back on the tried and true cliché—"only by experience." But that, while certainly meritorious, is not the only answer and is of no help to a newcomer to this field. What we need are some guidelines to follow. But keep in mind that there are many factors involved, not the least of which is your ability as an investor to improve the property, upgrade its management, and thus increase the profitability. This is not an easy task, and major problems can arise in an investment property which are nearly impossible to overcome in a reasonable amount of time and after spending a reasonable amount of money.

Overload of Debt

In periods of high inflation and relatively easy but expensive money, it is not unusual to find a property owner enticed into overborrowing, either in the beginning or later with second and third mortgages. Often the money obtained with later financing is used to acquire an entirely different development. The property operates at a very high "break-even" point. This means it takes high occupancy, 93 percent to 95 percent for an apartment, just to meet its obligations. A slight decline in occupancy can be disastrous if the owner is not prepared to pick up the losses. Heavy debt loads have been "the way to go" with single-family rental housing and many other commercial investment properties. The expectation, of course, is that inflated property values will ultimately produce a handsome profit. It certainly has worked in a number of cases, but it has meant adding cash to the investment each year to sustain the costs. Be sure the debt load is such that either the property can sustain the cost or you, as the owner, can add your own cash to hold on to the property until inflation does produce that profit. Any bet on inflation alone to produce a profit has to be classed as speculative.

Physical Condition

Most of us can cite horrible examples of investment property that has been allowed to deteriorate so badly that it is nearly worthless. The reasons are many: the death of an owner and an estate managed by unqualified people; a remote owner with little interest in property maintenance and maybe too much trust in a poor or dishonest manager; a subsidized housing project that has become the victim of vandalism. Although some of the very best buys can be made in run-down buildings, if you are not knowledgeable in construction problems, best let these places go to someone else. It is so easy for repair costs today to exceed the initial cost of construction. Only a really experienced person should invest in a property requiring extensive renovation.

Property Location

One of the reasons that a building may be offered at what appears to be a good price for its size and utility is that the market for its type of service is moving away or has already disappeared. No amount of renovation, improvement of management, or advertising is going to bring the property back to profitability. Yet, a careful analysis is needed on this point. Location has a direct relation to the price of the services offered. For example, if an apartment building is not in the best location, can it be purchased at a price that will allow a substantial reduction in rents? Price will always attract customers. Has the highway bypassed a reasonably good motel and brought a substantial drop in room occupancy? Can it be bought at a low enough price to offer reduced rate accommodations? There are many travelers not interested in the prestige associated (by some) with $40 to $80 per-night rooms. Market study and common sense is needed to determine potential profitability.

CONCLUSIONS

There are many ways to enter the real estate investment field. It does take some cash and a willingness to accept management and maintenance responsibilities. The first-time investor should acquire property well within his or her financial means, then build on the increasing property value plus the successful track record of property operation. The better acquisition deals are usually made by those who can offer some cash and who have a good record to justify favorable refinancing.

Acquiring Real Estate

BUYING RIGHT

One of the obvious keys to success in real estate investment is to buy a property at a good price. If because of the circumstances of the sale, the property is plainly undervalued in relation to its income levels or in relation to what similar properties are being sold for, there is little problem. However, most transactions are not so obvious. Normally, both parties to a transaction seek an advantage for themselves. And certainly, a "good deal" is one that satisfies the special desires of each party.

The burden is on the buyer, or investor, to perceive an advantage that justifies a payment of cash and acceptance of debt in exchange for the property. There must be an advantage to the buyer greater than a rise in value of the property equal to the inflation; otherwise there is no real gain. What the investor should look for is a property that can increase beyond the inflationary growth because of (1) the physical improvement of the property itself and (2) the increase of population in the surrounding area. The large investor has a distinct advantage in building new and perhaps in being large enough to construct a development that in itself attracts population growth. But this is not a deterrent for the small investor. The trick in your particular area may be to watch carefully the direction that large investment companies move and follow them.

One more thought in regard to growth areas. These have occurred in the past because of an overall growth in population. With birth rates leveling out, however, future growth areas will be brought about by shifts in population: a movement to be closer to the job, a movement to the inner city rather than out to far-flung suburbs. And each local area will present a different pattern for this form of growth.

While the punch line definition of a successful real estate investment is as simple as whether or not you make a profit, let's look at some of the underlying information that affects this result. That person with the greater knowledge of property values, financing procedures, and the intricacies that are involved in real estate transactions is the one most likely to assure his or her profit at the closing table.

THE REAL ESTATE MARKET

Real estate does not have an organized market as is found with many other investment forms. Probably only collectibles and art objects are more demanding in the search needed to make the most profitable investment. To find suitable property some people watch all newspaper ads, some cruise the neighborhoods where they are seeking to invest, noting "for sale" signs, and many "list" their needs or desires with one or more trusted real estate brokers. Contacts with friends, associates, and business people can be productive. A "want ad" is also a means of generating contacts. Is there a best way to handle the problem? Unfortunately, no. It depends so much on the individual investor, the type of work that he or she does, the contacts available, and the local market situation. The following suggestions are based on experience in dealing with the real estate market in several different areas of the country.

Real Estate Brokers

Foremost on the list of possible sources of information leading to the best possible investment property are the local real estate brokers. It is not wise to shun this group for fear of paying a large commission or of being subjected to high pressure sales tactics. However, it is a good idea to do some initial exploration of the market on your own. Like people in all lines of professional activity, there are good and not so good. Keep in mind that a broker can perform a valuable service and the measure of cost is not necessarily in the dollar amount of the broker's commission. The astute investor will pay far more attention to what he or she is actually making out of a deal than to what the other fellow's gain might be. It must be human nature that many good opportunities are bypassed because of fear that someone else might make a profit also.

A broker has the advantage of a third party in negotiation. He can present negative factors as opinions of a client rather than his own and, thus, minimize personal involvement when it does little good. The sympathy a broker may offer to a seller over a negative factor can be surprisingly effective. When a buyer and seller deal directly with each other, it is possible to reach a confrontation stage before any real questions are resolved.

There are more serious questions concerning real estate brokers than commissions or pressure tactics—the latter activity should be dismissed with the same lack of courtesy by which it is offered. The search by an investor for suitable property needs to be as all-inclusive as possible. Brokers sell their "listed" property as offered by various clients, and sometimes exchange listing information, which is helpful to the investor. As a general rule, there is far more information exchanged between brokers on residential property than there is on commercial investment property. Investors should keep in mind, however, that some brokers are also interested in acquiring properties for themselves and can become effective competitors for the best investments. Remember too that no broker can provide a complete listing of all available properties. It is the nature of the business.

Listings

To better understand the stock in trade that a real estate broker works with, we need to examine the various types of listings that are most commonly used. This information is also relevant when the investor desires to dispose of property and may need a broker's help.

All states have real estate property laws, as well as licensing laws, that establish certain procedures under which properties can be sold by persons other than the owner. Obviously, private property cannot be offered for sale, advertised, or a "for sale" sign placed thereon, without the express permission of the owner. It is from this basic protection of private property rights that the various methods of listing property for sale have derived. If you, as an investor, are dealing with a broker who holds an exclusive listing, you are most certainly dealing with the right party for that listed property. The three basic listing forms in common use follow:

Open Listing. This is an agreement between a property owner and one or more brokers that allows the property to be offered for sale and generally assigns the commission due upon sale to that broker who first submits the successful prospect's name in writing to the seller. It is this type of agreement that discourages any one broker from spending his own money on advertising, and it also tends to inhibit buyers who fear a conflict between two or more brokers each claiming a commission. Also, with an open listing the owner retains the right to make a sale on his own and bypass the payment of a commission, providing the prospect is not one first contacted and reported by a broker.

Exclusive Agency.   This is an agreement between a property owner and just one broker to offer property for sale to the exclusion of other brokers. However, under this form of listing agreement, the owner still retains the right to make a direct sale and eliminate any commission paid to the broker.

Exclusive Right to Sell Listing.   This is an agreement with one broker to offer the property for sale on an exclusive basis for a limited period of time, usually about six months. Under this form of listing, if a sale of the property is arranged (not necessarily closed) by any other broker or the owner himself, the commission is still due to the listing broker. With the protection offered by an exclusive listing, a broker is able to advertise and promote the sale without fear of forfeiting the sales expense for someone else's benefit.

GENERATING INFORMATION

The search for a good investment should be a positive, aggressive one. Here are some suggestions on what you can do to uncover the best opportunities.

Newspaper and Magazine Ads

General advertisements, by owners or brokers, present a rich source of information, but it is a difficult field to cultivate for the best prospects. Good ads are designed to inspire interest without providing much solid information. The purpose, of course, is to encourage a personal contact. But it does provide a starting point for a search. You can discover, for example, which brokers appear to be most active in the particular field of your investment interest. A few calls on ads will give a general idea of what asking prices are in the current market. And the contacts can lead to some interesting and practical investment properties.

Neighborhood Search

This method is more commonly used when a person is seeking a home rather than investment property. The general neighborhood is a much more important consideration for a home than it is for an investment property. However, the idea of an area search is practical and can provide very helpful information. The importance of a personal inspection of the property under consideration cannot be overemphasized. It is one way of sorting out the good from the not so good properties. Further, by driving or walking through various commercial areas of the community, the prospective investor can gain a much better perspective on the quality and quantity of investment opportunities. While it is true that not all properties being offered for sale will carry a "For Sale" sign in a conspicuous place, quite a few do.

For various personal reasons, some sellers will not permit their property to be posted for sale with a sign. It can attract curiosity callers and others who are not seriously interested. One purpose in using a broker to handle a sale is to assess the prospect's qualifications before taking the time to show the property.

Personal Contacts

Word of mouth can be a powerful communication instrument. Be sure to let your friends and associates know of your particular interest in properties. If you have any contacts among mortgage lenders, let them know of your interest. This may help locate properties that have been acquired by lenders through foreclosure action. Lenders take no pride in having to foreclose a loan. It indicates that a mistake has been made or that a potential weakness exists in the assets of the lender—and publicity is not usually encouraged. Most of these distress acquisitions can be found on the down-slide of the housing and construction cycles. Favorable deals are often available for qualified buyers.

Want Ad Placed by Buyer

While a general advertisement in the local paper may produce a rash of nuisance calls from people with no practical suggestions—those who are attracted by the idea that here is someone with money to spend and maybe they can pick up their share—there is always the possibility that something useful will be developed. Such an ad would certainly attract calls from active real estate brokers who may have solid listings that they can offer. An ad is another method of acquiring the information you need to make a wise choice of investment properties.

CONCLUSIONS

Buying real estate requires a good knowledge of what properties are available for sale and a sorting out of the best information. Real estate brokers can be helpful if they are not competing for the same investments. An independent search through newspaper ads, neighbor-hood inspections, and personal contacts will help broaden the base of in-formation. Once a decision to buy has been made, the offer to the seller should be made carefully, objectively, and through a broker if deemed necessary and advantageous.

5

Minimizing Cash
Requirements

Few investment opportunities offer the smorgasbord of acquisition possibilities that can be found in real estate. There are many ways to structure a trade, depending entirely on the needs and capabilities of the buyer and seller. There are no minimum cash requirements as found in the margin requirements for purchasing securities, no interest rate requirements (other than state usury ceilings), and no minimum size requirements with some collectibles and certain savings certificates. The payment for real estate is a matter determined by the buyer and the seller.

METHODS OF MINIMIZING
CASH REQUIREMENTS

Many investment counselors consider the potential for making "no cash" acquisitions of real estate one of its major advantages. However, it simply does not follow that anything acquired with no cash down is a good deal. The nature of the property and the debt structure that is undertaken in the acquisition must also be considered. A property overburdened with debt may continue as a liability and never become an asset.

Nevertheless, if one can use another's money or assets to his own advantage, it is certainly worth exploring. There are many ways to minimize the initial cash needed to acquire real estate. All have been used in practice, and many need special circumstances for practical application. But the ideas suggested may be combined or adjusted to fit your local situation.

Mortgaging Out

One of the more obvious methods of eliminating a cash requirement is to obtain a loan for 100 percent (or more) of the acquisition price. Can this be done? Yes, in certain situations, and it is neither illegal nor in violation of banking regulations. Two possibilities come to mind. First, if leases from good tenants can be obtained (new construction) that produce an income which, when capitalized, exceeds the cost of construction, the loan amount can be based on the value of the leases. Or, if expiring leases can be renegotiated to increase the gross income sufficiently for an existing building, refinancing may be sufficient to buy it with no additional cash. Both situations will give an appraiser the basis for revaluing the building from an income approach. Second, unimproved land substantially increases in value when it is dedicated to a productive use, such as for building lots or for an apartment project. The justification for the lender to make a so-called 100 percent loan is that the appraised value has become sufficient to justify a loan that on the lender's books may amount to an 85 percent or 90 percent loan. Just make sure the debt service can be handled if the economy slows a bit.

A slight variation on the mortgaging out method is to obtain a second (or third) mortgage, if possible. There may be some advantage in retaining an existing mortgage if it can be assumed at a lower interest rate than current market.

Trading Services for the Down Payment

If the buyer has any professional qualifications that may be offered as personal services to the seller, the value might be applied to the acquisition cost. (Note: The value of such services is taxable income to the *buyer* under IRS rules.) If the buyer is also a real estate broker, the value of the sales commission may be accepted as a part or all of the cash consideration. If the buyer is qualified in a trade, such as plumbing or carpentry, an offer to undertake certain repairs for the seller may be acceptable instead of cash. The latter form of services are acceptable as a form of down payment by both the FHA and VA and are usually referred to as *sweat equity*.

Seller-Assisted Financing

When the seller must sell, or perhaps is holding out for a maximum market price, there is a possibility that he or she may provide financial assistance to the buyer. While sellers usually are selling with the expectation of receiving at least some cash, there are situations where the seller expects to reinvest the proceeds of the sale anyway. In this case, why shouldn't the seller offer a secured investment in his or her own property to the buyer? The seller may be willing to finance all, or part, of the equity requirement, taking a second or junior mortgage to the existing financing.

Junior Mortgage Financing

A close corollary to the seller-assisted financing is the same sort of equity financing, only from an institutional lender. Most real estate, particularly seasoned properties, has enjoyed an increase in value that provides a substantial equity interest for the owner. Where state laws, banking regulations, and the institution's lending rules all permit, junior mortgage loans can be found to help pay off the seller. The risk is greater than for a first mortgage loan, and the interest cost will be correspondingly higher.

Borrowing on Other Collateral

While this is not quite the same as using "someone else's assets," it is an avenue that may be overlooked. Many people accumulate assets without realizing their true worth. Lenders make loans with a variety of collateral; here are some assets that could serve as collateral to raise additional cash.

- The equity in your home.
- Securities if listed on an exchange and publicly traded.
- Savings accounts or other savings certificates.
- Certain types of trust funds.
- An assignment of rental receipts.
- Additional signatory parties for the note (such as another family member, a good friend or two).
- Cash value of a life insurance policy.

Borrowing from Unconventional Sources

While most mortgage loans are made by institutional lenders, every community has lesser known sources that generally do not advertise or promote their lending interests. Loans are really secondary to their primary purpose for existence. Consider these suggestions:

- Advertise in local papers for a private loan.
- Ask a family member who may have investment cash.
- Some trust fund arrangements allow the beneficiary to borrow their own money from the trust.
- Credit union—not an "unconventional" source as since 1978 they can make 30-year mortgage loans but to members only.
- Religious or fraternal group that you may belong to (and some you do not have to belong to).
- A hospital, university, or other entity that holds endowment funds for investment (particularly if you have been a generous contributor).
- The real estate broker who may consider loaning his or her commission.

Property Exchange

If the investor has other property holdings, it may be possible to arrange an exchange. This minimizes the cash requirements as well as defers capital gains taxes. (See Chapter 17 Tax Advantage Transactions.)

Benefits from Leases

The seller of a home, or a business property, who does not want to vacate immediately but needs an assured sale may be willing to close the transaction and allow the next six or eight months rental payments which would be paid by the seller to the buyer as a part or all of the cash down payment.

Another more complex procedure would be for the *buyer* to arrange for a *sale* of the land underlying the building to be acquired by a third party. Simultaneously, the buyer arranges to lease back the land from the third party purchaser. The proceeds of the land sale can be used as all or part of the down payment needed to acquire the building-only portion of the property.

Structuring the Deal Advantageously

There are several methods that may be used to arrange the acquisition in a way that utilizes certain values of the acquired property as a part of the consideration.

Future Profits. An assignment of a portion of the acquired property's future profits might have an appeal to a seller who believes strongly in his or her own property. In this way, the seller has an opportunity to gain a higher price if the market continues to escalate. When payment for the property itself is made *contingent* on the future income from the property, the procedure is called a *performance second mortgage*. If the property does not produce the projected income, the acquisition cost is thus reduced.

Use of Closing Credits. If the income property has substantial closing credits available, such as taxes, insurance, rental payments, these credits may be offered to the seller as a part or all of the down payment. The trick is to time the closing so as to take full advantage of the maximum credits that may be available.

Assumption of Debt. If the seller is overburdened with excessive debt, he or she may offer some cash or other consideration to the buyer in exchange for relief from the obligation. Care needs to be taken in such circumstances that you do not step into the same hole.

Down Payment in Installments. Rather than put up the full down payment at closing, the seller may agree to accept this payment in a series of installments which allows the buyer more time to collect the necessary cash.

Adjustable Rate Mortgages. The use of repayment procedures other than constant-level, fully amortized loans is on the increase. Depending on the market, lower interest costs may be achieved by allowing the lender to adjust the interest rate at periodic intervals. (See the discussion of adjustable rate mortgages in Chapter 11.)

Graduated Payment Mortgages. These forms can be fully amortized or partially amortized procedures. For commercial loans the more common method is to allow, say, a 30-year amortization payment with a 10-year term. This form is also called a *balloon note*. When the initial payments are lower than needed to amortize, the method is called *soft paper*. The simple advantage is that less cash is needed in the earlier years of ownership.

CONCLUSIONS

All these procedures are directed toward reducing the need for cash. They do not necessarily increase the profitability of a property—the reverse is likely to be true. But it may allow an acquisition and pave the way for future profitability. When negotiating to acquire property it is difficult to know exactly what is motivating the seller and what might be acceptable consideration. There is a story that the elder Henry Ford showed up at his factory one day driving a new Cadillac. When asked the reason, he responded, "You know, no one ever tried to sell me a Ford!" It doesn't hurt to ask.

The acquisition of real property can be accomplished in many ways. If the intent of the buyer is to reduce cash requirements, he or she should consider the following:

- Mortgaging out.
- Trading services for the down payment.
- Seller-assisted financing.
- Junior mortgage financing.
- Borrowing on other collateral.
- Borrowing from unconventional sources.
- Making a property exchange.
- Using benefits derived from leases.
- Structuring the deal to the buyer's advantage including using the property's future profits, taking advantage of any closing credits, recognizing the benefit to the seller of relief from debt, or arranging for lower initial payments that increase later.

6

The People Involved

Reference is frequently made to various specialists who are involved in some measure with real estate transactions. Most potential investors are acquainted with lawyers and their qualifications and with real estate brokers and how they operate. But what about escrow agents, accountants, surveyors, appraisers, and mortgage loan representatives? What qualifications should you look for and what help should you expect? Since all of these services represent a certain professionalism, the most common qualification is the individual's local reputation. But if your contacts are somewhat limited, this chapter is devoted to pointing out the basic services and qualifications offered by the many people who can become involved with your real estate transaction.

LAWYERS

Of the various professions involved in handling real estate, certainly an attorney represents the most demanding. The educational requirements are high: at least three years of specialized study beyond a Bachelor's degree and an exhaustive qualifying examination. The rewards for success are good. The degree awarded is a "J.D.," Doctor of Jurisprudence, which compares with the Ph.D. of academic excellence, plus a state issued license to practice law. The license is a general one, meaning qualification to practice any form of law that the attorney is offered or prefers. There are specialized groups, mostly represented by peer groups, and each attorney generally finds one or two areas of the law to be of more interest. There are specialists in corporate law, marine law, banking law, securities law, workman's compensation law and many, many others. The point is that not all lawyers are interested in or qualified to handle the details of real estate law. So make sure you select an attorney who has the expertise and interest in your field.

An attorney is a necessity whenever legal title to property is conveyed. With only a few limited exceptions, lenders will not undertake a mortgage loan unless the necessary instruments have been prepared by an acceptable attorney. In most states any conveyance of land is considered the practice of law and must be handled by a licensed attorney.

It is in the *negotiation* for a property investment that the buyer may use discretion as to the employment of an attorney. A realistic businessman's approach to this question runs along the line that there are business matters and there are legal matters involved with any negotiation—don't let the two conflict! An attorney by training looks for potential problems. He operates on the premise that it is better to avoid a problem than have to resolve it later. The difficulty arises when all the attorney finds are problems and few solutions. It is with the preliminary negotiations and the general concept of how a transaction can be structured that the business approach can be more effective. Once the basic plan is agreed upon, the attorney is needed to draw up a clear agreement that avoids as many potential problems as possible.

REAL ESTATE BROKERS

References are made throughout this book to the various services that are provided by competent brokers. As a group, they are a valuable source of information for an investor because of their familiarity with the market arena.

The qualifications to be a real estate broker vary widely in the different states. All states have licensing requirements that call for minimum educational standards and special examinations. Most states offer two levels of licensing—as a salesperson and as a broker. The normal rule is that no one may offer another's property for sale or lease unless properly licensed in the state in which the land is located. Licensing requirements usually include an understanding of the ethics involved with real estate transactions and the handling of escrow money. However, it is still the individual agent's personal reputation that provides the best guide to the standards that are upheld.

There are some national organizations that offer certain designations which indicate special qualifications in the real estate field. A discussion of the major ones follows:

National Association of Realtors (NAR).   An organization of state associations and 1,780 local Boards of Realtors. Only members are authorized to use the designation *Realtor,* which is a registered name (with the first letter "R" always capitalized). To belong, a member must subscribe to a strict code of ethical practices and faces expulsion if the code is violated. The Association offers extensive educational programs through its nine professional institutes, societies, and councils. It operates its own press and publishes numerous books, pamphlets, and articles in the field of real estate. It employs a full-time staff in Washington, D.C. to serve as a spokesperson for the real estate industry. This group furnishes information and testifies before Congress and various regulatory agencies. NAR offers a valued designation of GRI (Graduate, Realtors Institute) to those who pass an extensive training course.

Other designations are offered by organizations affiliated with the National Association of Realtors. The Realtors National Marketing Institute (RNMI) runs educational programs to qualify members for designations as CRB (Certified Residential Broker) and CCIM (Certified Commercial Investment Member). The Society of Industrial Realtors offers its SIR designation (Specialist in Industrial Realty), and the Farm and Land Institute (FLI) offers an AFLM qualification (Accredited Farm and Land Member).

National Association of Real Estate Brokers (NAREB).   A national organization of brokers whose members carry the designation of "Realtist."

American Society of Real Estate Counselors (ASREC).   A growing segment of real estate professionals are now confining their efforts to counseling clients on a fixed fee basis. Like a real estate broker, the counselor's knowledge and advice can be valuable to the investor, particularly a newcomer to the field. Working as a consultant on a fixed fee basis, the counselor does not have the same financial incentives to close a particular sale and may be more objective in his or her approach to problems as they arise. ASREC offers the special designation of CRE (Counselor, Real Estate) to those who qualify through experience, education, and examination.

Institute of Real Estate Management (IREM).   The importance of competent management of income properties cannot be overemphasized. There is a special designation for the professional in this field, CPM for Certified Property Manager.

If you, as an investor, have a special interest in any of these areas, achieving a professional designation can be very educational and personally satisfying.

ACCOUNTANTS

Almost anyone who is familiar with bookkeeping methods can call himself an *accountant*. But only the person who meets certain educational requirements and is able to pass an exhaustive testing procedure is allowed to identify himself as a CPA (Certified Public Accountant). Each state grants the designation in accordance with its own requirements. Only a CPA may prepare an *audited* financial statement. An audited statement is one prepared from figures that have been verified by the accountant and is presented in a generally accepted form for the business under audit.

Some states offer a lesser qualification for accountants, such as the designation of *Public Accountant*. This procedure usually allows entry to the profession with lower requirements and can be an encouragement for younger persons seeking to become CPAs.

The need for accurate financial information is important for every investment, and the competence of the person preparing the information is critical. In a later chapter the various problems associated with obtaining financial information are dealt with in greater detail.

APPRAISERS

Professional evaluation of real property is essential for investor guidance and is the basis for obtaining a mortgage loan. For an appraiser, there are trade groups, or peer associations, that grant certain designations for persons who meet their education, experience, and testing requirements. An appraiser's professional designation is a key to acceptability for many lenders.

The organizations and designations granted are as follows:

- *American Institute of Real Estate Appraisers (AIREA)*.
  RM—Residential Member.
  MAI—Member, Appraisal Institute (highest designation).
- *American Society of Appraisers (ASA)*.
  ASA—American Society of Appraisers.
- *Society of Real Estate Appraisers (SREA)*.
  SRA—Senior Residential Appraiser.

SRPA—Senior Real Property Appraiser.
SREA—Senior Real Estate Analyst (highest designation).
- *Appraisal Institute of Canada (AIC).*
AACI—Accredited Appraiser Canadian Institute.
- *National Association of Independent Fee Appraisers.*
IFA—Independent Fee Appraiser Member.
IFAS—Independent Fee Appraiser Senior Member.
IFAC—Independent Fee Appraiser, Counselor.
- *National Association of Review Appraisers.*
CRA—Certified Review Appraiser, Senior Member.

MORTGAGE LOAN REPRESENTATIVES

There are few professional designations among the many people who work in the mortgage loan industry as loan officers, loan representatives, loan supervisors, loan managers, or any other title denoting expertise in the lending field. The origination of loans is handled by commercial banks, savings and loan associations, by mortgage companies, and many other sources. Each has its own trade groups, devoted to the general problems within the industry.

The oldest trade association, dating back to 1914, the Mortgage Bankers Association (MBA), has emphasized the special requirements and knowledge necessary for proper handling of mortgage loans. It offers the professional certification of CMB (Certified Mortgage Banker).

A more recent entry into the field of mortgage loan trade associations is the American Association of Mortgage Underwriters (AAMU) organized in 1976. The Association has chapters in several eastern cities and offers three designations to those meeting prescribed education and experience requirements:

- C.M.U.—Certified Mortgage Underwriter (8 years experience, both residential and commercial).
- C.R.M.U.—Certified Residential Mortgage Underwriter (5 years experience, residential only).
- A.M.U.—Associate Mortgage Underwriter (3 years experience in either commercial or residential underwriting).

For the investor, a good lending officer's qualifications are of less practical concern than the question: Do I get the loan or not? The lending institution or company is of greater importance than the individual.

ESCROW AGENTS

While the term *escrow agent* is used differently in different parts of the country, the focus here is on the person involved with the settlement procedures used to close a real estate transaction. An escrow agent may be a highly qualified attorney or an inexperienced clerk. Because there are no professional designations for this specialized field, the investor is best advised to place his or her trust in the integrity and reputation of the institution behind the person handling a settlement.

OTHER DESIGNATIONS

- Architecture:
  American Institute of Architects.
  AIA—American Institute of Architects.
- Insurance:
  American Institute for Property and Liability Underwriters.
  CPCU—Chartered Property Casualty Underwriters.
- Securities/Syndication:
  Real Estate Securities and Syndication Institute (RESSI).
  CRSS—Certified Real Estate Securities Sponsor.
  CRSM—Certified Real Estate Securities Member.
- Management:
  Building Owners and Management Association (BOMA).
  RPA—Real Property Administrator (Office buildings).

THREE

Financing Real Estate

The Regulated Lenders

THE CHANGING MORTGAGE MARKET

Mortgage financing crossed a threshold of change with the passage by Congress of the landmark Depository Institution Deregulation Act, effective March 31, 1980. Prior to passage, it had become increasingly evident that the traditional sources of long-term capital would no longer be able to provide mortgage money in the face of growing competition for borrowed funds. As the decade of the 70s faded, the demand for funds soared, spurred by a number of activities in addition to the oft blamed federal deficit.

There is little question that the substantial peacetime deficits incurred by federal government fiscal policies have contributed to the increased cost of money and to inflation. But this is only one of the causes—and a deficit financed through the sale of Treasury bills to the general investing public is not nearly so inflationary as a deficit financed by the Federal Reserve Bank. The Fed, as the Federal Reserve Bank is popularly known, has the authority to credit the bank account of the United States Government out of "thin air"—actually, in exchange for a Treasury issue of government bonds or notes with only the good faith of the government supporting the issue. When the Federal Reserve buys government bonds from the U.S. Treasury, it is simply creating more money. An expression often used for this paper for paper transaction is "monetizing the federal debt," that is, exchanging the government's debt instruments (the bonds) for money it can spend. When the Fed moves to buy government bonds, thus increasing the overall supply of money, it creates concern in financial markets. The reason is that an excessive increase in the money supply is directly related to a potential increase in inflation. So the money markets interpret a growth in the money supply as encouraging inflation and lenders hold out for higher interest rates.

But the actions of the government and the Fed in their money management maneuvers cannot carry all the blame. Another very important element in the growth in demand for borrowed funds stems from the proliferation of government loan programs—not the making of loans, but the underwriting of a wide variety of loans for businesses, farmers, students, utilities, and also for home buyers. (*Underwriting* means that the government insures or guarantees repayment.) It is not the purpose of this discussion to judge the merits of the various loan underwriting programs, only to point out that through these programs, many borrowers enter the market for loanable funds who might otherwise not be eligible. The increase in demand has been substantial, and the pool of money available for loans has not enjoyed a proportionate increase.

Besides government deficits and government underwriting of loans, a third element has moved forward to demand a greater share of the available money for loans. This is consumer credit, which has grown to great size by the availability of credit cards. Buying on credit has become the "way to go"—even on vacation trips.

To satisfy this increase in demand for funds, lending institutions scrambled to raise more money themselves. With their own assets limited, they in turn borrowed money in order to loan it out at ever higher rates. In order to remain within the constraints of banking regulations, the lenders borrowed their money through the sale of Certificates of Deposit (C/Ds). Banks and savings associations attracted large depositors by offering high interest rates for $100,000 and larger C/Ds because the interest rates allowed for them had been deregulated. While it is a matter of perception, the banking industry classified these large denomination certificates as deposits, while many of those holding the C/Ds considered them a type of security, in essence, a loan to the bank. Banks also expanded their borrowing activity through the direct sale of securities, such as bonds and promissory notes, to the investing public.

As the margins between the unrestricted interest paid on large C/Ds, compared with smaller savings certificates, became more apparent, the next step was creation of money market mutual funds. These funds simply pool small investors' money into large blocks so as to loan the money in the form of large C/Ds to the banking institutions. The high interest rates that the banks have been able to pay for these funds have carried all rates upward. The obvious attraction for the small investor to earn possibly 15 percent on a few thousand dollars in a money market fund that would otherwise lay in a savings account at 5 1/2 percent or 6 percent has had its impact. By the early 80s money market funds were drawing new investment cash at the rate of several billion dollars per week.

What has been the impact of these changes on the money normally flowing into the mortgage market? For one, few lending institutions are still willing to place their own deposit assets in long-term loans at fixed interest rates. Three methods have developed to allow lenders to continue making mortgage loans: they can (1) pass the new loans on to the financial markets through the sale of mortgage-backed securities; (2) sell the loans directly to secondary market investors (such as the Federal National Mortgage Association or the Federal Home Loan Mortgage Corporation) who can raise their money in the financial markets; and (3) keep only those loans in house (called *portfolio loans*) whose interest rates can be adjusted as may be indicated by a market index.

With this background in mind, we can take a closer look at traditional sources of mortgage money. These sources include the major institutional (regulated) lenders: savings associations, mutual savings banks, commercial banks, and life insurance companies, plus the non-institutional mortgage companies. This group of lenders is knowledgeable in the mortgage field and can be expected to continue their dominance. They can make money from origination fees and service charges earned from handling mortgage loans. This is true even though their own source of money is shifting away from the traditional savings accounts to the financial markets. What this means is that mortgage lenders must compete for funds against all other forms of credit demand. This includes the powerful demand for funds by the U.S. Treasury, which is not subject to any legal, political, or economic limits with respect to the interest it can pay. In an overburdened credit market, the U.S. Treasury can easily crowd out business and consumer loans, which have practical limits as to the interest that can be paid.

In mortgage finance, probably the greatest change is being made by the thrift institutions—savings and loan associations and the mutual savings banks. Savings associations in the past have invested over 80 percent of their assets in residential mortgage loans, largely because of tax incentives. Mutual savings banks, on the other hand, have placed over half of their assets in mortgage loans, particularly FHA/VA loans, simply because they were good investments. Now the pattern is changing. Fixed interest rates and long-term mortgage loans have produced income levels much too low when compared with the steady rise in the cost of funds for the lending institution. The Deregulation Act of 1980 allowed lending institutions to diversify their activities into other financial fields, and many have made just such a move.

Following is a discussion of the primary sources of money and the kind of mortgage activity that they undertake. The term, *primary source*, needs some explanation. This is the market, the companies, the lenders, that an individual can approach to borrow money. The primary market makes loans to borrowers and charges an origination or finance fee for the work of assembling a loan package. The cost of the money borrowed is expressed as an interest rate plus a discount. The primary market is the loan originators. Many of the loans so originated are funded by the lender, who retains the note as an asset. These are called *portfolio* loans. However, many of these loans are sold to large investors, such as life insurance companies, FNMA, or mutual savings banks. Companies or investors who buy these loans are called the *secondary market*. Real estate investors normally have no contact with the secondary market. However, its influence is great and growing. As an increasing share of mortgage money flows from the financial markets (the money invested for the short term in stocks, bonds, Treasury bills, large C/Ds, and commercial paper), the secondary market reflects the new money costs. Whether or not a loan originator retains a loan in its portfolio or sells the loan, the principal concern of the real estate investor is the cost and conditions under which the loan is made. And this is spelled out by the loan originator. Now, let's look at the major loan originators.

SAVINGS AND LOAN ASSOCIATIONS

First in the field of mortgage lending is the savings associations. In Colonial America, savings associations grew from voluntary organizations whose members pooled their savings to enable qualified members to borrow from the pooled funds to buy a house or perhaps a farm. The various states undertook to charter and regulate these organizations. Later, the Internal Revenue Service recognized the importance of encouraging home ownership and allowed a unique tax exemption. Any savings association that held not more than 18 percent of its assets in commercial loans (that is, nonresidential), could transfer its earnings to a surplus account, make it available for more loans, and defer income taxes. Earnings distributed to the stockholders or owners of the savings associations are considered taxable.

The substantial tax incentive made residential loans the dominant activity for savings associations. At their peak in 1979, they held just one-half of all the residential loans in this country.

The combination of substantially diminished earnings from older, fixed interest rate loans plus the new rights under deregulation to engage in other forms of banking activities, such as issuing credit cards and handling estates, is reducing the savings associations' dependence on mortgage loans. Still, savings associations remain the number one source of mortgage funds and should be high on the list of any real estate investor seeking mortgage financing.

While there is a growing tendency for savings associations to merge or be taken over by larger banking or conglomerate-type financial groups, those that continue are following three paths:

1. *Traditional*—a continuation of the same mortgage lending activity of the past with most loans held in their own portfolio.
2. *Seller/Servicer*—to undertake a role similar to mortgage companies. Loans are made with aggressive selling techniques and almost immediately sold to secondary market purchasers.
3. *Family Financial Center*—an expansion into many financial services formerly offered only by commercial banks. Mortgage loans are still an important investment, but the institution's earnings are much more broadly based than in the past.

In most areas of the country, savings associations have not been so active in handling FHA and VA types of loans. Traditionally, savings associations have made their own conventional loans using their own mortgage instruments and retaining the loans in their own portfolios. FHA/VA loans required different handling procedures and were considered more the marketing area for mortgage companies. As savings associations became more involved with the sale of their loans to secondary market purchasers, the need for uniform mortgage documentation became apparent. As procedures became more standardized, the FHA/VA loans began to offer some opportunities for lenders. As a result, savings associations have taken more interest in them.

MUTUAL SAVINGS BANKS

Like savings associations, mutual savings banks grew from a need to protect savings and to use the money for making loans. Mutual savings banks are not so restricted in their powers to invest assets as are savings associations. However, because of the security, and what in the past has been a fair return, most mutual savings banks have favored long-term mortgage loans.

While mutual savings banks have been partially deregulated by the 1980 Act, it is not likely that they will pull away from mortgage lending. It is a field in which they are very knowledgeable and have many well-established relationships with primary lenders throughout the country.

This type of bank is only found in the northeast states and in Washington, Oregon, and Alaska. Some 75 percent of mutual savings assets are found in the two states of New York and Massachusetts. These areas are generally "cash rich" (that is, deposits are greater than the need for mortgage money), and for years mutual savings banks have purchased loans from lenders in the southern and western growth areas of the country. As mutual banks expand their services as is now permitted, they will most likely reduce their investments in out-of-state loans and increase their activity within their local market area by offering other credit services.

COMMERCIAL BANKS

Largest of all lenders with more loanable funds than any other institution are the commercial banks. However, their main lines of credit have been extended more to consumer loans and to business borrowers than to longer term mortgage loans. This pattern, too, is changing. As commercial banks become more familiar with the marketing of mortgage loans, many can be expected to expand their role in mortgage financing. *Marketing loans* for a commercial bank can mean selling loans to such major purchasers as the Federal National Mortgage Association, or it can mean selling a mortgage-backed security directly to investors as does the Bank of America. The collateral for a mortgage-backed security is a diversified block of mortgage loans whose monthly payments are passed through a trustee on to the holder of the security. Thus, the expression, *pass-through security*, is applied to this procedure. In this way, banks can profit from the fees charged for originating a loan plus the service fees for handling the monthly payment collections without committing their own funds to the loans. In addition, they provide a further service for their customers.

When a commercial bank makes mortgage loans from its own assets, there are three types that are most common.

Construction Loans

This is a specialized form of mortgage loan used by a builder as interim financing. Incidentally, *interim financing* means a loan made with the expectation that it will be repaid from the proceeds of another loan rather than from, say, the income from the property. A construction loan is a good example of an interim loan, but any loan repaid by another loan qualifies as interim.

Construction loans are short term—usually six to 30 months, depending on the size of the project. Considerable construction expertise is required to manage the funding and the repayment. Not all banks make this type of loan. It is considered a high-risk loan and commands one of the highest interest rates in the mortgage field. The risk stems from whether or not the builder has the ability to complete the project within the time limits and with the money allocated. Factors other than the builder's capabilities are involved, such as the weather, labor conditions, subcontractors' abilities, and delivery of materials. The cost of this type of loan is usually based on an interest rate that *floats* over prime. The rate may range from prime rate up to six percentage points over prime. Every time the prime rate is moved by the banker, the cost to the builder is adjusted, either upward or downward.

Warehouse Credit Lines

Another form of mortgage loan handled by commercial banks is the line of credit extended to mortgage companies. Unlike savings associations and other depository institutions, mortgage companies have no deposit assets with which to fund their loans at closing. To obtain the needed cash, mortgage companies usually establish a line of credit with a local commercial bank. As the mortgage company arranges to close loans, it uses the line of credit to provide funds. The mortgage notes are assigned to the commercial banker as security for the loans.

After a block of loans has been accumulated by the commercial banker, the loans are sold to a secondary market purchaser. Delivery to the purchaser is often made directly by the commercial banker who accepts payment for the account of the mortgage company. The loans so held by the commercial banker pending sale to a purchaser are in effect held *in warehouse.*

The line of credit is generally short term—from 6 to 18 months—and is not intended as permanent financing. Because of the good security and the credit support of the mortgage company, warehouse credit lines are generally granted at or near the prime rate of interest. Fluctuating interest rates are a problem for mortgage companies. When prime exceeds mortgage market interest rates, as it has often done in recent years, mortgage companies may easily lose money as long as loans are held in warehouse. To offset this cost, many mortgage companies have added still another charge, a *warehouse fee,* to the cost of a loan. This charge may be one quarter to one half of a point and is collected when the loan is closed. On the other hand, when prime is less than the mortgage interest rate, the mortgage company will profit.

Direct Mortgage Loans

In spite of the earlier emphasis in this section given to down playing the role of commercial banks in mortgage lending, this is still a major activity by many banks. Differences in practices develop from local customs and from the size of the institution. Generally, small banks in small communities are more apt to grant long-term mortgage loans than big city or regional banks. However, commercial banks consider 15 to 20 years a fairly long term, and they tend to favor the commercial building loan over a residential loan. The reason is that commercial loans usually command a higher interest rate than do the more marketable residential loans.

As mentioned earlier, commercial banks are in the process of redirecting their lending practices. Many, no doubt, will enter the long-term residential market but with loans that provide for an adjustable rate repayment plan and can be sold in the secondary market. Real estate investors should stay in touch with their commercial banker to learn what new types of credit become available.

LIFE INSURANCE COMPANIES

The average real estate investor could call on a small life insurance company to request a loan, but would have difficulty contacting any of the large ones. Life insurance companies are all state chartered and, therefore, must meet differing investment requirements. But this does not present problems because first mortgage real estate loans are universally permitted. Company policies differ. Generally, small insurance companies see greater advantage in making mortgage loans within their own market area. Some even encourage the borrower to take life insurance with the loan and thus gain a policyholder as well as a secured loan.

The large insurance companies follow a different path. With greater resources and better access to the specialized talent needed for real estate development and management, these companies prefer to make real estate loans only to such projects that permit them to participate in the ownership. Joint ventures between large insurance companies and major builders and developers are common in the big cities. Or, in some cases the insurance company will undertake its own development project as part of its investment portfolio.

There is a middle ground, however, between the large joint ventures and the direct loans that some insurance companies will make. This middle ground is represented by the participation-type loans. Partly as a hedge against continued inflation and partly to increase the yield from a loan beyond the level of a fixed interest rate, insurance companies offer loans that allow a share in the profits. Participation loans fall into two major categories:

Income Participation

The lender shares in the cash flow from the property for a limited period of time, seldom longer than the term of the loan. The participation is usually based on a percentage of the gross rental receipts. A variation might, for example, disallow participation under the initial rental struc- ture, but require 25 percent of any rental increase to be paid to the lender.

Equity Participation

The lender receives rights in the property that may endure beyond the term of the loan and represent a true ownership in the real estate. The lender may pay only a token price for the equity interest but gains a share in the cost recovery allowed on the total value of the project. A profitable sale of the property results in a capital gain for the lender (as well as for any other owners). For an investor with development experience and a need for cash, an insurance company can make a good partner.

FEDERAL AND RELATED AGENCIES

Government programs to provide funds for mortgage loans fall into three categories:

1. *Direct loans*—mostly to benefit low income or distressed families.
2. *Underwritten*—the government underwrites all or a portion of an in- dividual loan, such as FHA, VA, and FmHA programs, thus allow- ing a borrower access to credit markets that otherwise might not be available.
3. *Mortgage pools*—the sale of securities, backed by a diversified block of individual mortgage loans whereby monthly payments on the loans are passed through to the security owners. The securities are guaranteed by agencies of the federal government, principally GNMA, FHLMC, and FmHA.

For the average real estate investor, *direct* government loans are not available. These are limited to disaster victims, displaced families, and in some cases, to owner-occupants (not investors) in low-income neighborhoods.

On the other hand, federal *underwriting* programs offer some opportunities to the investor. Both the FHA and the FmHA provide loan assistance for projects that further the agencies' goals. The VA confines its aid to veterans, and the home loan program is limited to owner-occupants. The FHA has several good programs to encourage investment in multifamily housing, nursing homes, clinics, and mobile home parks. The availability of these programs varies from time to time and from area to area. Approvals often depend on an allocation for a given area. It is worthwhile to explore all open programs currently offered in the local HUD/FHA offices.

In areas where there is a proven need for more apartment units, the FHA may offer its Section 221 (d) (4) which can provide an insured commitment for up to 97 percent of the project's total costs, including financing charges plus mortgage insurance for the construction loan. Where need exists for housing for the elderly and disabled, FHA Section 221 (d) (3) offers a developer less than market interest rates for financing. These mortgages are usually purchased by the Government National Mortgage Association as a part of their assistance functions authorized by the government.

There are several programs that provide underwriting assistance for rehabilitation work on existing apartment stock. One of the interesting programs is Section 223 (f) which permits a developer to buy an older multifamily project, plan a rehabilitation program, and obtain FHA mortgage insurance on the total package (purchase price plus rehabilitation). With the mortgage insurance certificate issued, the developer can then work with an investment banking firm specializing in FHA program financing, who can arrange to sell the mortgage to a secondary market pool. Rehab costs cannot exceed the lesser of 15 percent of the value or $3,000 per unit. A practical minimum amount on this type of financing would be $3,000,000. This is another type of *mortgage-backed security*, only in this instance, the collateral is a single mortgage rather than a diversified block of loans.

Underwriting programs offered by the Farmers Home Administration expanded substantially in the late 1970s. FmHA was established in 1946 and remains under the jurisdiction of the Department of Agriculture. Generally, it makes and insures loans to those farmers and ranchers who are unable to secure credit from other sources. The range of lending activities includes:

1. Financing of houses for low-income farmers, including a subsidy program for qualified applicants.

2. Financing rural housing for the elderly.
3. Financing the purchase and/or the improvement of farms.
4. Financing the construction and/or the rehabilitation of farm homes and outbuildings.
5. Financing rehabilitation programs for rural communities.
6. Financing the purchase of property by tenant farmers.
7. Administration of rural resettlement projects.

8

Mortgage Companies

Mortgage companies serve as intermediaries between lending institutions and the borrower. As a group, they are often referred to as *unregulated lenders*. While they have no deposit assets to work with, as do the regulated lenders, they aggressively seek lenders willing to make loans and work with borrowers to match their needs with suitable lenders. They perform an invaluable service as a kind of "lubricant," encouraging a smooth flow of mortgage funds.

HISTORICAL BACKGROUND

From its origin as a brokerage-type service arranging loans, the mortgage banking industry has grown to a major business, handling well over half the mortgage loans in this country. As early as 1914, the people in this business formed a trade organization, known as the Farm Mortgage Bankers Association, indicating the original emphasis placed on farm loans. The name was changed to its present title of Mortgage Bankers Association of America in 1923, and it now has members from every state and a large permanent staff.

The Association serves as a communications and information center for the industry. Educational programs are sponsored to keep the many persons employed by mortage bankers up to date on an ever-changing business. And a constant effort is being made to improve the methods and procedures of the industry.

In the early years of this century, mortgage bankers arranged for the sale of their own bonds and used these funds to buy small home and farm mortgages. Because of the thrift-conscious nature of these farmers and homeowners, mortgages were amazingly free of defaults and provided a widely used medium of investment.

The 1920s brought an increase in mortgage company financing of income properties such as office buildings, apartments, and hotels, perhaps with the firm conviction that a mortgage loan was as secure as gold. And the mortgage companies even referred to the small denomination bonds that they sold to the general public for mortgage financing as *gold bonds.*

However, the Depression, triggered by the collapse of prices on the nation's largest stock exchange in October 1929, showed up many basic weaknesses in the mortgage loan system. In the next two to three years most of the mortgage companies that had issued their own bonds, as well as those that had guaranteed bonds for other development companies, were faced with massive foreclosures. Unable to meet their obligations, they were forced into bankruptcy.

From these ruins has arisen a far more enlightened and professionally sound industry—one that today not only arranges for permanent financing of all types of mortgage loans, but also uses its own resources to fund the loans initially, sometimes handles the interim or construction financing, and finally services or administers the repayment of the loan for the permanent investor.

MORTGAGE BROKERS

There is a significant difference between the services offered by *loan brokers,* and those offered by mortgage bankers working within the mortgage industry. Brokers limit their activity to serving as intermediaries between client-borrowers and the client-lenders. While brokers are capable of handling all arrangements for the processing or *packaging* of the loan, they do no funding and have no facilities to service or administer a loan once it has been made. There are some loan-wise individuals who prefer to work on their own as brokers and carry their loan applications to a mortgage banker for verification and funding. They earn a portion of the normal one point finance fee plus an application fee.

Other types of mortgage brokers are companies operating on a national scale who primarily arrange purchases and sales of mortgage loans between originators and investors, or between investor and investor, and in so doing, greatly aid the free flow of mortgages across state lines in the private mortgage market. These brokers seldom originate a loan and do not service them. They are a part of the secondary market in some of their operations.

Occasionally, a mortgage banker, or even a savings association will broker a loan for a customer. Money may not be readily available through regular channels, or the loan request may be for something that the lender cannot handle with its own funds. The lender may then turn to other sources and earn a brokerage fee for handling the loan. This type of extra service is more commonly found in small communities.

The lines between a broker, a mortgage banker, and a lender are not always clearly drawn, as brokerage service may be handled by any one of them. Brokerage is essentially the service of processing the loan information for the borrower and arranging for a lender to make the loan. Good brokerage work is done by professionals who respect the confidential nature of the information they must obtain and who earn their fees by knowing which lenders are presently seeking certain types of loans.

MORTGAGE BANKERS

The *full-service* facility offered by the mortgage banker today developed from both the need for a new approach after the Depression collapse and from the desire of the Federal Housing Administration to conduct its programs in conjunction with private industry. The economic pressures of 1930–1931 had dried up lendable funds, construction had been halted, and many banks had closed their doors. The shortage of available funds made the mortgage banker an intermediary for the only remaining sources of cash—cash from insurance companies, from a few large savings banks, and from the Federal National Mortgage Association. And the growth of the FHA resulted in the need for more servicing or loan administration by the mortgage bankers. More than half the mortgage companies operating today were founded after World War II, and in the 1950s four-fifths of all federally underwritten loans held by life insurance companies, savings and loans, and FNMA were serviced by mortgage bankers. The upward trend has continued, and if the government ventures further into the field of real estate financing, it undoubtedly will move through the channels that it helped to create—channels that have helped the government programs to succeed, that is, the mortgage banking industry.

THE LOAN PACKAGE

All lenders prepare *loan packages*. A loan package is a collection of the various pieces of information, the legal instruments, and other paperwork needed to evaluate a loan applicant, and if approved, to provide complete documentation for underwriting the loan. Mortgage companies are, perhaps, more adept at assembling this information because they must do so for a variety of lenders with differing requirements. Following is a list of the ordinary requirements that a loan representative for a mortgage company would assemble in the preparation of a home loan package:

Information required on the property

1. Earnest money contract on the sale, which should provide proper legal names of seller and purchaser, legal description of the property, and any special terms.
2. An appraisal by a qualified person.
3. A land survey by a registered surveyor.
4. A title opinion from the attorney for the title company that will issue the title insurance.

Information required on the borrower (mortgagor)

1. Information questionnaire covering legal names, address, children, employment (for both husband and wife), assets and liabilities, and income and expenses (including fixed payments).
2. Verifications of employment.
3. Verifications of assets and debts.
4. Credit report from accepted agency.
5. Letters of explanation if unusual circumstances are involved.

The mortgage company then adds to this assemblage a cover letter or a report (FHA and VA have a special analysis form). The report summarizes pertinent details and includes an analysis of the borrower's income, from which is subtracted calculable living expenses and installment or monthly payments already committed to show the cash available for debt retirement. Lenders each have varying requirements as to how this analysis should be presented, and the mortgage company is expected to know precisely what is needed.

For larger loans, the same general information is required but in much greater depth. Usually this borrower is a corporation or partnership, and the loan package would require complete company information, financial statements, and corporate resolutions, if applicable. If the loan involves a project to be constructed, the package must include complete plans and specifications plus an assurance of the contractor's capability. A completion bond is required of the contractor under FHA procedures but is not always used in conventional financing. There is a growing list of certifications needed, such as the status with labor unions, nondiscrimination pledges, and statements relating to the project's impact on the neighborhood and the environment. Any special participation agreements required by the lender must be worked out in advance of the loan commitment.

A loan package assembled for initial closing under FHA procedure with multifamily projects includes 30 to 40 separate instruments, with all plans and data. Often the loan package is assembled under the guidance of an attorney who specializes in such requirements and can knowledgeably represent the sponsor to the FHA and its attorneys at the closing.

MONEY COMMITMENTS

Without deposit assets, mortgage companies rely on the promises (commitments) of major lenders for funds. These commitments can be made in several different ways. Following is a discussion of each of the principal methods used within the industry to assure loan originators lendable funds.

Forward Loan Commitment (Sales and Servicing Contracts)

Since most mortgage bankers represent various institutional investors, some form of understanding or agreement is used to spell out the terms. Such an agreement between a lender and a mortgage company is called a *sales and servicing contract*. The agreement states the type of loan and conditions under which the lender will accept a loan and also describes the services that must be provided by the mortgage company along with the fees charged for these services.

The lender, by terms of the agreement, offers to provide a specified amount of money to the mortgage company for certain classes of loans at a fixed interest rate. The mortgage company is allowed to charge a service fee for handling collections, providing the escrow services, paying taxes and insurance, and for representing the lender if problems occur during the transaction. This service charge, which varies from one-tenth of 1 percent to one-half of 1 percent of the loan depending on the amount of servicing required, is a direct addition (add-on) to the interest rate. For example, presuming that a lender, such as an eastern savings and loan association, agrees to accept a mortgage company's loan for an interest rate of $13^1/_2$ percent and the mortgage company requires $^3/_8$ percent for servicing the loan, then the quotation submitted by the mortgage company to the borrower would be an interest rate of 13$^7/_8$ percent. In this example, the 13$^1/_2$ percent rate is referred to as *net* to the lender. The lender then sets up a time limit during which the mortgage company may exercise its rights under the commitment, which usually extends from three to six months. This type of commitment can be termed a *forward* commitment, and depending on the relationship between the mortgage company and the lender, it is not unusual for the lender to require a commitment fee.

The commitment fee, when required, is usually 1 percent (or one point) of the total commitment payable upon issuance of the agreement by the lender. Generally this fee is refundable when the commitment is fully used. However, if the mortgage company does not use the full amount of the commitment, it may be required to forfeit a portion of the fee. For example, if a mutual bank makes a $1 million commitment to the M Mortgage Company for four months and the mortgage company deposits $10,000 as a commitment fee, then if at the end of the four-month term, only $750,000 of acceptable loans have been made, the mortgage company may have to forfeit the unfulfilled portion of the fee, or $2500.

Under the forward commitment procedure, a mortgage company may be allowed to submit loans one at a time to the prime lender, but since this is a burdensome procedure, most agreements call for a minimum amount, say $250,000, in a group of loans at any one time. Unless the mortgage company has considerable capital of its own, it will resort to a *warehouse* line of credit with a local commercial bank to carry the loans until the minimum shipping package has been reached.

Immediate Commitments

Another method employed, and one that accounts for the greatest volume of commitment money, is the immediate or direct purchase of loans from the mortgage company by an institutional lender. Under this procedure the mortgage company funds large volumes of loans with its own capital and credit lines and periodically offers the loans in multimillion dollar blocks to the institutional investor. Immediate delivery usually means within 90 days.

A lender with surplus money to invest will tend to accept a lower net interest rate on a large block of loans where it is possible to make an immediate purchase. In this manner the lender's money is earning interest sooner. Under a forward commitment procedure, the lender may be reluctant to tie up money for future months since interest rates may change.

The large blocks of loans available by means of immediate purchase procedures are of great interest to big investors who must move their money in wholesale lots. Most large investors will not undertake a purchase of less than $1 million in loan totals from any single mortgage company.

Mortgage companies are generally able to retain the servicing contracts for residential loans when they are passed on to the institutional lenders regardless of the type of commitment—forward or immediate purchase. The amount of the servicing fee is determined in advance with the forward commitment but can vary somewhat with an immediate purchase commitment. With the latter, the servicing fee to be earned by the mortgage company would amount to whatever the differential is between the interest rate at which the loan was made to the borrower and the net rate acceptable to the secondary lender.

In the large commercial loans, the servicing may be passed on to the secondary lender, or a fee for this service may be negotiated with the mortgage company. While the FHLB has dropped its requirement that a servicing agent be located within 100 miles of the mortgaged property, many major lenders prefer local representation.

Future Commitments

While some of the terms used to describe the various types of money commitments are not always consistent in various parts of the country, probably the most confusing is the difference between a forward commitment and a future commitment. The *forward* commitment as described in the preceding section states a maximum amount for the commitment, then provides for the use, or withdrawal, of that money *during the term* of the commitment. The *future* commitment is a pledge of money, all of which will be made available at a *later specified date*. The future commitment may use terminology such as "on or before July 31, 19—" or "not before 18 months nor later than 24 months from the date of this commitment agreement." It is the future commitment that is used in making a permanent loan for a building yet to be constructed.

Delivery of the mortgage under a future commitment may, or may not, be mandatory. If delivery of the mortgage is not mandatory, the holder of the commitment may find a lower cost source of money for the permanent loan elsewhere and simply forfeit the commitment fee.

A future commitment almost always costs a nonrefundable commitment fee, which is negotiable. Normally it will be one to two points. The reason for the fee is that the lender is agreeing to have money available for a loan, perhaps one or two years from the date of commitment, and usually at a fixed rate of interest. The lender feels entitled to a fee for this promise to deliver. As interest rates have become more volatile, future commitments are tending to be tied to a leading indicator of the capital market rather than held to a fixed rate.

It might be well to recall here that the long-term capital market fluctuates far more slowly than the short-term money market. The long-term investor is more interested in the *average* return on the total investments and thus can accept periodically small increases and decreases from new investments. The movement of rates, upward or downward, affects only a small portion of the overall portfolio at any one time. These investments over or under the average return are the *marginal* investments.

Take-Out or Stand-By Commitments

A take-out or stand-by commitment is actually a backup promise to make a loan. It is more popular in periods of tight money and can be applied to any kind of loan on a projected building, residential property, or income property. It is a commitment that is really not intended to be utilized but is available if needed.

To exemplify a take-out commitment in operation, let us assume that a builder wants to construct an apartment complex. But the money situation is tight, and the city already has too many apartment units with a decreasing occupancy rate. Let us also assume that the major lenders have withdrawn from further apartment loans for the time being. However, the builder owns a piece of land in an area of the city that is growing and shows a real need for more apartment units. In such a case the builder might seek stand-by financing in the form of a take-out commitment from a mortgage company, a real estate investment trust, or another type of lender. A take-out commitment is issued at a higher than market interest rate and lasts for a longer term than the average construction loan commitment. The builder may be allowed three to five years to exercise the rights. To obtain this type of commitment, the builder must pay from two to four points in cash at the time the commitment letter is issued. This assurance of a permanent loan, even though it is at uneconomical rates, is used as a backup to obtain a construction loan.

The real idea of the take-out commitment is to enable a builder to proceed with the construction of a building, allowing perhaps a year to achieve good occupancy, and with a proven income, then obtain a more reasonable permanent loan and simply drop the higher cost take-out commitment. The builder would, of course, forfeit the initial commitment fee. The idea has worked well when everything has clicked and the market analysis has proved accurate. It has also caused some disasters when it hasn't worked.

The idea of take-out commitments has moved into the field of house construction loans as a better protection to the construction lender than a speculative house loan. A commitment for residential house loans would be made at 80 percent of the appraised value of the finished house (usually the same amount as the construction loan itself), to be exercised within one year and at a cost of one point, payable when issued. Sometimes the mortgage company that issues the take-out will allow a portion of the commitment fee to be applied to the origination fee if the mortgage company also handles the home buyer's permanent loan. Unlike a take-out commitment for a commercial project, the take-out on a house loan is used by the issuing mortgage company to help secure the *permanent* loan when the house is sold. The borrower then would be the new house buyer.

Permanent Loan

The permanent loan is the final mortgage loan with repayment extended over many years. It can be made from a future commitment or an immediate one. Conventional loans are made for a period of time extending to 30 years, while some federally underwritten loans extend to up to 40 years.

Commercial projects should have a permanent loan assured (or a valid take-out loan commitment) before a construction loan will be released. The construction lender wants to know how he or she will be repaid when the building is completed. Only a few builders are financially strong enough to give this assurance without a loan commitment to support them. If a builder is capable of handling the construction costs with personal resources, it is far easier to obtain permanent financing upon completion of the project when the building can be inspected and the income potential more easily ascertained. Such a strong builder would also save paying the commitment fee that would be necessary if the permanent financing were handled as a future commitment rather than immediate.

The permanent loan for a single-family residence is made to the buyer. It may be in the form of a future commitment made prior to actual construction, or more commonly, in the form of an immediate commitment for an existing house.

WAREHOUSING OF MORTGAGE LOANS

In order to accumulate the volume of mortgages needed to satisfy a sales and service contract or to work with immediate sales of blocks of mortgage loans, the mortgagee (mortgage company) must use its own cash to make the initial funding of a loan at closing. Or, as most mortgage companies do, it borrows short-term money at a local commercial bank to provide the cash.

Warehouse lines are established by mortgage companies on a fully secured basis; that is, each loan advanced by the commercial bank is secured by a note and mortgage assigned to the bank by the mortgage company.

While the credit-worthiness and capabilities of the mortgage banking company will have been fully cleared by the commercial bank before a line of credit is established, there is still a concern as to what will become of the accumulated loans as interest rates fluctuate. If the commercial bank accepts, for example, $1 million in home loans, which were made at a 14 percent interest rate, and the rate then begins to climb upward to 15 percent, can the loans be sold without a loss? The answer, of course, is negative unless the loans have previously been committed at a price to yield 14 percent.

Under these conditions, small mortgage companies seek to protect themselves and their warehouse line with a forward commitment; that is, a sales and service contract with a major lender or, perhaps, an FNMA commitment. As discussed earlier in this chapter, the commitment by a permanent lending source to accept a fixed amount of certain types of loans over a period of four to six months not only assures the mortgage company of its sale of loans but provides assurance to the commercial bank that the loans in warehouse will be liquidated at an established price.

It is by means of this assurance to small mortgage companies, and to some of the giants, that the Federal National Mortgage Association has played such a dramatic role. If a small mortgage company is simply unable to find any lenders willing to furnish a forward commitment because they themselves are short of cash, the mortgage company can then turn to FNMA and acquire, for example, a $200,000 commitment under the free market system procedure by making a noncompetitive offering and accepting the weighted average yield.

The large mortgage companies are capable of playing a different game with their warehouse lines. In the multimillion dollar business of handling large blocks of residential loans and some commercial loans, the commercial banks know that their large mortgage company customers are quite capable of selling big blocks of loans and absorbing substantial losses, if necessary, in an adverse market. Medium to large mortgage companies may have lines of credit at one or more banks totaling from $10 million to $100 million. As the mortgage company makes loans each day and places them in the warehouse line, one or more of the company's officers will be watching the secondary market and discussing possible loan sales with the larger lenders. This procedure is somewhat like a speculation game, for when the market is right the mortgage company may sell off $10 or $20 million in loans at a price that provides a slight additional profit to the mortgage company. In these large volumes, a very slight movement of loan prices has a tremendous effect on the gain (or loss) on the sale.

In view of all this shifting around of the actual note and mortgage, what happens then to the people who borrowed the money to buy a house? They are relatively unaffected and, in most cases, do not know about the movement of the note. This is because the responsibility for the proper servicing of the loan is normally held by the originator of the loan who handles the collections and escrows the necessary tax and insurance money as an agent for the holder of the note. The originator earns a service fee for this work and provides a continuity to the borrower who continues to make monthly payments to the same office.

9

Other Sources for Loans

The regulated and unregulated lenders discussed in the previous two chapters are the obvious sources of money. They are visible to the general public and making loans is their business. However, there are a number of other, less well-known sources of loan money that need to be sought out. There are, for example, fraternal organizations, endowment funds, pension and trust funds, and religious groups in every community that do make loans, even though lending is not their purpose for existence. Primarily these organizations exist for the protection of a body of assets and are not pressed to earn top dollar on an investment. Many do make mortgage loans, perhaps only to members or maybe at no greater than a 75 percent loan to value ratio; but they are worth exploring. This chapter discusses a number of these other sources of loan money.

Fraternal Organizations

A number of brotherhood- and sisterhood-type organizations have long offered to their members some form of insurance coverage. Over the years their pool of assets has grown, and many no longer confine their loan activity to members only. If you do happen to belong to such an organization, find out about its lending policies. If not, explore the local phone directory and contact your friends for information on which groups are active in your community.

Religious Groups

Individual churches are not a practical source of mortgage funds: most all have a greater need *for* money. However, the general assembly of a group of churches, a state organization, or a national administrative body may very well have money to lend. Most such groups assess their local church membership to build funds that satisfy long-term goals; that is, to acquire land for future expansion or to help build or renovate member churches. All have established pension and retirement funds for their ministers. Further, such organizations often have personnel who are knowledgeable in the area of land transactions. Mortgage loans represent good security for their assets in a familiar field. It is true that more favorable consideration might be given to a substantial contributor to the church, but this need not always be the case. Of prime importance to the administration of any pension or trust fund is the protection of its assets and not the highest market yields.

Union Pension Funds

The inherent interest of many unions in the betterment of their members has led a few into the business of providing home purchase loans at less than market rates from their pension funds. Such loans give good security, a reasonable return to the fund, and a lot of help to the beneficiaries. An examination of the union you may belong to or questions about activities of these organizations in your local area can prove advantageous.

Local Government Pension Funds

For reasons similar to those discussed with respect to union pension funds, some government pension funds are now making lower cost loans to help people buy homes. Government pension funds are less likely to limit applicants to their own members than are union funds, but this could be a restriction. Another point to remember is that these loans are not always made for a full 30-year term. The term may be shortened to, say, 10 years, but the amortization is allowed as a 30-year loan. Also, these lenders may offer a lower interest rate for a limited span of years, say, 5 or 7 years, then offer an adjusted interest rate that reflects the movement of a national interest rate index. The primary purpose of this type of lender is to assist a home buyer in a very difficult market time. They are not engaged in big time mortgage lending.

Title Companies

Because of their close association with the real estate industry and their considerable knowledge of the field, some title companies have developed direct loan departments or subsidiary companies that handle loans. These affiliated companies act both as primary sources in lending their own funds or those raised from the sale of mortgage bonds and as correspondents or agents for other major lenders.

Endowment Funds, Universities, Colleges, Hospitals

As a group, endowment funds prefer to maintain their assets in high-grade stocks and bonds that have a good record for security, are considered to be more liquid, and, most important, require less administrative attention than a portfolio of mortgage loans. However, many endowments are passed on in the form of land and other real property, and these have required more expertise in the mortgage loan field. The endowment funds can and do assist in the development of their own land by experienced developers, and they are increasing their activities in mortgage lending with such encouragements as the GNMA mortgage-backed security.

Foundations

Foundations have been established primarily by corporations or by wealthy families as a means of continuing charitable or other purposes through the use of income earned from the foundations' investments. The attitude of foundations toward mortgage lending is somewhat similar to that of the endowment funds. They are primarily interested in investing in high-grade stocks and bonds but are not adverse to mortgage loans, particularly if a purpose of special interest to the foundation can be served.

Foundations have been under substantial legal attack as to their tax obligations and sometimes for the controversial use of their tax-free funds. However, they do represent a limited pool of investment capital that can be used in the mortgage market.

Individuals and Others

Statistically, "individuals and others" hold about 13 percent of all mortgage debt in this country. This statistic, as compiled by the Federal Reserve, encompasses mortgage companies, real estate investment trusts, state and local credit agencies, and credit unions in addition to in-dividuals.* The actual dollar amount of mortgages in the hands of in-dividuals cannot be accurately determined as there is no reporting procedure for this type of loan. However, financing by individuals as a necessary help in order to sell a property has become increasingly impor-tant. Methods used to encourage an owner to accept a note in lieu of cash in order to close a sale is high on the list of creative financing procedures. For the real estate investor, owner financing can result in lower finance costs and easier qualification procedures. Care must be taken with such financing, however, as initial payment requirements can be deceptively low; for example, only interest payments may be required for the first year, but then the principal balance may be due within a year or two. In-dividuals do not look with favor on long-term loans when the motivation is the sale of a property.

Real Estate Investment Trusts (REITs)

A relatively new source of mortgage money was encouraged in 1960 when Congress passed the Real Estate Investment Trust Act. The pur-pose of the Act was to provide more capital to satisfy the growing demand for long-term investment money by opening the field to the individual small investor. In order to encourage a person to buy stock in a corporation that qualified itself as a real estate investment trust, Con-gress exempted the trust from income taxes, provided that at least 90 per-cent of the profit is distributed each year as dividends. Also, the income must be derived from real property investments to qualify for the tax ex-emption. However, the dividends are taxable to the investor.

The idea was not enthusiastically received at first, but by 1970 many investment trust issues were placed on the market and sold very well. The trusts are formed primarily by leading banks and insurance companies, and many are traded on the nation's stock exchanges. A few of the well-known companies operating in this field are Massachusetts Mutual Mortgage, Northwestern Mutual Life Mortgage, Bank American Realty, Equitable Life Mortgage, MONY Mortgage, Mortgage Trust of America, and many others.

Most of the trusts are controlled by a board of trustees responsible for the integrity of the fund. Actual management of the investment port-folio is contracted to a professional money management team. The management company is paid a fee for its services, usually about 1 per-cent of the total assets per year. The managers are all experienced lending officers who have worked with or are well-known to the sponsoring bank or insurance company.

---

*Federal Reserve Bulletin, "Mortgage Debt Outstanding" A39.

Two basic types of REITs have developed—equity and mortgage. The original purpose of Congress was to encourage investment in the real estate field as owners and operators of income properties. The profit of equity REITs was derived mostly from the operation of income-producing properties they would buy. In the late 1960s, a newer concept developed known as the mortgage type. These newer trusts specialized in the financing of properties and made their profits from the interest income on their mortgages. They operated under the same tax incentives as the equity type.

It was the mortgage type of REIT that created the surge in popularity between 1969 and 1971. Underwriters encouraged banks and insurance companies to establish the trusts because the shares could be easily sold and produced good underwriting fees. Loans were easy to make in the real estate boom period of the early 1970s. The REITs borrowed heavily from banks and other lenders to support their demand for more money to lend to construction and development projects. Developers often found a source of mortgage money plus a partner in the REITs to build apartments, office buildings, and shopping centers. Between 1969 and 1973, the relatively new industry increased its assets from about $1 billion to nearly $20 billion.

Serious problems began to surface by 1974 after the bank prime rate had soared past 12 percent and some construction loans on large projects were reaching 18 percent interest rates. The unanticipated high interest costs faced by many of the builders (most construction loans pay interest rates that float from one to six points over the prime rate) consumed the construction money before the projects could be completed, and many failures resulted. By 1975 some of the largest REITs in the country were reporting as much as 25 percent of their loans "not accruing interest." (This is a more optimistic way of describing loans in default.) The sagging record forced REIT stock prices down to less than book value in some cases and destroyed the market for any new issues. At the same time, major lenders were withdrawing their support for the REITs, and many of them faced the same bankruptcy procedures that their builders had faced earlier.

Only a few of the REITs have actually been forced out of business, more have sought mergers with larger REITs, but most of them have survived the shakeout because they became the equity owners of properties forced into foreclosure, and those properties recovered value in the reviving market. The original purpose is still sound—to provide capital for real estate projects and to enable the small investor to participate in large, well-managed projects. Those REITs that became too heavily involved in mortgage loans were often forced into an equity position. But it may be a long time before REITs can again sell new stock issues to raise additional capital.

Commercial Credit Companies

One of the newest entrants into the field of mortgage lending is the commercial credit company. For many years such companies as Consumer Credit Corporation, a subsidiary of Data Resources, and Household Finance Company have made primarily small consumer loans, both secured and unsecured. The security may have been furniture or appliances. With the change in the bankruptcy laws in 1979, it became much easier for a person to declare bankruptcy and still retain a substantial portion of his or her assets. Small consumer loans suffered some major setbacks. One result has been that companies engaged in the business began demanding additional collateral for loans, usually a pledge of real estate. Thus, second mortgage loans on home equities grew, and consumer finance companies gained expertise in mortgage lending.

The next step—making first mortgage loans—was easy. Consumer credit has never been "low cost"; that is, it usually carries add-on–type interest. So the entry of these companies into mortgage lending will not bring any cost advantage to borrowers. They will simply be one more potential source for a loan. Funding of these loans is expected to be accomplished through the sale of mortgage-backed securities.

Credit Unions

Many credit unions have long had the authority to make intermediate-term mortgage loans for periods of up to ten or twelve years. A big change occurred in the competitive position of credit unions with regard to long-term mortgage loans when Congress passed a law in 1977 authorizing federally chartered credit unions to make first mortgage loans with up to 30-year terms. In 1978, the National Credit Union Administration (NCUA) implemented the law and further authorized federally chartered unions to sell their loans in the secondary market. In order to qualify for making the 30-year loans, federally chartered unions must show a minimum of $2 million in assets. Many state-chartered credit unions have benefited from policies of expanded state lending authority based on the federal requirements.

Credit unions are restricted to making loans only to their own members. And because of the more complex nature of a mortgage loan (as compared, say, with a car loan), the lack of experienced personnel within credit unions has hampered growth. However, the larger unions are capable of maintaining trained personnel in this field and should now be able to offer full-service residential mortgage loans.

10

Costs of Borrowed Money

FINANCING CHARGES

There may have been a day when the cost of borrowed money could be defined with the simple word *interest*. Unfortunately, this is no longer true; interest is just one of the charges to be considered, albeit, the largest one. Almost all loans today are funded at a discount; that is, the amount funded at closing is less than the face amount shown on the note, which can result in a substantial increase in money costs. In addition, obtaining a real estate loan can involve a number of fees or charges in addition to the basic cost of interest and discount: some are in payment of services rendered in processing the loan, and others are simply a method of increasing the return for the lender. An application fee, for example, is almost always charged, but a warehouse fee may or may not be collected. Some fees, like a commitment fee, are subject to negotiation while others, like an origination fee, are charged at the same rate to all applicants. The real estate investor should be able to distinguish the various fees that are involved. Following is a discussion of the additional fees that may be encountered in financing a real estate investment.

Application Charges

A nonrefundable *application charge* is standard practice among lenders who handle residential loans. This charge covers the cost of a credit report, a property appraisal, and the time spent reviewing the application itself. With commercial- or investment-type loans, the procedure varies with the applicant, the loan, and the lender. Most commonly, the lender imposes a nominal charge to help offset the cost of reviewing an application and to discourage frivolous and repeat applications. With a commercial loan application, the applicant is expected not only to pay an application fee, but also to furnish a property appraisal, pay for a credit report, and supply such additional information as the lender may request.

Commitment Fees

A *commitment fee* is a one-time charge made by a lender. In return, the lender promises to fund a loan at a future date. A commitment fee is most commonly assessed when a permanent loan will be funded at the completion of construction. A commitment agreement normally takes the form of a letter from the lender which, when signed by the borrower and returned with the commitment fee, becomes a binding promise for a loan at a specified future date. Commitment fees are generally from 1 percent to 2 percent of the loan amount.

The value of a permanent loan commitment to an investment builder is such that some mortgage lenders will offer *standby* commitments to assist in obtaining a construction loan. This form of commitment normally calls for a higher-than-market interest rate, a shorter-than-normal term, and two to four points in commitment fees. (A *point* is 1 percent of the loan amount.) It *is* a bona fide loan commitment, but intended, as its name implies, to be used as a backup or standby promise, enabling a builder to first complete construction of a project and then obtain a more favorable loan commitment.

Origination Fees

An *origination fee* is a mortgage lender's charge for processing a mortgage loan. It may also be called a *brokerage fee* or *finance fee*. This charge averages between 1 percent and 2 percent of the loan amount. Usually a portion of this fee is paid to the mortgage company's loan representative as a form of commission for the work involved in preparing the loan application and obtaining all required information.

Finance Charges

There are a number of ways for a lender to increase his yield from a loan. The nomenclature varies—some lenders are more imaginative than others! Whatever you call it, however, the bottom line is that this fee is designed not to compensate for a service, but rather to increase the yield from a loan. Following are some examples:

- *Funding fee.* At the time a loan is funded, the lender may assess a fee which is simply deducted from the loan's proceeds.
- *Renewal fee.* When a borrower asks to renew a mortgage note for an additional term, the lender may demand a renewal fee, usually one point. This kind of fee is commonly found in construction loans to small home builders. If the six-month term for a house construction loan is not sufficient to complete construction and sell the house, the builder-borrower may obtain an extension of time and pay a renewal fee.
- *Assumption fee.* When a new owner assumes an existing mortgage loan, the lender incurs some additional expense in reviewing and approving the assumption agreement. Hence, an additional fee is justified. Many lenders also reserve the right to increase the interest rate when a loan is assumed.
- *Warehousing fee.* When a mortgage company borrows money from a commercial bank to fund loans at closing, the interest paid is usually prime rate or a float at one or two points over prime. In years past, the prime rate normally remained at something less than the rate charged for mortgage loans. This is no longer "normal" as prime has frequently escalated to higher rates than mortgages. When this occurs, mortgage companies are faced with an additional cost while a mortgage loan is held in *warehouse*; that is, held as collateral by the commercial bank pending sale to a secondary market purchaser. To offset this cost, mortgage companies are adding a warehouse fee, which normally amounts to $1/4$ to $1/2$ percent of the loan amount.

INTEREST AND DISCOUNT

Real estate investments are usually financed with the help of mortgage loans. In addition to the one-time commitment fees and finance charges discussed in the preceding section, the continuing cost of borrowed money includes both interest and a one-time charge for a discount (if applicable). First, we look at interest rates, then, at the loan discount.

Interest rates are fairly simply by themselves—a fixed percentage of the loan amount becomes due on specified dates. It is the method of calculating interest rates that creates complications. Two basic kinds of interest rates are used in finance:

- *Simple interest* is based on a fixed rate, or percentage, of the loan amount, calculated on an annual basis. For example, 9 percent per annum translates to $90 each year for each $1,000 of the loan amount.
- *Compound interest* is a procedure whereby, at specified intervals ranging from one day to one year, the earned interest is added to, or compounded with, the principal. The added interest then earns additional interest. Compound interest is most often associated with the payment for a savings account. More recently, it has become a necessary part of the interest calculated when graduated payment, or variable rate mortgages, produce negative amortization. With these mortgage payment methods, the monthly payment may be insufficient to pay all of the interest due. So the unpaid interest is added to the principal balance, requiring the borrower to pay interest on the unpaid interest.

Mortgage Loan Amortization

The amortization of a mortgage loan is normally calculated as a fixed monthly payment for a specified number of years. This fixed payment system calculates the interest charge for one full year on the outstanding loan amount at the beginning of the year, then divides that interest into 12 payments, adding sufficient payment against principal to pay off the loan by the end of the loan term.

EXAMPLE

$1,000 loan at 11% per annum, payable monthly over 30 years. Monthly payment is $9.52 (from amortization tables).

First year calculations	
Annual payments—12 × $9.52	$ 114.24
Less: Interest charge—11% of $1,000.00	− 110.00
Paid on principal balance	$ 4.24
At the end of first year— Principal due $1,000.00—$4.24	$ 995.76

Second year calculations	
Annual payments—12 × $9.52	$ 114.24
Less: Interest charge—11% of $995.76	− 109.53
Paid on principal balance	$ 4.71
At end of second year—	
Principal due $995.76 − $4.71	$ 991.05

The principal due at the end of each year can be readily converted to a percentage figure with the information found in a "Remaining Balance Table." Using the figures above, the principal due at the end of the first year is $995.76, or 99.58% of the original loan amount. At the end of the second year, the $991.05 principal due converts to a remaining balance equal to 99.11% of the original loan amount.

Another, and more accurate, method of calculating the amortization (reduction in principal balance) of a mortgage loan is to amortize monthly.

Interest Cost on Long-Term Loans

The interest cost of a long-term mortgage loan is calculated no differently from that of a short-term loan if both are using simple interest computations. The mortgage loan's large amount and longer repayment term create an impression of excessive interest cost. However, that impression is not precisely accurate as can be seen in the following example.

EXAMPLE

Interest cost for a small loan of $1,000 for 10 years at an 11% simple interest rate:

Monthly payment: $13.78 × 120 months	$1,653.60
Less: Amount of original loan	− 1,000.00
Interest cost over 10-year term	$653.60

Interest cost for a mortgage loan of $40,000 for 30 years at an 11% simple interest rate:

Monthly payment (P & I): $380.93 × 360 months	$137,135
Less: Amount of original loan	− 40,000
Interest cost over 30-year term	$ 97,135

While the interest rates are exactly the same, the shorter term loan shows a much lower interest cost as a percentage of the loan amount.

This is due to the term of the loan, not the way the interest is computed.

> Interest cost for the short-term loan:
> $653.60 divided by $1,000 = 65.36%
> Interest cost for the long-term loan:
> $97,135 divided by $40,000 = 242.84%

Daily Interest Calculation

A few types of mortgage loans, principally construction loans and warehouse credit lines (extended to mortgage companies by commercial banks), often use an annual interest rate reduced to a daily charge. Even this calculation can be made in two ways:

1. *360-day year.* Almost all institutional lenders calculate the daily rate based on a 360-day year.

$$\$1,000,000 \text{ at } 9\% \text{ per annum} = \$90,000$$
$$\frac{\$90,000}{360} = \$250 \text{ daily interest cost}$$

2. *365-day year.* Federal agencies and a few institutional lenders calculate the daily rate based on a 365-day year.

$$\frac{\$90,000}{365} = \$246.57 \text{ daily interest cost}$$

Obviously the difference per day is not a significant item in smaller loans, but it can become a substantial amount of money if the calculations concern multimillion dollar construction loans!

There's one more point to remember when dealing with interest costs calculated daily: the lender expects to be paid for the day the money is advanced *and* the day the loan is paid off. For example, when a construction loan is paid off through the funding of a permanent loan, the borrower must almost always pay interest to *both* lenders for the day of refinancing. An exception is the case where one lender makes both loans.

Installment Loans

While most mortgage loans are paid off in monthly *installments*, this nomenclature is usually used to describe short-term personal loans, such as loans for furniture or a car. For an installment loan, a bank may use a simple interest calculation, as previously described. More commonly, banks use the *add-on* procedure.

Add-on calculation

For a $5,000 car loan, the lender may use an interest charge of 8 percent for a term of three years:

$$\$5,000 \times .08 = \$400.00 \times 3 \text{ years} = \$1,200$$

Principal due	$5,000
Interest due	1,200
Amount of note due	$6,200

$$\text{Monthly payment } \frac{\$6,200}{36} = \$172.22$$

The truth-in-lending laws (regulation Z of the Federal Reserve Bank) require that the lender specify the exact financing cost that is being charged to the borrower, which, in this example, would be 14.55 percent,* considerably more than the 8 percent used in the calculations.

This example describes a car loan. But the same procedure is often used in short-term mortgage loans of second- or third-lien stature. Home improvement loans may also use the add-on procedure for calculating interest.

Rule of 78

When an installment loan is paid off prematurely, the calculation of *interest due* is not always based on simple interest earned as of the date of payoff. Many installment loan agreements provide that the loan may be paid off at any time during its term, with interest calculated in accordance with the *Rule of 78*—but the mathematics are not detailed in the agreement. Lenders may describe the procedure as a method of rebating unearned interest on an installment loan.

The following schedule details the *Rule of 78* method of calculating the premature payoff of a 12-month installment loan for $1,000 at 8 percent interest, or $80.00 interest per annum.

Truth-in-Lending Tables, Financial Publishing Co., Boston, Mass.

Months		Interest Due for Each Month or Part Thereof	
12	1st month	12/78 × $80	$12.31
11	2nd month	11/78 × $80	$11.28
10	3rd month	10/78 × $80	$10.26
9	4th month	9/78 × $80	$ 9.23
8	5th month	8/78 × $80	$ 8.20
7	6th month	7/78 × $80	$ 7.18
6	7th month	6/78 × $80	$ 6.15
5	8th month	5/78 × $80	$ 5.13
4	9th month	4/78 × $80	$ 4.10
3	10th month	3/78 × $80	$ 3.08
2	11th month	2/78 × $80	$ 2.05
1	12th month	1/78 × $80	$ 1.03
78			$80.00

Note: Interest accrues on the first of each month, not at the end of the month. In the above example, if the loan is paid off *during* the second month, interest due would be: $12.31 + $11.28 = $23.59.

Interest Paid on Savings Accounts

Since the Depression years, government regulations have set a maximum limit on the interest rate that can be paid by regulated lenders to their savings account customers (Federal Reserve Regulation Q). These interest rate controls are being phased out and are scheduled for elimination by 1986.

The interest rate has been so uniform and widely accepted that little thought is given to how the interest is actually paid by the lender. Recent studies have found a wide disparity in these calculations. Following are the major conditions that create these variations:

- *Date of deposit.* Lenders may decide to pay interest from the first day of deposit, from the first quarter of the next month, or the first of the next quarter. So variations in the date a lender commences the payment of interest should be examined.
- *Date of withdrawal.* A similar disparity exists in how the time span for actually earning interest is measured by the institution. The investor should find out how the withdrawal date affects the interest paid. Is the period for computing interest paid figured to the date of withdrawal, or was it concluded at the end of a previous month?
- *Amount on deposit.* Does the lender pay interest on the daily balance, the minimum balance during the month, or minimum balance during the quarter?

The most beneficial method of calculation for the depositor is one that pays interest each day on that day's balance. Some lenders follow this plan, plus compounding the interest each day; while others stick with a quarterly payment of interest. In years past, a daily calculation would have been impractical, but with today's computer technology, it is no longer a problem. The disparity mentioned here exists mostly with passbook savings accounts—savings certificates are much more clearly defined as to time span and deposit amount.

Loan Discount

A *loan discount* is a reduction from the face amount of a note retained by the lender at the time of funding the loan. It is measured in points—again, one point equals 1 percent of the loan amount. It is another cost of borrowed funds.

The purpose of a discount—like that of interest—is to provide a yield for the lender. But a discount is a one-time charge and to convert this into an annual percentage amount requires a time span—a number of years—before the loan is paid off. Since most long-term mortgage loans are paid off prior to the full term, lenders generally consider 12 years as a standard to calculate the yield provided by a discount.

Discounting has long been used in the securities market. The purpose there is to adjust the yield on fixed-interest bond issues so that they can be bought and sold in the open market. With the exception of FHA and VA loans, a national market for mortage loans is a fairly recent development. Since the early 1950s, the fixed-interest FHA-VA loans have been discounted to adjust their yields to prevailing market rates. As trading in existing mortgage loans expanded between lenders (called the *secondary market*), conventional loans were added to the market along with FHA and VA loans, and the use of discounting increased.

Neither mortgage loans nor bonds are always discounted. If the interest rates called for on the mortgage notes or bonds are higher than current market rates, the loan may well be sold at a premium, that is, for more than face value. For the real estate investor, there are no premium payments. The real estate investor is a borrower of mortgage money, not a purchaser of mortgage loans.

Because it is the combination of discount and interest rate that determines the lender's yield, the borrower may elect (1) to pay more in discount points to obtain a lower interest rate or (2) to secure a lower—or no—discount by accepting a higher interest rate.

Continuing inflation has begun to affect the relative use of loan discounts versus interest rates. Inflation adds to the cost of money as well as of commodities. The problem arises in states where usury limits are being approached or surpassed by current market interest rates, since these laws *do* consider a discount as part of the cost of borrowed money.* The current interpretation of the laws, however, *does* permit the lender to spread the discount over the full term of the loan. Thus, a one-point discount on a 30-year loan would increase by .033 percent the interest cost subject to usury laws.

$$\frac{1.0\%}{30} = .03333\%$$

The lender's use of larger discounts designed to increase his yield without violating usury limits is more advantageous in 30-year residential loans (normally paid off in 10 years or less) than in shorter term commercial loans (often held for the full term of the loan).

---

*NOTE: State usury ceilings on most first mortgage residential loans were preempted by Act of Congress in 1980.

11

Loan Repayment Methods

The stable pattern of fixed interest rates and constant-level mortgage payments began to deteriorate in the mid-1970s. Two basic problems faced the lending industry and its regulators. One was to provide a better means for lending institutions to compete for loanable funds against other higher interest-yielding investments. The other problem, really brought on by the first, was the inability of first-time home buyers to enter the housing market with its ever higher monthly payment requirements. To solve these problems a way was needed to change mortgage loan repayment procedures.

NEW MORTGAGE PAYMENT PLANS

While the fully amortized mortgage loan with constant-level payments is still widely used for both residential and commercial loans, many new procedures are being adopted. Some are intended to benefit the lender coping with the unstable and escalating cost of funds; others are designed to benefit the borrower by permitting lower monthly payments in the early years of loan repayment. First, we will examine procedures that stem from the method of amortization—variations that have long been used in mortgage loans. Following this, the major new mortgage designs will be considered which include adjustable (or variable) interest rates, graduated payment plans, and shared appreciation methods. To better understand the explanations, we should review some basic terminology. *Term* means the length of time over which there remains an outstanding balance on the loan. *Maturity* is that point in time when the loan must be paid in full. *Amortization* is the periodic repayment of the principal balance, plus interest as it comes due. Three general forms of amortization are described briefly. The partially amortized mortgage loan is then discussed more fully.

1. *Straight mortgage loan.* Only interest is paid over the term, with the entire principal amount due at maturity.
2. *Fully amortized mortgage loan.* Periodic equal payments (usually monthly) include principal and interest computed so that the loan is fully paid at maturity.
3. *Partially amortized mortgage loan.* Periodic payments are not sufficient to completely amortize the loan by maturity, requiring a lump sum payment (often called a *balloon* payment) at maturity to complete repayment of the principal.

PARTIALLY AMORTIZED MORTGAGE LOANS

Balloon Notes

A note that calls for a partial reduction or no reduction of the principal amount during the term of the loan, with the remaining balance due in full at maturity, is called a *balloon note.* This procedure has two basic purposes:

1. The *borrower* is allowed to make smaller payments in the early months or years of the term and then repay the balance at a later date when his income has increased or his asset value has expanded to permit a more profitable liquidation.
2. The *lender* may classify the balloon note as a short-term loan if the balance becomes due in three years or less. It is sometimes assumed that if the borrower makes timely payments on the note during the term of the loan, then the lender will allow a renewal of payments at the time the loan matures. This procedure is often followed, but the lender is under no obligation to renew, regardless of a good payment record.

Interest-Only Agreements

Another form of balloon note permits repayment of only interest in the early years of the mortgage term. After several periods of interest payments, the principal becomes due. This is also called a *straight mortgage loan*. The principal may become due in full at the end of the interest payment term. Or, a second series of payments may be expected, this time covering both principal and interest. This form of financing has a special appeal for land speculators purchasing undeveloped property for a quick turnover. The low cash requirements for the first few payment periods are tax-deductible interest. And if the property can be resold before the principal payment falls due, the profit margin is escalated because of the small amount of cash required for the original purchase. For the seller, such a sale produces an immediate income of interest payments on what might not otherwise have been a revenue-producing asset. Furthermore, the interest is generally close to the market rate and is based on a top price for the land. Should the buyer fail to make the payments, the seller would repossess the property (assuming the seller has retained a mortgage for security), thereby earning some interest along with any forfeiture of down payment.

Amortization Schedule Longer Than Loan Term

Another procedure that can create a partially amortized loan has long been used with commercial loans. The lender offers a loan term of, say, 10 years, but allows payments to be made based on a 30-year amortization schedule. At the end of 10 years, the principal balance due is still close to 90 percent of the original loan amount. The agreement may provide for a renewal for another term at an increased payment rate, or the loan may become payable in full. The loan term and the amortization schedule used are subject to negotiation between the lender and the borrower, and any number of mutually beneficial arrangements are possible.

The market for long-term loans of all kinds has been declining as uncertainty has increased in financial markets. So it is probable that shorter term loans will be more popular (at least with lenders), and longer term amortization schedules will be used to help reduce the repayment impact on the borrower.

NEW MORTGAGE DESIGNS

In an effort to cope with fluctuating and ever higher interest rates, the banking system regulators have been approving new mortgage designs. The private lending institutions have added their own ideas for payment plans to best protect their own earnings margins and at the same time have a marketable mortgage instrument. The result has been a proliferation of mortgage designs that has brought considerable confusion into the field. During 1981, the secondary market purchasers of mortgage loans introduced an adjustable rate mortgage plan that affects all residential loans. *Secondary market* in this instance means principally the large mortgage purchasers: the Federal National Mortgage Association and the Federal Home Loan Mortgage Corporation. What these two purchasers decide to accept for loan commitments at their various auctions becomes something of a standard for all residential loans. These standards do not apply, however, to commercial loans.

In order to better understand how mortgage loans can be designed to allow an adjustment in the interest rate during the term of the loan, or graduated payments in the early years, or even combinations of the two, the following discussion will cover the essential mortgage provisions.

Adjustable Rate Mortgages

The removal of interest rate ceilings on passbook savings accounts over the past few years, plus the effects of inflation on lender's expectations, has brought about a need for greater flexibility in the earnings side of loan portfolios. Lenders have responded with a number of methods that result in a better match between the lenders' cost of funds and their income from the investment of those funds. The regulations that limit what a lender may offer come from both federal and state agencies—and they differ considerably. For the most part, the lending institutions are limited to rules that apply to first mortgage residential loans. Greater flexibility is allowed for commercial loans. The investor should understand the basic procedures used, any of which may be incorporated in the commercial loan instrument.

The tools used to bring about interest rate adjustments are discussed next.

Term of the Loan.   The term of the loan may be for a long period, say 30 years, and it may provide for periodic interest rate adjustments at predetermined intervals during the term of the loan. The alternative method is to offer a short-term loan, say 3 to 5 years, and then offer to renew the note or ask the borrower to pay it off in full. The renewal of an existing note allows the lender to set a new interest rate at whatever the current market might be at the time of renewal. After all, it is a new note and not subject to renewal except at the option of the lender. If the short-term loan carries with it some obligation on the part of the lender to renew the note, it may be called a *rollover* mortgage. In such a case, the note is normally renewed using a predetermined interest rate index to arrive at the new rate. If the lender is obligated to renew a note, there is also an obligation to disclose the index to be used for establishing the new interest rate. The short-term loan, when renewed, carries with it some legal problems as to the need for a title insurance endorsement and the submittal of a new truth-in-lending statement to the borrower. These questions generally do not arise with the long-term loan that is subject to periodic interest rate adjustment. Under the latter procedure, the lender is considered to have an obligation to continue the loan (it is not being renewed, only the interest rate is changed) even though the borrower may have demonstrated a poor payment record.

Interest Rate Change.   Regulations that apply to residential loans usually carry limitations on how much of a swing the interest rate will be permitted. That is, How much can the rate be increased or decreased at any given time in the loan term? Commercial loans are generally not subject to the same limitations as are residential loans. However, for either type of loan, a key element in determining the new interest rate at the time of rate adjustment is the index of interest rates that applies—which should be noted in the mortgage instrument.

Interest Rate Index.   The purpose of selecting a major indicator as a base for interest rate adjustments is to protect the borrower against an unreasonable or unfair change in the rate by the lender. There are a number of interest rate indices that can be used. And with a commercial loan, it can be whatever index is agreed upon between the lender and the borrower. Following are some of the principal published indices available in this country:

1. FHLB's average mortgage rate on previously occupied houses.
2. FHLB's average mortgage rate on new homes.
3. FNMA's auction rate on mortgage purchase commitments.
4. Average cost of funds—FSLIC insured institutions—all districts.
5. Three-year rate on U.S. Treasury securities.
6. Five-year rate on U.S. Treasury securities.

The first three indices would be most appropriate for a residential loan. The fourth index, "average cost of funds," bases the rate change on the cost experience of savings institutions. It is not a sensitive indicator as savings associations' cost of funds is most likely to continue a slow creep upward as interest rate ceilings are removed (over a six-year period that began on March 31, 1980). The last two indices might be used to set the pattern for a commercial loan interest rate adjustment.

How an Index is Applied.   There are several ways that lenders can use to calculate the interest rate adjustment triggered by a movement in the agreed-upon index. Whatever the method selected, it will be incorporated as a part of the mortgage agreement. The major procedures are as follows:

1. The index itself may be applied directly to the loan. For example, an indicator such as the FNMA most recent auction rate on mortgage purchase commitments may be used with no change in the published rate.

2. The index may be indicated with an addition of one or two percentage points added to it. For instance, if the FHLB's average mortgage rate on previously occupied homes is used, it may be with the addition of a percentage point or two.

3. A base rate plus the movement of an index may be used. In this procedure the lender selects an initial interest rate to apply to the loan. Then the indicator is noted at the time the loan is initiated and again at the time the rate becomes subject to adjustment. Whatever the change (the difference between the initial rate of the index and the rate at the time of a change), it is added or subtracted from the initial interest rate charged for the loan to determine the newly adjusted rate.

4. The lesser of two indices may be used wherein two published rates are selected; then whichever of these two reflects the lower rate at the time the mortgage rate becomes due for change, this becomes the new rate. The same procedure could be used with the *higher* of the two rates becoming the new interest rate.

So far, all regulations applicable to interest rate adjustments make an increase in the rate *optional* with the lender, even though justified by the index. However, if an index indicates a reduction in the rate, that reduction is *mandatory* for the lender.

Mortgage Payment Change.   In residential loans there is another variable that most likely will not be found in a commercial loan. This is a limitation on how frequently a change can be made in a monthly payment amount. For example, in Texas the interest rate may be changed on a residential loan every 6 months, but the mortgage payment amount cannot be changed more often than once a year. Further, the time period for a mortgage payment change can be extended for up to 5 years, at the lender's option. When an interest rate is changed and the payment amount remains constant, it means that the allocation of that payment between principal and interest is changed. This inevitably results in a change in the term of the loan. There are loans outstanding now that call for an interest rate change every 6 months with the monthly payment remaining constant for 5 years. Such a loan may have some interesting consequences when one considers the fact that on a 30-year loan, about ¹/₄ percent increase in the interest rate changes the allocation of money between principal and interest so that nothing is paid on the principal. Likewise, if the loan term is for 40 years, an increase of only ¹/₈ percent eliminates any payment to reduce principal. This type of loan agreement can easily result in what is called *negative amortization*—when the principal balance is increased periodically by the addition of unpaid interest, rather than periodically reduced, which is the definition of amortization.

Rate Based on Prime Rate.   Commercial banks have long used their published prime rate as the base rate for business loans. *Prime rate* is usually defined as that rate a bank charges to its most credit-worthy customers. It is not a regulated rate and varies over the country with individual banks. In practice, the rate has become a base on which the bank floats almost all of its business and some personal loans, sometimes *above* the prime rate, sometimes *below*. For instance, a business loan may be priced at "prime plus 2"—if prime rate is set at 14 percent, the rate for the loan is 16 percent. In this way, commercial banks have managed to maintain a margin of earnings more consistent with the fluctuating cost of funds than have the thrift institutions (savings associations and mutual savings banks). The thrifts have been burdened with a large investment in older, long-term loans paying interest rates at somewhat less than the current market cost of funds.

Banks have always applied the prime rate to their shorter term mortgage loans, such as warehouse lines of credit for mortgage bankers and construction loans to contractors. However, the prime rate has not generally been used for the longer term direct mortgage loans, most likely due to the complexity of frequent changes applied to fully amortized loans. Even so, it is another method that could be used to make periodic adjustments in the interest rate for such a loan.

Graduated Payment Plans

Several of the new mortgage designs are intended to help the first-time home buyer by permitting a reduction in the monthly payment amount during the early years of the mortgage term. The purpose is to match the borrower's income to the lower first-year payment. This provides easier qualification for more buyers, or possibly the acquisition of a larger house than might otherwise be justified.

Two basic methods are used to accomplish this purpose: the graduated payment mortgage and the pledged account mortgage.

Graduated Payment Mortgage (GPM). An arbitrary reduction is made in the early payment amounts, which normally results in a payment insufficient to pay any principal and only a part of the interest due for the month. Periodically the unpaid interest is added to the principal balance and earns additional interest. As previously mentioned, since amortization of a loan is the periodic *reduction* of the principal balance, when the balance is *increased*, it is termed *negative amortization*. The payment amounts are increased each year for a period of 5 or 10 years until they reach a level that fully amortizes the loan within its original term. It is this method that has gained popularity through the FHA Section 245(a) and (b) programs identified as GPMs (Graduated Payment Mortgages). When traded in the secondary market, this mortgage plan is known by the acronym *jeep* (not *gipem* as originally proposed).

The down payment for a GPM-type mortgage is increased in proportion to the reduction of the initial monthly payments. The reason is to prevent the periodic additions to principal from increasing the loan amount to a sum greater than the initial value of the property.

Pledged Account Mortgage (PAM). The same purpose is accomplished with PAM as with the GPM design, but without the negative amortization feature. What would otherwise amount to the down payment is deposited in a savings account pledged as additional collateral to the lender. The additional collateral allows the lender to make nearly a 100 percent loan (based on the property value) and to pay off the seller. The pledged account (which belongs to the borrower but is pledged to the lender) is then used as a source of supplemental funds to help make the monthly payments. Each month during the early years, the borrower makes a payment that is less than needed to fully amortize the loan. And each month the lender withdraws a portion of the pledged savings account, adds the interest earned for the month, and applies this amount to the borrower's payment to achieve a constant-level, fully amortized payment.

Comparison of GPM and PAM Mortgage Designs. Both the GPM and the PAM mortgage designs were approved as conventional loans by the Federal Home Loan Bank Board as of January 1979. They are intended for use with residential loans, primarily to assist home buyers. However, these plans, particularly the PAM, could find limited application for smaller income property loans when the income in the early years of ownership may be insufficient to cover larger constant-level payments. Like the requirement for the home buyer, there would have to be some reasonable assurance of future increases in the borrower's (or the property's) income for loan qualification.

From the lender's viewpoint, there is an obvious advantage in PAM over the GPM procedure. PAM allows for monthly payments that cover all interest due plus a reduction of principal; in other words, it repays on a fully amortized schedule. GPM, with its negative amortization feature, is not as acceptable for the lender as it does not pay all the interest in the early years. In effect, the lender continues to advance funds for the payment of interest by adding the amount to the principal balance periodically. There is another advantage in PAM for the lender: the pledged savings account adds to the lender's deposit assets.

Both GPM and PAM require generally higher down payments than would be required for a mortgage with a constant-level repayment plan. For the GPM, the reason is to prevent the negative amortization increase in principal balance from exceeding the value of the property. For PAM, the reason is in part to obtain the cash needed to create the pledged account. While the amount required to be deposited in the pledged account under PAM is a precise figure (the withdrawals are calculated to exactly exhaust the fund over the period that payment supplements are made), lenders are not limited to this amount in their buyer qualifications. It is not unusual for the lender to require that the deposit amount be set up *prior* to closing and that an additional down payment be made at closing.

The GPM plans most widely used follow the FHA patterns, which are periodically changed in an effort to keep abreast of the residential market for loans. Generally, these plans call for annual increases in the payment amounts until a level is reached at which the loan payments fully amortize the remaining balance due.

PAM REPAYMENT PLAN

One of the more widely used plans to calculate the initial cash requirements and the amount of monthly payment for a pledged account mortgage plan has been developed by Allan H. Smith of FLIP Mortgage Corporation. The complex calculations required are resolved with a computer program which is what FLIP Mortgage markets. Following is the computer calculation for a house costing $70,000, a mortgage loan of $62,100 for 30 years at 14 percent interest, with a cash requirement of $20,000. To repay a $62,100 mortgage loan over 30 years at 14 percent normally requires a monthly payment of $735.81. By using a pledged account mortgage plan, the FLIP generated figures permit borrower qualification of income at a monthly payment figure of $380.05; substantially less than the $735.81 amount. Here is how the calculation is handled:

First, a series of information input questions are asked.

Price of home: $70,000

Housing expense to income ratio allowed: 28%

Housing plus non-housing expense to income ratio: 36%

Applicant's annual income: $35,000

Estimated maximum rate of income growth: 7.5%

Length of supplementary period: 5 years

Term of mortgage loan: 30 years

Annual interest rate: 14%

Mortgage insurance premium: None (LTVR less than 80%)

Property tax rate per annum: 1%

Additional annual housing expense: $150

Annual non-housing expense: $2,400

Cash down payment: $20,000

Annual interest rate on pledged savings account: 5.5%

Second, calculations based on the above information show a pledged account requirement of $12,132.73 which must be deposited with the lender in an insured passbook type savings account. Since the lender is requiring $20,000 cash from the borrower (this figure is negotiable with the lender) the difference of $7,867.27 ($20,000 minus $12,132.73 equals $7,867.23) is applied to the down payment for the house. The house costs $70,000, so the $7,867.23 down payment reduces the mortgage loan to a rounded off figure of $62,100. (The small difference between the two amounts is $32.73 and must be added to the down payment by the buyer.)

Third, with a pledged account on deposit with the lender in the amount of $12,132.73, the borrower authorizes the lender to make monthly withdrawals from the pledged account to *supplement* the borrower's monthly payment amounts. Interest earned on the pledged account (at the passbook savings rate) is added each month to the amount of principal withdrawn. Level payments are made for a 12-month period and then the supplementary amount is reduced while the borrower's payment is increased in a corresponding amount so that each month the lender receives what amounts to a full payment that will amortize the loan within the 30-year term. Following is a break-down of the buyer's monthly payment plus supplemental withdrawals to pay the $62,100 loan in this example:

Beg. of Year	Buyer's Monthly Pmt. for Yr.	PLUS	Pledged Acct. Principal	PLUS	Interest on Pledged Account	EQUALS	Total Monthly Payment
1	380.05		308.64		47.12		735.81
2	441.29		263.12		31.40		735.81
3	507.14		210.29		18.38		735.81
4	577.92		149.40		8.49		735.81
5	654.01		76.91		2.19		735.81
6	735.81		-0-		-0-		735.81

Fourth, the lender initially holds as security for the loan a house worth $70,000 PLUS control of the pledged account which adds to the collateral in the amount of $12,132.73. Thus the initial risk exposure of the lender is reduced to a loan-to-value ratio of only 71.38 percent. As the pledged account is reduced during the five years of withdrawals, the risk exposure climbs to a high (for this example) of 87.32 percent, well within the lender's risk limits. Following is the annual change in mortgage balance and loan-to-value ratio:

Beg. of Year	Mortgage Balance	Pledged Account Balance	Net Mortgage Balance	Cost of House	Loan-to-Value Ratio
1	62,100	12,133	49,967	70,000	.7138
2	61,955	8,429	53,526	70,000	.7647
3	61,788	5,272	56,517	70,000	.8074
4	61,598	2,748	58,849	70,000	.8407
5	61,378	955	60,422	70,000	.8632
6	61,125	-0-	61,125	70,000	.8732

Note: Figures in the above example used with permission of FLIP Mortgage Corporation, Newtown, Pennsylvania 18940.

Why pledge a portion of the $20,000 cash requirement in a pledged account? Wouldn't it be better to use the entire $20,000 to reduce the mortgage loan to $50,000 (the $70,000 price of the house less $20,000 equals $50,000)? The answer is clear: a $50,000 loan at 14 percent interest for 30 years requires a monthly payment of $592.44. Using the FLIP calculation for a pledged account mortgage, the initial monthly payment drops to $380.05. Obviously, more borrowers could qualify at the lower monthly payment amount.

12

Variations in Financing Methods

With high interest rates, the cost of owning a home using borrowed money has become far more expensive. Variations in repayment plans may provide some temporary help but do nothing to overcome the basic cost of the borrowed funds. Another method being used to assist a buyer acquire property is the purchase of partial ownership interests, which still allow full possession. While this concept has been utilized in home acquisitions, it can be used with commercial properties as well. Variations include rental of the land rather than purchase, shared appreciation mortgages, and shared equity participations.

LAND LEASES

Historically, land leases have been considered low risk and often command rentals at rates less than the cost of financing. A land lease is most advantageous to the property user if it can be arranged at a lower cost than a purchase. In some areas of the country, homes are being sold with the seller retaining outright ownership of the land and arranging for a long-term lease of the land to the home buyer. The buyer needs to borrow less money if he or she is purchasing only the building.

To exemplify such a lease arrangement let us assume that a buyer wants to purchase a $100,000 property. The land is valued at $40,000, and the building at $60,000. A 30-year loan at 14 percent interest for $40,000 (the cost of the land) amounts to a monthly payment of $474. If the seller will accept, say $250 per month rental on the land, the buyer can reduce his monthly payment by $224. A leasehold mortgage loan can then be arranged to handle the purchase of the building itself. Payment on the land lease would normally be made to the lender as an escrow deposit with the money passed on to the landowner at periodic intervals. Thus the lender has an assurance of proper payment in a manner similar to that used in the handling of property taxes. The lender's security for the loan would be a leasehold mortgage. As described here, the land is not subordinated to the leasehold. (See Chapter 37.)

Why would anyone agree to lease, say a $40,000 tract of land, for less than a going market rate of return? There could be several reasons:

1. The lower total monthly payment might qualify a buyer with smaller income and enable the property to be sold.
2. The land value most likely represents an inflated market value figure rather than the original cash cost amount.
3. The land remains within the family as a tangible asset.
4. Appreciation to both land and the improvements thereon ultimately accrue to the benefit of the landowner when the lease expires. Thus, the true rate of return could be much greater, depending on the effect of inflation. (*Note:* There are land leases where the landowner agrees to reimburse the tenant for the appreciated value of improvements when the lease terminates.)

Lease with Option to Buy

A lease may be arranged for the whole property (or the land if it only is leased) which grants the tenant a right to purchase the property at a set price within some specified time period. The purpose could be to allow possession immediately without a long-term, high-cost monthly payment commitment. The hope is that better financing might be arranged at a later date.

Caveat for the seller

If a personal residence is transferred under a lease with option to buy and the option is not exercised in less than a year, the IRS has ruled that the lease terminates the seller's qualification for a personal residence. The house becomes rental property and no longer is eligible for deferment of the capital gain tax upon sale.

REVERSE ANNUITY MORTGAGE (RAM)

The reverse annuity is another of the mortgage plans approved by the FHLBB as of January 1, 1979. However, it does not finance the acquisition of real estate as the other forms do. Rather, the reverse annuity utilizes the collateral value of a home as a means of financing living expenses for the owner. The basic purpose is to assist older homeowners who are pressed to meet rising living costs with fixed retirement or pension forms of income. With the use of a reverse annuity, the increased value of the home may be utilized without the owner being forced to sell it.

Where state laws permit (the owner's homestead rights may preclude this form of mortgage), a lender can advance monthly installment payments to the homeowner, using a mortgage on the home as security. The FHLBB rules governing the writing of RAMs require extensive disclosures to reduce the possibility of misunderstandings by the homeowner. Among the requirements is that a seven-day rescission period be allowed the borrower should a change of mind occur. Another is that a statement must be signed by the borrower acknowledging all contractual contingencies that might force a sale of the home. Repayment of the loan must be allowed without penalties, and if the mortgage has a fixed term, refinancing must be arranged at market rates, if requested, at maturity of the loan.

Interest on this type of loan is added to the principal amount along with each monthly payment made to the borrower. For a savings institution, the monthly pay-out of loan proceeds with interest added to the principal presents an altogether different cash flow problem. The concept of reverse annuity is new and will require some years of testing before many institutions will decide to offer it.

FINANCING WITH JUNIOR MORTGAGES

A mortgage is a lien. A lien is a claim on property for payment of some debt, obligation, or duty. There can be more than one mortgage claim against the same property, so long as state laws or existing mortgage provisions do not prohibit it. Multiple mortgages present no problems for a lender unless a default occurs in the payment, resulting in a foreclosure. Under a forced sale, the foreclosed property may not bring enough money to pay off all of the claims. So a system of priorities is necessary to determine which claims have precedence. Sale proceeds are distributed not in proportionate shares for each claimant, but through a priority list that indicates which claimant is to be paid in full first, which comes next, which third, and so forth.

Lien priorities become important in the event of foreclosure against the mortgaged property. Foreclosure procedures vary under the separate state laws but are always difficult, costly, and usually time consuming. Lenders are extremely interested in avoiding foreclosures and cooperate with the borrower whenever possible to avoid this step. It is most important that the borrower communicate with the lender and extend his full cooperation whenever unanticipated problems arise. The lender is obligated to protect his own legal position should foreclosure become imminent but can more readily grant forbearance to a cooperative borrower. The foreclosure process is not considered in this text; the determination of lien priorities is considered, however, as is the application of proceeds under foreclosure.

State law prescribes the order of priority for distributing proceeds from the sale of a foreclosed property, usually handled by public auction. A general outline for such cases is as follows:

1. *First priority.* Administrative costs of the foreclosure proceedings, including attorneys' fees.
2. *Second priority.* Taxes, including property taxes and claims by the federal government.
3. *Third priority.* Secured claims, which include mortgages and other liens of record.
4. *Fourth priority.* Unsecured claims, which are those not recorded.

It is in the third category—secured claims—that the rights of mortgage holders lie. Within this category, the determination of priority is made either by date of filing (recording) or by written agreement between the parties involved (subordination).

Mortgage lenders are careful to examine the county record of claims before a loan is closed. If any claim is outstanding, the lender asks that it be paid off or that it be subordinated to the lender's own mortgage. The purpose is to assure that the lender's mortgage is not superseded by the claim of another. The date—down to the time on that date—that the claim or lien is filed of record in the county where the land is located controls the priority of the lien.

When a lender makes a mortgage loan with the knowledge and acceptance that there is at least one mortgage claim of record, the new mortgage is said to be *junior*, that is, of lower priority than the earlier claim. It may be the second or third mortgage in the order of priorities. Some states do not recognize a mortgage claim against certain kinds of property, such as a homestead, unless special requirements are met. Where state laws allow junior liens, the procedure is widely used as a method of borrowing additional cash based on the increase in equity value in the property.

Because of a junior mortgage's lower priority, the lender's risk is considerably greater than with a first mortgage. Consequently, the interest cost is higher—and the loan term shorter—than would be available for a first mortgage loan on the same property. A junior mortgage can be used to obtain purchase money for acquisition, or it can be used to obtain cash for improvements or for other uses not related to the property itself. The security that is pledged is the equity in the property; that is, the difference between the market value and the balance due on the existing mortgage loan or loans. Debt service for a junior mortgage is usually substantially larger—proportionately, at any rate—than for a first mortgage, because of its generally shorter term and higher interest rate. The cash flow for the owner is thus reduced, which diminishes the value of the additional cash provided by the second or third mortgage financing.

A popular purpose of a second mortgage is to assist in the financing of a property's equity when an existing loan is assumed. Some lenders specialize in this form of loan because it provides higher yields than are normally available from first mortgage loans. When financing is handled by the *seller* of a property, some states permit a *vendor's lien* to be created, which is an implied lien even without a mortgage. When the mortgage loan, made by any lender, is for the *purchase* of property, it is sometimes called a *purchase money mortgage* and in some states carries a favored priority position.

All regulated lenders are subject to rules regarding the acceptance of loans other than first mortgage priority; many are restricted to making only first mortgage loans.

WRAP–AROUND MORTGAGE

A wrap-around mortgage, like a second mortgage, provides additional financing for an existing property. It is an especially appealing inducement for the seller to assist in financing the property sale. Instead of using a second mortgage note for the amount of required additional financing, the wrap-around procedure creates a new note that acknowledges and includes (thus "wraps around") the existing first mortgage note. For a wrap-around mortgage to succeed, the first mortgage note must be assumable; to be most effective, there should be a reasonable differential between the interest rate on the existing mortgage and the current market rate. The inducement works when the holder of the wrap-around note can earn something like 2 percent or more interest on the existing first mortgage. The same additional yield can be obtained with a second mortgage by simply increasing the interest rate—only the "packaging" is different with the wrap.

EXAMPLE

Wrap-Around Mortgage

Here is an example of how this procedure works. Assume that an existing property is being sold for $150,000. Assume an existing first mortgage balance of $70,000 at an interest rate of 9 percent and a current market rate of 12 percent. The buyer is reluctant to invest the $80,000 cash required for the equity interest. The maximum new loan available to refinance the older property is $110,000 at 12 percent interest, leaving a cash requirement of $40,000 to purchase. A second mortgage, due to its greater risk, can be found for only $35,000 at 14 percent interest, which would thus require $45,000 cash to purchase ($150,000 purchase price, less $70,000 first mortgage, less $35,000 second mortgage leaves $45,000 cash requirement). If the seller is not pressed for cash and plans to invest his profits for a reasonable return anyway, he could have an interest in assisting the financing of a sale. Under these conditions, the seller might make a wrap-around mortgage loan for $130,000 at an interest rate of 11 percent. The seller (or a designated trustee) would receive the installment payments on the $130,000 wrap, out of which he would pay the installment on the first mortgage loan (which has a balance due of $70,000). The seller earns the difference between the 9 percent rate on the first mortgage and the 11 percent rate on the wrap-around, plus the full 11 percent rate on the $60,000 portion that the seller is financing. The terms of the wrap-around agreement provide for a mortgage on the property which, in effect, gives the seller a second mortgage security. There is another possible advantage for the seller in a wrap—the favorable financing that it can provide might induce a higher sales price that could otherwise be realized. For the buyer, the property may be acquired for $20,000 cash (or less than might otherwise be possible) and at a less-than-market interest rate for the total financing.

Other Aspects of the Wrap-Around Mortgage

The new buyer does not accept direct liability on the existing note, rather the liability is to the holder of the wrap-around mortgage. To do otherwise could place the buyer in obligation on two notes covering the same indebtedness The way this is handled is in the normal language of a wrap mortgage; the buyer accepts the property "subject to" an existing mortgage obligation. Thus, the debt is acknowledged, but liability for it is not accepted. If liability is accepted on an existing note, the buyer would "assume" the obligation.

If the holder of the wrap mortgage fails to make timely payments on the existing mortgage, there is a possibility of foreclosure. Consequently, the new buyer needs some protection. This can be provided by making monthly payments on the wrap to a trustee rather than to the holder of the wrap. The trustee, which could be a bank, takes the responsibility for disbursement of the payment due on the existing mortgage.

A key element in the wrap procedure is to have an existing loan that can be assumed with little or no increase in the interest rate. Both FHA- and VA-type loans can be assumed without any escalation of the interest rate. Most conventional loans require the lender's approval for a transfer of property rights, and this usually means an adjustment of the interest rate to near current market levels. It should be noted that state legislatures are looking into the right of a lender to increase an interest rate when a loan is assumed (or the property is transferred without a pay-off of the existing loan). At this writing, seventeen states restrict lenders rights to call a loan but the trend of recent court decisions favors lenders exercising their contractual rights.

The text has pointed to advantages in the wrap procedure for both buyer and seller in a seller-assist financing deal. However, this is not the only way a wrap can be handled. Many mortgage lenders undertake wrap-type financing as a method of increasing their own yield on a mortgage loan. Whether seller-assist or lender-financed, a wrap can be an effective sales tool for packaging a property transaction.

Another common use for the wrap-around procedure is in the refinancing of existing properties. If additional financing is needed, the lender may prefer to secure the new loan by "wrapping" it with the existing loan.

SHARED APPRECIATION MORTGAGE

With this financing procedure, the lender accepts a lower interest rate for the loan in exchange for a share of the property appreciation within a limited number of years. For example, in exchange for a reduction of interest from a market rate of 15 percent to 10 percent for the loan, the buyer-borrower agrees to deliver a one-third share of any appreciation at the end of 10 years, or sooner if the property is sold. If the borrower does not sell within 10 years, the property is appraised in accordance with the loan agreement and the borrower must pay the share of appreciation due the lender. The appreciation is a net amount which does not include improvements made by the borrower. The lender's share is called *contingent interest*.

If payment to the lender cannot be made when due, the amount may be added to the principal balance of the original loan and a new payment (which may include a new interest rate) is established. In some states, the addition of what amounts to earned interest for the lender to a principal balance may not be acceptable. Some lenders, however, are making this form of loan in an effort to encourage home sales. The Federal Home Loan Bank Board has studied the procedure and has made a proposal for its use. The FHLB suggests that the lender's share of appreciation (contingent interest) be limited to 40 percent of the appreciated amount.

The obvious problem for a lender undertaking this form of a loan is the calculation of a rate of return. Since a large percentage of the interest to be earned is based on the rate of inflation, How does one project this calculation?

SHARED EQUITY MORTGAGE

Often associated with a shared appreciation mortgage, the shared equity mortgage is distinguished by the lender's participation as a part *owner* in the acquisition of property. The procedure may be used in a number of ways and for a variety of purposes. The following discussion focuses on two of the more popular ones.

Investor Syndicate

An individual, or a small syndicate, may purchase an equity in the property as a nonoccupant at the time of acquisition by putting up a share of the down payment and paying a share of the monthly payment. The buyer-occupant benefits from the lower cash requirements and, in exchange, agrees to pay the nonoccupant participant a reimbursement of the invested amount plus a share of the appreciation within a limited number of years, or sooner if the property is sold. The payment of the appreciation share may be called for in five to seven years and could be in the form of cash or a mandatory sale of the property for satisfaction of the obligation.

Employer Participation

To provide employees housing that can be afforded within a limited wage scale, an employer may agree to pay for a portion of the house. The employee is called upon to finance the other portion and is usually granted an option to buy out the employer's interest within a limited period of time. If employment is terminated, the employer may be obligated to assume the employee's obligations.

This concept has been successfully applied by Stanford University (California) and is also used by Tenneco (Houston) to encourage the transfer of employees to some of their more remote operations.

Dual ownership of real property can create some questions in states that grant homestead privileges, and this should be checked with competent legal counsel. In general, homestead rights accrue to the occupant of the dwelling, not to a participating investor.

TIME–SHARING OWNERSHIP

While the concept of time-sharing lacks the quality of ownership embodied in the other forms of ownership discussed here, it is growing in importance and needs to be understood.

Time-sharing ownership means the holding of rights to exclusive use of real estate for a designated length of time (such as two weeks or a month) each year. It is practical primarily in resort areas. There are two basic methods used to create time-sharing arrangements: one is through a long-term lease, and the other is through condominium-type ownership.

Long-Term Lease

Under the long-term lease arrangement, the developer, or promoter, acquires a hotel, motel, or an apartment building in a suitable resort area. For each unit in the building he sells, say, 25 two-week leases out of each year for 30 years. That leaves a two-week period unallocated that can be used for general maintenance work. The sale of the leases is calculated to pay for the building, and the lessee pays a proportionate share of the cost of the management, maintenance, and any services that are commonly provided. A specific unit may be assigned to the lessee, or he may be allowed to use any unit available on a first come, first served basis. In an arrangement of this kind, the leasehold interest should have the right to sell; thirty years is a long time for one vacation spot.

Condominium

The purchase of a condominium with this plan grants the owner the right to use the unit for a specified period each year. An example might be the sale of a unit to 24 buyers as tenants in common. Each holds the right to use the unit for two weeks out of each year. Or the arrangement could be a sale to 12 owners, each of whom has the right to use the unit for two weeks in the summer and two weeks in the winter.

Management and maintenance problems are somewhat more difficult with time-sharing as compared with full-time occupancy of a condominium. An ownership agreement is necessary to define user priorities, assign responsibilities for maintenance (probably a professional management company), and to detail the procedures to be used if an owner wants to sell his interest. Another matter of concern is the allocation of expenses and debt service if one or more of the owners fail to pay their share.

MORTGAGE BUY–DOWNS

A practice that has developed primarily among home builders is for the builder to pay the mortgage lender a portion of the interest in advance in exchange for a reduction of the early monthly payments to be paid by the borrower. It is a variation on the long-time practice of a builder buying a loan commitment in advance in order to assure the home buyer a more affordable source of loanable funds.

The older loan commitment procedure called for the builder to pay some points in advance sufficient to achieve a lower fixed interest rate over the life of the loan. With the more recent buy-down practice, the builder only pays sufficient interest in advance (the points) to reduce the mortgage payment for the first two or three years. For example, if the builder wants to offer a house that requires a $60,000 loan, the monthly principal and interest payment at 14 percent constant level amounts to $711. To make the house more attractive to the home buyer, the builder wants to offer lower initial monthly payments. Using round figures for easier understanding, the cost of the loan amounts to $600 per year for each 1 percent of interest charged. To reduce the loan payment amount to the equivalent of an 11 percent interest rate for the first year, the builder must pay approximately $1,800 (14 minus 11 equals 3: 3 times $600 equals $1,800) in advance interest to the lender. The result is a first year's payment amount of $571 which is $140 less than the original amount of $711 per month. The lower monthly payment allows easier borrower qualification. The builder may consider the buy-down cost as a part of the selling expense or may try to include it in a higher price for the house.

SELLER–ASSIST FINANCING AIDS

In 1982, the National Association of Realtors reported that 60% of the houses being sold carried some kind of financing by the seller. The numerous variations in repayment plans developed by sellers in an effort to sell houses has been loosely identified as "creative financing." The thrust of creative plans is to reduce the impact of high costs in the early years of repayment with the expectation that in a few years interest rates will return to a lower level and refinancing can then be accomplished at less cost. Thus, most of these plans provide for lower initial payments, a short term like 3 to 5 years, and a balloon at maturity. Unfortunately, expectations have not always been realized because interest rates did not fall as anticipated and refinancing in the depressed market of 1982 was difficult.

While nothing short of lower interest rates or lower housing costs will alleviate the underlying problem, there have been two new developments which offer substantial assistance to a seller who must offer financing assistance in order to sell a property. These are:

1. Default insurance offered on seller-assist first or second mortgage loan.
2. A plan offered by the Federal National Mortgage Association to buy (convert to cash) first or second mortgage loans taken by sellers.

The importance of these two aids now available to home sellers is that it brings professional lenders with all of their credit knowledge into the handling of this type of loan. Also, it offers to the seller an option to sell the loan on a fair basis for cash. Few home sellers are in the business of making mortgage loans and they no longer need to be placed in the position of an involuntary lender. Following is a discussion of the two kinds of aids available to home sellers.

Default Insurance for Seller-Financed Loans

In the Spring of 1982, private mortgage insurance companies offered to insure seller-assist loans against default by the buyer-borrower. Qualification of the applicant is generally the same as for regular private mortgage insurance. Default insurance is not offered directly to the home seller. It can only be obtained through an approved mortgage lender called a "servicer." The servicer acts as an agent for the *home seller* and handles the necessary qualification procedures for both the property and the buyer to obtain an insurance commitment certificate. Servicers work under a service contract with the insurance company. This contract may vary in the different states due to variances in state insurance requirements.

Underwriting Guidelines for Home Seller Coverage. While there is some difference in the coverage offered by insurance companies, the following are fairly standard guidelines for insuring seller-financed loans:

1. Each loan must be secured by a 1 to 4 family owner-occupied property.
2. The maximum loan-to-value ratio (LTVR) is 90 percent. This means a minimum of 10 percent cash equity by the buyer.
3. Qualification of the buyer-borrower's income is based on the same debt-to-income ratio as that applied to standard lender-financed loans. Generally, these limits are now being used:
   a. The total mortgage payment, including default insurance, cannot exceed 33 percent of the borrower's income.
   b. The total mortgage payment plus long-term installment obligations cannot exceed 38 percent of the borrower's income.
4. The same coverage that applies to standard lender financing also applies to seller-financed first lien mortgages and land contracts in most states.
5. Seller-financed second lien mortgages are also eligible for insurance coverage in most states with coverages ranging from 25 percent to 100 percent.
6. The application form and documentation needed to qualify a seller-financed loan for insurance is the same as that used for standard lender-financed loans. Generally, in the space calling for 'type of loan,' the applicant indicates "seller-financed."

Claim Procedures. In case of a default on an insured loan, the home seller is offered the same coverage as for standard lender loans for either first or second mortgage coverage. The claim amount includes the unpaid mortgage balance, interest to date of claim, reasonable attorney's fees, and property preservation costs. Following is an example of how a typical claim would be settled on a seller-financed wrap-around mortgage.

Homeseller: Insured Seller Financing

Sample Claim 3: Seller-Financed Wrap-around Lien

The sample claim shown below illustrates the default protection Homeseller offers. This example pertains to a seller-financed wrap-around mortgage or land contract with an underlying lien. The seller is responsible for maintaining the underlying lien.

Facts which apply to Example 3:

1. Purchase price	$85,000.00
2. Down payment	$10,000.00
3. Seller-financed original wrap-around loan amount	$75,000.00
4. Loan-to-value ratio	88%
5. Interest rate on wrap-around	14%
6. Wrap-around loan term	15 years
7. Original first mortgage amount	$50,000.00
8. Interest rate on underlying mortgage	8%
9. Original underlying mortgage loan term	30 years
10. 12 payments made	
11. 25% MGIC insurance coverage	
12. Six months (180 days) from initial default by buyer to date of claim, outstanding principal balance of first mortgage at date of claim	$41,905.50

Claim for Loss

1. Principal balance (from Amortization Table)	$73,414.50
2. Interest (180 days)	5,139.00
3. Attorney's fees	750.00
4. Real estate taxes advanced	600.00
5. Insurance premiums advanced	150.00
6. Preservation of property	450.00
7. Disbursements	300.00
Total Claim	$80,803.50

MGIC, at its option, would settle this claim through one of the following three methods:

Percentage Payment Option (25 percent coverage)

Under this option, MGIC would reimburse the servicer on behalf of the seller for 25 percent of the total claim or $20,200.88. The seller would retain title to the property.

Acquisition Option

Under this option, MGIC would either assume or pay off the first mortgage, taking title to the property. The outstanding balance on the first mortgage would be deducted from the total claim. MGIC would pay the balance of the claim to the servicer on behalf of the seller.

Total claim	$ 80,803.50
Less net of outstanding balance of the first mortgage at date of claim	− 41,905.50
Claim payment	$ 38,898.00

Pre-Sold Claim Option

Under this option, the property would be sold and the proceeds deducted from the total claim amount. MGIC would pay the balance of the claim to the servicer on behalf of the seller.

Total claim	$ 80,803.50
Less net proceeds of sale	− 68,000.00
Claim payment	$ 12,803.50

Reproduced with the permission of Mortgage Guaranty Insurance Corporation, Milwaukee, Wisconsin

How to Secure Insurance Coverage. Insurance coverage against default on a seller-financed loan can only be obtained through an approved mortgage servicing company, that is one holding a service contract with an insurance carrier. Who are these servicers? They would vary a little in different states but basically comprise those companies normally engaged in making residential mortgage loans. This includes mortgage companies, savings associations, mutual savings banks, and in some states, commercial banks. Not all mortgage lenders handle seller-financed insurance coverage so it is usually necessary to screen the local market. The home seller, or the listing real estate broker, can make the arrangements with the mortgage servicer company. In most cases it is a prudent step to turn buyer-borrower qualification over to a qualified professional. The mortgage servicer has all of the necessary instruments and documentation forms required by the insurance company and can see to it that they are properly completed and meet minimum standards. Credit reports and verifications are routinely handled by mortgage lenders which does relieve the seller of an important burden. The mortgage servicer charges a fee for preparation of the loan package. Further, the mortgage servicer handles monthly collections on behalf of the seller and earns a service fee for this continuing work also.

Secondary Market Purchase of Seller-Financed Loans

In June, 1982, the Federal National Mortgage Association (FNMA) announced plans to purchase seller-financed first and second mortgage loans. This step brings professionalism to the business of seller-financed transactions, opening the door to many home sellers seeking cash for the equity in their homes rather than take a mortgage note with relatively small monthly payments. As too many home sellers have learned, creative financing ideas that have enabled homes to be sold at inflation-induced prices have also created many problems. Buyers have often overburdened themselves with high monthly payments anticipating increased income or continuing price increases in the property itself. These expectations have not always been realized, resulting in loan defaults. So the advent of a secondary market purchaser willing to pay cash for a seller-financed mortgage note is most important. How does a home seller qualify a loan for sale to FNMA?

How the Program Works.   First of all, the home seller must contract an approved FNMA "seller/servicer" lender. These are mortgage companies, savings associations, mutual savings banks, or possibly commercial banks, who have qualified to do business with FNMA. While most mortgage lenders have met this standard, the home seller should screen the local companies and institutions—not all qualified seller/servicers will handle seller-financed transactions. Then the home seller arranges with the FNMA-approved lender to perform all the services associated with originating the loan. This includes necessary documentation such as credit and property appraisal reports. It relieves the home seller's problem of making a decision on the credit-worthiness of a prospective buyer. For this professional help, the seller/servicer will charge an origination fee. Normally, this charge is paid by the buyer-borrower as a cost of obtaining financing.

Eligible Loans.   The seller-financed loan can be a first or second mortgage so long as the documentation is originated by an FNMA-approved lender and meets FNMA's requirements at the time the loan is offered for sale to FNMA.

For first mortgage loans

For owner-occupied houses, financing can go as high as 95 percent of the current property value, or up to 80 percent if non-owned occupied. The maximum loan amount for a single family conventional mortgage is $107,000. (Two- to four-family homes have higher limits). Private mortgage insurance (see previous section) must be obtained on mortgages with loan-to-value ratios over 80 percent. The mortgage must be fully amortized over the term of the loan which cannot exceed 30 years. Both fixed-rate and FNMA standard adjustable rate mortgages are eligible.

For second mortgage loans

For owner-occupied houses, the total of the first and second mortgage cannot exceed 80 percent of the current property value, 70 percent for non-owner occupied property. At this writing the maximum loan permitted by FNMA on any one single family property is $107,000. Thus, if FNMA owns the first mortgage, the combination of the first and second cannot exceed $107,000. But if FNMA does *not* own the first morgage, then the second mortgage cannot exceed $107,000.

Private mortgage insurance is required if the combined first and second mortgages exceed 65 percent of the home value. PMI is required on the top 25 percent of the second mortgage.

There is greater flexibility allowed in repayment for a second mortgage loan than a first mortgage. Second mortgages may be fully amortizing (payments sufficient to fully pay the loan within its term), or partially amortizing with the remaining balance due at maturity (a balloon payment). Fully amortized loans may offer repayment terms of 3 to 15 years. Partially amortized loans may offer terms of 5 to 15 years with payment amounts calculated as though the loan amortized in a period up to 30 years. Since partially amortized loans do not pay the full amount of the principal within the monthly payment amount, the full balance due must be paid in a lump sum at the end of the loan term.

How to Sell the Loan to FNMA.   Whenever a home seller wishes to sell his or her loan to FNMA (convert it to cash), the seller/servicer who originated the loan must be notified. The seller/servicer can then determine just what the FNMA required yield is at that time. Generally, the FNMA purchase price is based on current mortgage market rates. If the interest rate on the mortgage is the same as, or higher than, prevailing mortgage interest rates at the time of sale to FNMA, the home seller will receive the full remaining principal balance of the loan. If the interest rate on the mortgage is lower than the prevailing mortgage interest rate, the seller will receive a discounted amount.

EXAMPLE:

If a first mortgage is being sold:	
Outstanding mortgage balance is	$80,000
Interest rate on mortgage is	13%
At the time of sale:	
FNMA requires	13%
Home Seller receives	$80,000*
OR:	
Outstanding mortgage balance is	$80,000
Interest rate on mortgage is	13%
At the time of sale:	
FNMA requires	15%
Home Seller receives	$71,288*
*Less lender fees to be subtracted.	

FNMA reserves the right to review the loan once again at the time it is offered for sale to FNMA to make sure it meets eligibility requirements. FNMA will also require a satisfactory payment record for the loan.

Cost to the Home Seller.   FNMA does not set fee requirements for charges made by the seller/servicer who acts as an agent for the home seller. The fees are negotiable and could include:

1. An origination fee for preparing the loan package and obtaining the necessary verifications.
2. A fee for selling the loan to FNMA should the home seller want to convert the loan to cash.
3. A service fee for collecting the monthly payments and handling the tax and insurance escrows. The service fee is usually stated as a percent of the loan amount and, if the home buyer is to pay this cost, the fee is normally included in the interest rate charged on the loan when initially negotiated.

In conclusion then, the home seller would be well advised to shop around among the seller/servicers to obtain the best prices even though the home buyer will most likely end up paying the fees.

FOUR

Property Taxes and Income Taxes

13

Property Taxes

Real property investments are subject to two basic types of taxes—one on the income earned and/or any gain realized from disposition of the property, and the other on the property value itself. First, we will consider property taxes, which are much less complex than those relating to income.

Property taxes are generally identified as *ad valorem* taxes; that is, the tax is levied according to the value of the property. These taxes are the principal source of revenue to support local government programs and services. The range of activities that are paid for by property taxes includes fire and police departments, street maintenance, public libraries, public hospitals, parks, flood control and drainage districts, and local welfare programs. Some state governments obtain a portion of their revenues from these taxes.

Determining the Amount of Taxes

Three steps are used to determine the amount of taxes levied against each parcel of land in a tax district: (1) each taxing authority determines its budget requirements for the year; (2) the taxable property within the district is appraised; and (3) the taxing authorities' needs are allocated against the total property value to ensure that each tract pays an equitable share. The process is not always smooth and raises numerous disputes as to what is equitable. Following is a discussion of these three steps.

Budget Requirements.   Each taxing authority prepares a budget for the following year. These authorities include counties, cities, towns, villages, school boards, sanitation districts, hospital districts, flood control districts, county road departments, and in some cases, the state. Revenues from other sources such as sales taxes, federal revenue sharing, business licenses, income taxes, and various fees are estimated and then deducted from the budget requirements. The balance needed must come from the property taxes.

Appraisal.   Each parcel of taxable land is appraised periodically by the county or state appraiser or, in some cases, by private appraisal companies under contract to the taxing authority. While the methods used to appraise are not uniform—some use fair market value, some replacement value less depreciation—the purpose is to establish a fair value for the tax assessment of each parcel. It is in this area of valuation that most taxpayers express objections if they feel they have been treated unfairly.

Assessment.   With an amount figured for the budget needs and the total value of the taxable property determined within the district, it is a simple matter of mathematics to decide for how much each parcel should be assessed. Practice varies as to assessment. Some districts use the appraised value as the *assessed value*, others use a percentage of the appraised value. Based on the assessed value, the authority calculates a *tax rate*—the amount of taxes that must be levied against each dollar of taxable value within the district. The tax rate can be quoted as a *mill rate* (1 mill equals one-tenth of a cent; a 50-mill rate would be 5 cents on each dollar of assessed value); or it can be expressed as dollars per hundred, or per thousand, of assessed value.

Delinquent Property Taxes

Property taxes carry a unique power under the law. They become a *specific lien** at the time the tax bill is enacted. The lien is released only upon payment of the taxes. The tax lien carries a high priority in the event of a foreclosure, exceeding the claim of a mortgage that may have been recorded many years earlier.

If a landowner fails to pay the property taxes when due, the tax lien

---

*A *specific lien* is a claim against a designated tract of land as contrasted to a *general lien* which is a claim against all property owned by the target of the lien.

can be enforced through the sale of the property at public auction. In some states, the landowner is allowed a *redemption* period that varies from six months to two years after foreclosure. During this period, the landowner may reclaim title through payment of the delinquent debt. For example, Texas law allows such a taxpayer two years for redemption of the property if foreclosure is for property taxes.

Property Tax Exemptions

In all taxing districts there is a large amount of land carrying an exemption from property taxes. This includes government-owned property (states do not tax federal land and vice versa), parks, schools, churches, public roads, hospitals, charitable organizations, military bases, and cemeteries.

The right to a property tax exemption may be used to attract industry to the local area—the added jobs should more than offset the loss of tax revenues. Further, some communities grant special property tax exemptions to senior citizens. In California and some other states, elderly homeowners are allowed to postpone the payment of property taxes and to let the assessments accumulate. Payment is made when the property is sold.

Special Assessments

Property taxes are not always used for the general welfare of all taxpayers. When the need for an improvement, such as pavement of a street, is deemed of special benefit to a local area, it is possible to form a special *improvement district*, or *assessment district*. In such a case, the cost of the improvement is borne by the taxpayers who directly benefit. A special assessment may be paid in full when it comes due, or the cost may be handled from the sale of a special bond issue that allows the taxpayer beneficiaries to repay the cost over a period of years.

Revenue Bonds

When the taxing authorities decide to invest in an improvement of a long-term nature, such as a new public hospital, the cost may be spread over a number of years with the use of revenue bonds. In such a case, the taxing authority issues a series of bonds to be sold through securities dealers, with the tax assessment pledged to the repayment of the bonds. Such bonds, issued under state or municipal authority, pay interest that is not subject to federal income tax. Because of this exemption, the bonds can be sold at much lower interest rates than would be normal for other corporate bonds.

Tax Limitation Measures

Sparked to some degree by the success of California voters in June, 1978, with the roll-back of property taxes under Proposition 13, many states have sought to place limits on the amount of property taxes that can be assessed. Some states place a limit on the amount of increase that can be assessed on property each year, while others place limits on how much the government can spend. The latter limits are usually placed at a maximum growth rate per year such as the 7 percent ceiling in Colorado or at a rate not greater than the state's actual economic growth as in Tennessee.

14

Ordinary Income

Income derived from real property is subject to taxation by the federal government and most states in basically the same manner as any business income. However, the information offered here is limited to the federal laws.

Ordinary and necessary expenses are deducted from the gross income for the tax year, and the difference is subject to taxation as *ordinary income.* If real property is disposed of and a gain or loss results, taxes are assessed at the *capital gain or loss* rates and procedures. (See Chapter 15.) There is a third type of tax-defined income identified as *earned* and *unearned* income. Earned income is that received for work performed during the tax year. Unearned income is generally that received from investments, which includes rent and royalty income. The distinction between earned and unearned income is used in the determination of social security taxes and credits for the elderly. It has also been used to set a higher maximum tax rate applicable to the taxpayer. While the distinction is important, consideration in this text will be limited to the tax definition of rent, which qualifies as unearned income (and, thus, is not subject to self-employed social security taxes).

DETERMINING ORDINARY INCOME

The gross income from a real estate investment, less ordinary and necessary expense deductions, results in the net income subject to ordinary income taxes. Deductible expenses may be grouped into the following general accounts:

- Salaries and wages
- Utility costs
- Repairs and maintenance
- Management
- Real estate taxes
- Insurance
- Interest
- Depreciation (or cost recovery)

Of the expense items in this list, only three deserve further examination. These are (1) repairs and maintenance, (2) interest, and (3) depreciation (or cost recovery). All three have special rules to help clarify what can be deducted. The other expenses are more easily distinguished and do not create so many controversial questions.

Repairs and Maintenance

Repairs are easily confused with property improvements. Repairs are deductible from ordinary income in the year paid while improvements must be capitalized and the cost deducted over a period of years. The IRS defines a repair as something that maintains a property but does not increase its useful life. An improvement can be an addition to the property which has a useful life of more than one year (and thus becomes a depreciable asset), or it can be something that *prolongs* the useful life of the property.

Maintenance expense is often confused with replacement of furnishings or equipment. The IRS classifies maintenance in the same way as it does a repair; it is deductible as an expense as long as it maintains the property but does not increase its useful life. The replacement of furnishings or equipment is considered an improvement providing the useful life is more than one year.

Caveat

For the investor, the depreciation, or since 1981, the cost recovery, of furnishings and equipment can present a problem in the initial evaluation of a proposed acquisition. The financial statement may lump the depreciation of personal property (furnishings, equipment, and so forth) with building depreciation. (Depreciation is normally shown on a balance sheet and a profit and loss statement, but *not* on an operating statement.) For tax purposes the distinction is inconsequential. But for the investor it is very important. The building structure may well appreciate in value, while the capital invested in personal property is most likely to be consumed in the operations. Expendable assets should be recognized as a real cost of doing business with the annual loss in value listed as an expense on the operating statement.

Interest Expense

Interest paid for the use of money is a deductible business expense but is generally limited to that amount actually due and paid during the tax year. There are some exceptions to this general rule for real property investments:

For unimproved land

When unproductive land is held, the taxpayer may elect to capitalize interest and finance charges each year rather than deduct these costs as an expense.

New construction

Under the 1976 tax revision, interest and taxes payable during a new project's construction phase *must* be capitalized and then amortized over at least a 10-year period.

Prepaid interest

A former inducement to invest in real estate was the allowance of up to five years' interest paid in advance as a deduction in the current tax year. Over a period of several years, this allowance has been eliminated. Only that interest actually due and paid within the tax year may now be deducted.

Excess investment interest

For property held for investment, if interest expense exceeds the property income, a portion of this expense may be disallowed. The meaning of "held for investment" is not clear-cut but generally indicates an investment requiring very little management by the taxpayer, such as would be found with a net lease property.

Cost Recovery Expense (Depreciation)

Since the beginning of income taxes, tax law has allowed an investor to recover at least a portion of a capital investment through deductions from income taxes. Up until 1981, real and personal property went through an increasingly complex procedure to determine useful life and to estimate the salvage value when the asset was no longer usable in the business. All of this has been eliminated for property acquired after 1981. (But the old rules still apply as to how deductions can be taken on property acquired prior to 1981.) The new procedure even introduces a new name—*Accelerated Cost Recovery System* (ACRS). There are several advantages in the new methods: (1) the recovery period (formerly identified as the useful life) has been defined for each of the major categories of property; and (2) the permissible deduction for each year is determined from a percentage table that allows greater deductions in the early years of ownership. Thus, the older methods of accelerated depreciation have become an integral part of the new laws. The advantage to the investor is that greater tax savings than previously allowed are now available from an investment.

Even before the enactment of the 1981 Tax Act, real estate offered a distinct advantage in the allowance of a depreciation deduction calculated on the total building investment rather than only the equity portion. In other words, depreciation, and now cost recovery, may be taken on buildings and personal property acquired with borrowed money. Since this deduction does not require an outlay of cash, such as a repair or interest expense does, it can create a dramatic reduction in the taxable income without reducing the spendable cash from an investment. It is not at all unusual for the owner-taxpayer to show a tax loss on a real estate investment while realizing a positive cash flow.

Cost recovery is allowable on business property, rental property, and personal property held for business purposes. It may *not* be claimed on a personal residence, its furnishings, a personal car, or other items used for personal purposes. To be recoverable, the investment must (1) have a limited and determinable useful life of more than one year and (2) be used in a trade or business or otherwise held for the production of income. Regardless of its use, land is not a recoverable investment because its life is not limited.

The new cost recovery procedures will be examined in greater depth in Chapter 16. However, it is urged that you as an investor consult with qualified tax counsel in these matters as the supplemental IRS rules and regulations for the new Tax Act are still being written.

CALCULATION OF ORDINARY INCOME TAX

Ordinary income is taxed at different rates for individuals and for corporations. For individuals, the tax rate depends on the income level, marital status, and exemptions claimed. For corporations, the rate is based on income levels only: the tax has several graduations up to a taxable income of $100,000 after which the rate remains at 46 percent (through 1984).

DETERMINING UNEARNED INCOME

The distinction between earned and unearned income is important to self-employed persons determining liability for social security taxes and for the calculation of the Over-65, Credit for the Elderly. Prior to the Tax Act of 1981, unearned income was subject to a higher maximum tax (70 percent) than earned income (50 percent). The Tax Act made both classes of income subject to the same 50 percent maximum tax.

Earned income is wages, salaries, professional fees, and other amounts received as compensation for personal services. Unearned income includes interest received, dividends, royalties, pensions, annuities, capital gains, and rental income.

Rental income

If the property owner provides services such as repairs and maintenance, or other services to the tenants which are an important part of producing the rental income, then up to 30 percent of the net profit (not gross rent) is considered earned income. If no services are provided, then the rental income is all unearned income.

15

Capital Gain or Loss

For many years the federal government and many states have levied income taxes on any profit made from the sale or disposition of an asset, whether or not the asset is used in a business or for personal purposes. However, the deductibility of losses is limited to only those assets used for business purposes (loss on a personal residence or a personal car is *not* deductible). The methods used to calculate the gain (or loss) from the sale of an asset has not changed much over the years; the rate at which the tax is levied has undergone some changes.

While the tax has been on the books for quite awhile, it has only been in recent years that many people have become aware of it due primarily to the rising value of so many assets, particularly a personal residence. Almost every time a house is sold, there is a need to calculate a capital gain tax and adjust for its deferment. The tax itself has always been there, it is the capital gain upon disposition that is much more noticeable now with the escalation of property values.

The IRS disallows capital gain treatment for any gain earned by a *dealer* in real estate. Nor can a dealer qualify for a tax-deferred exchange of property. The tax definition of a dealer is one who trades in the sale of property, such as lots, in the ordinary course of business. A dealer holds property in inventory and is thus selling his stock in trade. The definition is not always precise as the line is drawn when the taxpayer-dealer holds property *primarily* for sale to customers. Courts have held that *primarily* means "of first importance," not merely a "substantial" purpose.

To calculate the gain (or loss) in the disposition of an asset, the taxpayer must know two things:

1. The adjusted basis of value.
2. The realized selling price.

The gain has nothing to do with the amount of cash invested, the appreciation of value by itself, the manner of financing, or the method used to sell the property. The gain subject to tax is simply the *difference* between the adjusted basis of value and the realized selling price. So what is the *adjusted basis?* And how does one define *realized selling price?* These are tax definitions and are more fully explained next.

BASIS OF VALUE

The initial basis of value for a real property investment is determined by its method of acquisition. This basis is then adjusted by additions or deductions that are applied to the property in accordance with tax accounting requirements to arrive at the adjusted basis of value. The figure is not only important in the calculation of capital gain but is also a necessary component in the determination of the amount of an investment that can be deducted from taxable income as a cost recovery item.

While an outright purchase of investment property with a basis determined by the purchase price may be the most likely procedure, there are a number of other acquisition methods, each having a different consequence for the initial basis of value. Seven of the more common methods of acquisition are listed below with the calculation for the basis of value explained.

Purchased property

The basis for purchased property is the amount paid, including both cash and debt acquired. It makes no difference what percentage of the purchase price is paid in cash, what percentage is borrowed, or what percentage is assumed as an existing mortgage loan. The *total price* paid is the basis of value for tax purposes. If the buyer pays a fee to secure a mortgage loan, that fee cannot be deducted as an expense in the current tax year, nor can it be added to the basis and recovered. However, if the property is business property, the taxpayer can deduct the fee by amortizing it over the life of the mortgage. For example, a $1,000 fee on a 20-year mortgage loan is deductible at the rate of $50 per year.

Property purchased with other property (unlike property)

If the purchase includes payment with other than cash or borrowed money—such as a car, a diamond, stocks, or bonds—the fair market value of the property used to make the purchase becomes the determinant of the basis of value for the acquired property. However, if the basis for property used to make the purchase is less than the acquired property's fair market value, then the difference between the basis and market value must be reported as a gain by the buyer. For example, if a buyer pays for a building with shares of General Motors stock having a market value of $150,000, the basis for the acquired building is $150,000. But, say the buyer's basis in the General Motors' stock (meaning the initial cost of acquiring the stock) is only $90,000, then the *buyer* has realized a $60,000 taxable gain in the transaction ($150,000 minus $90,000 equals $60,000).

Property exchange (like property)

When properties of a "like kind" are exchanged, there may be no immediate tax consequences as any gain can be deferred. The method used to defer the taxes is derived from the transfer of the basis of value. In this procedure, the basis for the property *acquired* is determined by the basis of the property *given up*, with adjustments for any unlike property used to equalize differences in the equity. Real estate has a special advantage in this exchange procedure in that any property held for investment classifies as like kind and thus may be exchanged with capital gains taxes deferred. For example, an income-producing apartment may be exchanged for an unimproved tract of land as a like-kind exchange since both are considered investment properties. (See Chapter 17 for further information on property exchange.)

Inherited property

The basis for inherited property generally is the market value on the deceased's date of death. When an estate must file a Federal Estate Tax Return, the taxpayer has the option of using a market value of six months after the date of death as a basis of value.

Property received as a gift

The recipient of gift property assumes the donor's adjusted basis at the time of the gift. If the donor pays a gift tax on the property, the amount of this tax is added to the donor's basis and thus to the recipient's. However, the recipient's basis cannot be increased above the fair market value of the property at the time of the gift.

Property received for services rendered

The fair market value of the services rendered becomes the basis for property received in exchange for services. The fair market value of the property so acquired would also be ordinary income to the recipient since it is compensation for services.

Foreclosed property

If a seller of real property holds a purchase money mortgage as a part of the consideration and then is forced to repossess the property, the basis of value becomes the sum of the unpaid obligation, plus any recognized gain, plus the cost of repossession. If the repossession is of *personal* property, the tax basis is the market value of the property because the seller's gain or loss occurs at the time of repossession.

ADJUSTMENTS TO THE BASIS

The initial basis of value must be adjusted from time to time as additions or reductions occur in the value.

Additions to the basis of value include the following:

- Improvements with a useful life of more than one year.
- Additions such as the acquiring of more land adjoining the property. Parcels of land acquired at different times must have separate bases, even if they are contiguous and form one tract of land.
- Commissions, legal fees to defend the title, and title insurance costs if paid by the buyer. (*Note:* A sales commission paid by the seller can be added to the seller's basis, or it can be deducted from the sales price. The tax consequence is the same either way.)
- Interest, taxes, and carrying charges on unimproved land may be capitalized (added to the basis) at the *owner's option* each year the property remains unproductive.
- Interest, taxes, and carrying charges *must* be capitalized on new construction for amortizing in not less than 10 years.

Reductions in the basis of value include the following:

- Depreciation and/or cost recovery are the most important deductions taken from the basis of value each year. (No recovery is permitted for a personal residence.) Even if a property owner deducts *less* than the maximum allowable cost recovery for reporting taxable income, the basis must still be reduced by the full amount allowed.

- Sale or disposition of excess land or any portion of the property. In the case of a sale of excess land, the basis of value must be reduced by an allocation of the value between the property sold and the property retained.
- Casualty loss is the difference between the value of the property immediately before and after the casualty. The loss cannot exceed the adjusted basis at the time of the casualty. Insurance proceeds received in excess of that needed to repair the damage must be deducted from the basis of value.
- Payment to an owner for an easement reduces the basis of value by the amount of the payment.

REALIZED SELLING PRICE

Capital gain is the difference between the adjusted basis of value and the realized selling price. Let us next examine what is meant by the latter term. Essentially it is the selling price of the property, less those expenses incurred to bring about the sale.

Total consideration received

The selling price of the property includes all consideration received—cash, notes, mortgages, and the fair market value of any real or personal property received in the transaction. The sales price for any *personal property* is *not* included in the total consideration received.

Deduct selling expenses

Following is a list of selling expenses deductible from the sales price if paid by seller:

1. Sales commission.
2. Advertising paid for by the seller.
3. Legal fees incurred in the sale.
4. Loan placement fees or discount paid by the seller.

EXAMPLE

Calculation of Capital Gain

For this example, a small warehouse is sold for $122,500. The buyer is assuming an existing mortgage loan in the amount of $94,500, and paying $22,000 in cash plus a trailer house with a fair market value of $6,000 as consideration for the equity. The seller acquired the property initially for $58,250 and over the period of ownership purchased an adjoining tract of land for $9,000 and added a building to the property costing $21,000. Also, the seller sold the right of an easement across a portion of the land for $3,500 and during the ownership period took a total of $26,500 in cost recovery deductions. The problem is to calculate the capital gain resulting from the sale.

Consideration received in sale:		
Cash	$22,000	
Fair market value of trailer	6,000	
Assumption of mortgage loan	94,500	
Total consideration received		$122,500
Expenses incurred in sale:		
Sales commission	$ 6,000	
Legal fees	750	
Total expenses		6,750
Realized Selling Price		$115,750
Basis of value calculation:		
Initial basis of property value	$58,250	
Additions:		
Purchase of adjoining land	9,000	
Warehouse addition	21,000	
	$88,250	
Reductions:		
Sale of easement	$ 3,500	
Cost recovery allowed	26,300	
Adjusted Basis of Value		58,450
Capital Gain		$57,300

SHORT–TERM AND LONG–TERM GAINS AND LOSSES

The tax code distinguishes between long-term and short-term capital gains. The line is drawn (since 1978) at one year for the holding period of the asset disposed of. If an asset is held over one year, it classifies for long-term tax treatment upon sale.

Further, capital gains must be reported on the sale of both property held for investment and on property held for personal use. However, capital losses may only be taken on property that has been held for investment; losses are *not deductible* on property held for personal use (personal residence, car, boat).

Reporting on gains and losses, the taxpayer must consolidate the long-term and short-term gains and losses. Only one-half of the long-term losses are permitted to be deducted. Carryover provisions allow losses to be taken in successive years if they exceed the allowable maximum deduction for the current tax year.

Capital Gains Tax Rates

The net amount of long-term capital gain (as reduced by any allowable capital losses) is 60 percent exempt from income taxes. Only 40 percent of the gain must be added to the ordinary income of the taxpayer for taxation in whatever bracket the taxpayer's total taxable income justifies. The 1981 Tax Act made *no change* in the percentage of a capital gain that is taxed as ordinary income.

Related Parties

A *loss* on the sale or exchange of property is not deductible if the transaction is directly, or indirectly, between the taxpayer and related parties. However, any gain in such a transaction is taxable. Related parties under this requirement include:

- Members of the taxpayer's family.
- A corporation with more than 50 percent of the stock owned by the taxpayer.
- A trust created by the taxpayer or in which the taxpayer is the beneficiary.
- An exempt charitable organization controlled by the taxpayer or any member of his family.

16

Accelerated Cost Recovery System

Under the Economic Recovery Tax Act of 1981, a major change was introduced in tax accounting for capital expenditures. The new method, identified as the *Accelerated Cost Recovery System (ACRS)*, essentially replaces the *useful life* depreciation rules that have developed since the beginning of income tax laws. The older depreciation rules had become very complex, and been rendered ineffective by persistent inflation, making it difficult to recover the cost of capital expenditures. The benefits derived from the new procedures help reduce the impact of inflation by significantly increasing the rate of recovery of capital expenditures. This is done in two ways:

1. The useful life concept has been eliminated and replaced with a shorter recovery period time span.
2. Cost recovery percentages are mandated for each year and are designed to produce accelerated recovery in the early years of ownership.

Generally, taxpayers are permitted to apply the provisions of ACRS with property placed in service after January 1, 1981. Since ACRS reduces the recoverable lives of real property, the potential to convert ordinary income into capital gain is enhanced. This will increase the desirability of real estate as an investment.

There has been no basic change in the kind of property qualifying for cost recovery—it must meet the same tests that applied to depreciable property. These are as follows:

1. It must be used in business or held for the production of income.
2. It must have a limited and determinable useful life longer than one year. Thus, land cost cannot be recovered since it does not have a limited and determinable life.
3. It must be something that wears out, decays, gets used up, becomes obsolete, or loses value from natural causes.

Cost recovery, or depreciable property, used partly for business and partly for personal purposes, can be recovered by allocation, since only that portion used for business is deductible. Also, if the property is owned for a portion of the tax year, recovery is permitted for only that part of the year it is owned.

Cost recovery and depreciation are allowable deductions only if claimed on the tax return. If an investor, for any reason, fails to take the deduction and allows the three-year period for amending a return to expire, the deduction is lost forever. Even so, in computing the gain or loss on the sale of an asset, the IRS requires a reduction in the *basis of value* for cost recovery, whether or not it is taken as a deduction from income (thus increasing the gain subject to tax).

DEPRECIATION PROCEDURES REVIEWED

Because the nomenclature and methods that formerly applied serve as helpful reference points for the new procedures, and because property placed in service prior to January 1, 1981 must report depreciation in the same manner as previously committed to, this section undertakes a review of the principal elements employed by the useful life method of calculating depreciation deductions.

Under previous rules, the taxpayer needed to determine the following in order to calculate depreciation: (1) the basis of value, (2) the salvage value, (3) the useful life, and (4) a method of depreciation. Each of these requirements is explained as follows:

Basis of Value

The basis of value is determined initially by the method of acquisition. Purchase is the most common method used to acquire property, and the basis of value is easily figured as the amount paid for the property, including both cash and money borrowed for the acquisition. However, there are a number of other ways to acquire property, and each may result in a different basis. The procedures are the same as described in the previous chapter for the determination of capital gain.

Salvage Value

The maximum amount of depreciation permitted under the old rules was the difference between the basis of value and the salvage value. The preferred definition of salvage value is the estimated value of the property at the end of its useful life to the taxpayer. This determination is made at the time of acquisition and is not adjusted later, regardless of price level changes. The amount of salvage value depends on how the property is used, how long it is used, and the policy of the taxpayer in disposing of assets. If the policy is to dispose of an asset while it is still in good operating condition, the salvage value could be relatively high. If, on the other hand, the policy is to use something until it is no longer usable, the salvage value could be considered its junk value.

Useful Life

The useful life of depreciable property is an estimate of how long the taxpayer expects it to be useful in the trade or business. This is the length of time over which depreciation deductions can be taken. It is not so much how long a piece of property will last, but how long it will continue to be useful.

A number of things affect the useful life of a property and should be considered in making an estimate; these include:

1. How often the property is used.
2. How old it was when acquired.
3. How often it is repaired or parts replaced.
4. The climate in which it is used.
5. Normal technological progress and economic changes that may shorten its useful life.

There is no standard of useful life that applies to a particular type of property, because it may vary from user to user. The experience of the individual taxpayer should be considered in making the determination, and where this experience is lacking, an industry-wide experience may be substituted.

IRS Depreciation Guidelines. While the IRS set no specific requirements for the determination of useful life, other than that it be
reasonable and relate directly to the taxpayer's special usage, there were
some guidelines published. Under the name of Asset Depreciation
Range, the IRS offered a suggested lower limit in years of useful life, an
average called the Asset Guideline Period, and an upper limit. For real
estate investments, the guidelines were generally on the lengthy side and
not widely used.

Methods of Depreciation

The taxpayer formerly could use any one of a number of depreciation
methods so long as it met certain IRS rules and requirements. Four
methods of depreciation were most commonly used—(1) straight line, (2)
component, (3) declining balance, and (4) sum of the year's digits. These
are explained briefly, along with their present status.

Straight line

The basic procedure for calculating depreciation was to divide the total
amount of permissible depreciation by the number of years of useful life.
This resulted in a constant amount of depreciation each year. For example, a $20,000 property with a useful life of 10 years could be depreciated
at the rate of $2,000 per year ($20,000 divided by 10), disregarding any
salvage value. The depreciation *rate* for such a property would be 10 percent per year (100 divided by 10 = 10 percent). Straight line is still an acceptable option for taxpayers under ACRS procedures—the option
spreads the depreciation (or cost recovery) deductions over a greater
number of years than do the four "accelerated recovery periods" also permitted.

Component

A straight-line method that previously allowed the taxpayer to separate
the building into its basic cost components (such as walls, roof, floors,
heating and air conditioning) and allocate different useful lives to each of
the components. The method allowed room for considerable conjecture
on the part of the taxpayer as to just what value could be attributed to
each of the components and how to measure the separate useful lives. In
the last few years of its usage, component depreciation was limited by the
IRS to new construction—buildings that could more easily be separated
into their component costs. The new Tax Act of 1981 now *prohibits* the
use of component depreciation.

Nevertheless, it is quite possible for an investor to encounter component depreciation in an analysis of properties placed in service prior to 1981. For this reason, an example of how component depreciation is computed follows.

Use of the component method requires the deduction of salvage value from the adjusted basis *before* a depreciation rate is applied.

EXAMPLE

A building with an adjusted basis of $90,000 and a salvage value of $9,000 (total depreciation allowed = $81,000) is broken into seven component parts. Each component is assigned a proportionate share of the total depreciation amount (percent of building), a respective value (*value*), and a useful life. The useful life is converted into an annual percentage rate, and the annual depreciation for each of the components is computed in the last column.

Component	Percent of Building	Value	Life	Annual Percent	Annual Depreciation
Shell	40.0	$32,400	40 yrs.	2.5%	$ 810
Roof	7.5	$ 6,075	12 yrs.	8.3%	$ 504
Floor	7.5	$ 6,075	12 yrs.	8.3%	$ 504
Plumbing	12.0	$ 9,720	12 yrs.	8.3%	$ 807
Electrical	15.0	$12,150	10 yrs.	10.0%	$1,215
Heating & Air Conditioning	15.0	$12,150	10 yrs.	10.0%	$1,215
Paving	3.0	$ 2,430	8 yrs.	12.5%	$ 304
Totals	100.0	$81,000			$5,359

Declining balance

This method was formerly approved for certain classes of property and allowed accelerated depreciation deductions in the early years of ownership. *Accelerated* means a rate of depreciation greater than that allowed by a straight-line rate. The new ACRS "Accelerated Recovery Tables" automatically allow cost recovery (depreciation deductions) at percentage rates commensurate with the older declining balance formulas, with a switch to straight line at the optimum point in the ownership period. Therefore, declining balance procedures are no longer necessary for the investor interested in greater deductions in the early years of ownership. However, the older procedures can be more fully explained by citing an example showing calculations on next page.

There is an important drawback to accelerated deductions—any depreciation taken with an accelerated procedure, *including that permitted under ACRS*, is subject to certain recapture provisions. This means that upon disposition of the property, any gain resulting from depreciation or cost recovery taken at accelerated rates may be taxed at ordinary income rates rather than as a capital gain. (See later section on "Recapture.")

When applied to approved types of property, all declining balance methods of computation are made the same way with three different accelerations permitted—125 percent, 150 percent, and 200 percent. All start with a properly computed straight-line base rate. In the following example, a building is valued at $90,000 with a useful life of 25 years—the annual straight-line depreciation rate is 4 percent. Under declining balance procedures, salvage value is *not* deducted before the depreciation rate is applied. Following is the basic calculation method:

To compute accelerated rate:		
Straight-line rate	4%	
at 125% declining balance (DB)	× 1.25%	
Accelerated rate	5%	
To appy accelerated rate:		
Building value	$90,000	
$90,000 × .05 =	4,500	Deduct 1st yr. depreciation
Value, beginning of 2nd yr.	$85,500	
$85,500 × .05 =	4,275	Deduct 2nd yr. depreciation
Value, beginning of 3rd yr.	$81,225	
$81,225 × .05 =	4,061	Deduct 3rd yr. depreciation
Value, beginning of 4th yr.	$77,164	
$77,164 × .05 =	3,858	Deduct 4th yr. depreciation
Value, beginning of 5th yr.	$73,306	
$73,306 × .05 =	3,665	Deduct 5th yr. depreciation
Value, beginning of 6th yr.	$69,641	

Note that each year's depreciation amount is deducted from the property value, thereby establishing a new basis of value for the next year's depreciation calculation. An important point to remember is that while salvage value is not deductible from the basis of property value before applying the accelerated depreciation rate, the taxpayer may not depreciate a property below its salvage value. It is possible, by using accelerated depreciation, to come to the end of a useful life term without having deducted the full amount of available depreciation (which is the adjusted basis of property value, less the salvage value). To permit the use of all depreciation to which a taxpayer is entitled, a switch to a straight-line rate was permitted at the taxpayer's option.

Sum of the year's digits method

Another accelerated depreciation method that was acceptable to the IRS in certain situations is the *sum of the year's digits* method. The "digits" are the years, and the basic denominator of the rate is the sum of the years used as a useful life. If useful life is five years, for example, the sum of the digits is $5 + 4 + 3 + 2 + 1 = 15$. To calculate the applicable depreciation for the first year, the equation would be: $5/15 \times$ property value = depreciation. A simple formula for the sum of the years is:

$$\frac{(\text{n years} \times \text{n years}) + \text{n years}}{2} = \text{sum of the years}$$

Thus, if the useful life is 25 years, the sum of the years is:

$$\frac{(25 \text{ years} \times 25 \text{ years}) + 25 \text{ years}}{2} = 325 \text{ years}$$

To compute depreciation each year under this method, the number of years of remaining useful life is used as the numerator of the key fraction with the sum of the years as the denominator (which, of course, remains constant). This fraction is then multiplied by the depreciable base of property value to arrive at annual amounts of depreciation. For this method, the basis must first be reduced by the property's salvage value.

If the property has a 25-year useful life and a depreciable value (after deducting salvage value) of $81,000, the computation is as follows:

Year	Fraction Applied		Depreciable Value	Annual Depreciation
1	25/325	×	$81,000	$6,228
2	24/325	×	$81,000	$5,978
3	23/325	×	$81,000	$5,735
4	22/325	×	$81,000	$5,484
5	21/325	×	$81,000	$5,233

. . . and so on for each succeeding year.

DEPRECIATION PROCEDURES COMPARED

To assist in making the transition from the older depreciation methods based on the taxpayer's selection of a useful life for depreciable property to understanding the new concept of assigning *recovery property* to four classes (each with a specific recovery life), the following general comparison is offered.

Under the old rules, the *total* amount of depreciation that could be taken was limited to the difference between the adjusted basis of value and the salvage value of the property. Since salvage value was determined by the taxpayer in accordance with some rather generalized rules, there was always a question as to what might be the proper amount. Under the new ACRS law, salvage value is not a consideration.

Also, under the old rules, the *period of time* over which a property could be depreciated was left in some measure to be determined by the taxpayer. This was done by allowing flexibility in the selection of a proper useful life for the property. Since the useful life helped determine the amount of annual depreciation, this, too, became a subject of controversy with the IRS. ACRS attempts to simplify the problem by mandating four recovery periods: (1) three years, (2) five years, (3) ten years, or (4) fifteen years. The recovery period that applies depends on the type of property. ACRS also allows the taxpayer several optional time periods of greater length, providing the deductions are taken in accordance with straight-line depreciation procedures.

The old rules allowed the taxpayer to select any method of depreciation among a number approved by the IRS. The method used had to be reasonable and applied consistently—which left more open questions for taxpayers. The four methods of depreciation most commonly used in the past were (1) straight line, (2) component, (3) declining balance, and (4) sum of the year's digits. Further complications developed in selecting a method because the IRS would not permit all methods to be used with all types of properties. As the rules on depreciation developed over the years, distinctions were made between which method applied to new or used property and to residential or commercial property. ACRS has simplified a portion of this problem by eliminating any distinction between new and used properties—the same rules apply to both. But there are still distinctions made between residential, commercial, low-cost housing, and rehabilitation costs.

INTRODUCTION TO ACRS

The sweeping changes that have been enacted in the Tax Act of 1981 drastically alter the methods that may be used to recover (deduct) the cost of capital expenditures. To help accomplish this, new terminology is used to identify the elements of the Accelerated Cost Recovery System (ACRS). In general, property is no longer depreciated—its cost is recovered. *Useful life,* construed as a period of time over which deductions may be taken, has given way to a *recovery period*. Four basic recovery periods have been created, plus several longer optional periods, with specific assignments of property to each of the four periods. Each of the four periods has a recovery table which spells out in percentages the amount of deduction that can be taken for each year (or month in the case of real property). The following discussion explains the principal elements of ACRS and points out the distinctions between applications affecting personal property and real property.

Classes of Recovery Property

For use with ACRS deductions, recovery property means depreciable tangible property that is used either in a trade or business or is held for the production of income. The classes of recovery property, as defined here, are focused primarily on the needs of a real estate investor. The class lives in terms of years refers to the Asset Depreciation Range (ADR) guidelines approved by Congress in the Revenue Act of 1971. Each item of recovery property is assigned to one of the following classes:

- *3-year property*. Cars and light trucks. Property with an ADR life of 4 years or less.
- *5-year property*. Machinery, office equipment, furnishings, and large trucks. Generally, it is not 3-year or 5-year property—it is property with an ADR life of 5 years or more.
- *10-year property*. Depreciable real property with an ADR class life of 12.5 years or less. Theme park structures, prefab or manufactured housing, long-lived utility assets.
- *15-year property*. Depreciable real property that does not have an ADR class life of 12.5 years or less.

Application of Statutory Recovery Rates

ACRS uses a statutory percentage to be applied to the unadjusted basis of value in determining the amount of recovery deduction. There is a distinction between personal property and real property as to how the percentages are applied.

Personal Property.   In Table 16–1 the annual recovery percentage for the first year is based on a "half-year" convention which allows one-half year's recovery in the year of acquisition but *no* recovery deduction in the year of sale. The same recovery period must be used for all personal property of a class for which an election is made. Once made, the election is

TABLE 16-1

ACRS Statutory Percentages*

Recovery Year	Classes of Property			
	3-year	5-year	10-year	15-year
1	25	15	8	5
2	38	22	14	10
3	37	21	12	9
4		21	10	8
5		21	10	7
6			10	7
7			9	6
8			9	6
9			9	6
10			9	6
11				6
12				6
13				6
14				6
15				6

*NOTE: Table applies to personal property, and for the 15-year class, to public utility property.

revocable only with the consent of the IRS. Personal property assigned to the same class but placed in service in other tax years, or personal property in other classes, may use either applicable ACRS deductions or a straight-line ACRS deduction based on a different allowable recovery period.

Real Property.   The IRS has developed by regulation a different set of applicable percentages which are based on a month-by-month deduction in contrast to the annual percentage applied to personal property. This means that real property qualifies for a deduction for *each month* the property is in service, including the year of acquisition and of disposition. The real property percentages are based on the 175 percent declining balance method over 15 years, with a switch to straight-line recovery at the optimal crossover point (Table 16–2). Tables for low-income housing apply the 200 percent declining balance method, also switching to straight line (Table 16–3).

TABLE 16-2
15-Year Real Property Table (other than low-income housing)

Year						Month Placed in Service						
	1	2	3	4	5	6	7	8	9	10	11	12
1st	12%	11%	10%	9%	8%	7%	6%	5%	4%	3%	2%	1%
2d	10%	10%	11%	11%	11%	11%	11%	11%	11%	11%	11%	12%
3d	9%	9%	9%	9%	10%	10%	10%	10%	10%	10%	10%	10%
4th	8%	8%	8%	8%	8%	8%	9%	9%	9%	9%	9%	9%
5th	7%	7%	7%	7%	7%	7%	8%	8%	8%	8%	8%	8%
6th	6%	6%	6%	6%	6%	7%	7%	7%	7%	7%	7%	7%
7th	6%	6%	6%	6%	6%	6%	6%	6%	6%	6%	6%	6%
8th	6%	6%	6%	6%	6%	6%	6%	6%	6%	6%	6%	6%
9th	6%	6%	6%	6%	6%	6%	6%	6%	6%	6%	6%	6%
10th	5%	6%	5%	6%	5%	5%	5%	5%	5%	5%	6%	5%
11th	5%	5%	5%	5%	5%	5%	5%	5%	5%	5%	5%	5%
12th	5%	5%	5%	5%	5%	5%	5%	5%	5%	5%	5%	5%
13th	5%	5%	5%	5%	5%	5%	5%	5%	5%	5%	5%	5%
14th	5%	5%	5%	5%	5%	5%	5%	5%	5%	5%	5%	5%
15th	5%	5%	5%	5%	5%	5%	5%	5%	5%	5%	5%	5%
16th	—	—	1%	1%	2%	2%	3%	3%	4%	4%	4%	5%

TABLE 16–3

15-Year Property Low-Income Housing Table

	Month Placed in Service											
Year	1	2	3	4	5	6	7	8	9	10	11	12
1st	13%	12%	11%	10%	9%	8%	7%	6%	4%	3%	2%	1%
2d	12%	12%	12%	12%	12%	12%	12%	13%	13%	13%	13%	13%
3d	10%	10%	10%	10%	11%	11%	11%	11%	11%	11%	11%	11%
4th	9%	9%	9%	9%	9%	9%	9%	9%	10%	10%	10%	10%
5th	8%	8%	8%	8%	8%	8%	8%	8%	8%	8%	8%	9%
6th	7%	7%	7%	7%	7%	7%	7%	7%	7%	7%	7%	7%
7th	6%	6%	6%	6%	6%	6%	6%	6%	6%	6%	6%	6%
8th	5%	5%	5%	5%	5%	5%	5%	5%	5%	5%	5%	6%
9th	5%	5%	5%	5%	5%	5%	5%	5%	5%	5%	5%	5%
10th	5%	5%	5%	5%	5%	5%	5%	5%	5%	5%	5%	5%
11th	4%	5%	5%	5%	5%	5%	5%	5%	5%	5%	5%	5%
12th	4%	4%	4%	5%	4%	5%	5%	5%	5%	5%	5%	5%
13th	4%	4%	4%	4%	4%	4%	5%	4%	5%	5%	5%	5%
14th	4%	4%	4%	4%	4%	4%	4%	4%	4%	5%	4%	4%
15th	4%	4%	4%	4%	4%	4%	4%	4%	4%	4%	4%	4%
16th	—	—	1%	1%	2%	2%	2%	3%	3%	3%	4%	4%

Straight-line ACRS Election

If the accelerated rates for deductions allowed under the statutory percentage tables are not acceptable, the taxpayer may elect to claim straight-line ACRS deductions over the regular recovery period or optional longer recovery periods. Again, there is a difference in the application between real and personal property.

Personal Property.   The optional recovery periods for application of straight-line rates are as follows:

For Recovery Class	Taxpayer May Elect Recovery Period
3-year property	3, 5, or 12 years
5-year property	5, 12, or 25 years
10-year property	10, 25, or 35 years
15-year property	15, 35, or 45 years

Under this election, the half-year rule applies; that is, a half-year recovery can be claimed for the year the property is placed in service and in the year following the end of the recovery period. If disposition is made before the end of the recovery period, no deduction is allowed for that year.

Real Property.   The optional recovery periods under the straight-line ACRS election are 15, 35, and 45 years. Application is made on a month-to-month basis for the time the property is in service. One additional important point—in regard to real property, the taxpayer is not confined to using the same recovery period for all property in the same class as is required for personal property. The election as to recovery period can be made by the taxpayer on a property-by-property basis. Revocation of such an election can be made only with the consent of the IRS.

ACRS eliminates component depreciation, generally requiring composite depreciation of the entire structure. However, there are components, such as low-income rehabilitation expenditures, that a taxpayer may properly elect to amortize separately from the building. Also, if the taxpayer makes a substantial improvement to the building, it is treated as a *separate building*. In such a case, the taxpayer may use an accelerated ACRS deduction or a longer recovery period with straight-line ACRS deduction for the improvement, regardless of the ACRS method or recovery period that is used for the rest of the building. An improvement is defined as a substantial improvement if (1) the amounts added to the capital account over a two-year period are at least 25 percent of the adjusted basis (disregarding depreciation and amortization adjustments); and (2) the improvement was made at least three years after the building was placed in service. For example, a taxpayer claiming a straight-line ACRS deduction over a 35-year recovery period for a building may claim the accelerated ACRS deduction for a substantial improvement over a 15-year recovery period.

EXAMPLE

To compute the amount of deduction, the straight line rate is applied to the unadjusted basis of property value. To calculate a straight-line percentage, divide 100 by the number of years in the recovery period. For example, if the taxpayer elects a 35-year recovery period, the straight-line rate is 2.8571% (100 divided by 35 = 2.8571). As an alternative method of calculation, the amount of annual deduction can be determined by dividing the unadjusted basis of value by the number of years in the recovery period. If the unadjusted basis is $200,000 and the recovery period is 35 years, the deduction for each year amounts to $5,714.29 ($200,000 divided by 35 = $5,714.29). Remember, the application of these straight-line rates under the ACRS rules *does not* consider a salvage value—the application is against the total of the unadjusted basis of value. Under the previous method of depreciating property, straight-line rates could only be applied to the difference existing between the basis of value and the salvage value; that is, salvage value must be deducted before figuring depreciation amounts.

Unadjusted Basis of Value. The unadjusted basis of value that is recovered under ACRS is the basis of the property unadjusted for depreciation, amortization, or depletion. The unadjusted basis does not include (1) that portion of the basis for which there is an election to amortize, such as expenditures to rehabilitate low-income housing, and (2) that portion of the basis for which there is an election to expense the cost for personal property used in trade or business, rather than claiming an ACRS deduction. The unadjusted basis for computing ACRS deductions is that determined in the year the property is put into service. Further IRS regulations will be issued to disclose how to compute ACRS deductions in the case of basis redeterminations.

Allocation of the Basis of Value. When buildings are acquired in lump sum transactions, it is necessary to separate the cost of the land from the building. The purpose of the separation is to permit cost recovery solely on that portion of the acquisition that qualifies for this deduction, since land cost cannot be recovered. With new buildings, this is seldom a problem because the land is acquired separately and achieves its own basis from the method of acquisition.

So long as the allocation of the property cost between land and building is fair and reasonable, the IRS can accept the taxpayer's decision. However, it is subject to IRS scrutiny as the taxpayer might have a tendency to make a higher allocation to the depreciable property amount to achieve larger deductions in future years. There are several ways that help produce an allocation acceptable to the IRS:

1. The purchase contract may specify the prices for major components of the property. If the allocation is reasonable and negotiated at "arms length," a solid justification is provided.
2. An appraisal by a professional (not the taxpayer) gives good evidence of how a lump sum purchase price can be allocated.
3. The taxpayer may use an *ad valorem* tax assessment of the property. The tax assessment usually distinguishes between the value of the land and the value of the improvements thereon. The same ratio of values applied to the acquisition cost would give a sound basis for the allocation between land and buildings.

It is also important that an allocation of the acquisition cost be made between buildings and *personal property* acquired at the same time for use in the business. The reason, of course, is the substantial difference in recovery periods that applies to buildings versus personal property. The IRS expects the taxpayer to establish proper recovery periods for each asset during the first tax year.

Antichurning and Antiavoidance Rules

To prevent a taxpayer from transferring property between related persons or controlled companies for the purpose of utilizing the accelerated cost recovery procedures allowed under ACRS, certain rules are designed to disallow the tax advantages. If the main purpose of a transfer is to avoid antichurning rules, the property is excluded from classification as recovery property.

More specifically, ACRS qualification does not apply to real property if (1) the taxpayer or a person related to the taxpayer owned the property during 1980 (the year before ACRS methods were allowed), (2) the property is leased back to a person who owned the property during 1980 or to a person related to that person, or (3) the property is acquired in nonrecognition transactions, such as certain like-kind property exchanges, rollovers of low-income housing, involuntary conversions, repossessions, or in return for property the taxpayer or a related person owned during 1980. For these purposes, a person is considered related to the previous owner if there exists ownership of 10 percent of a corporation or partnership, if there is a family or fiduciary relationship, or if common control, meaning ownership of more than 50 percent of the business, is present.

RECAPTURE OF DEPRECIATION

Since 1962, the Internal Revenue Code has included a special tax requirement applicable to the portion of a gain that is attributable to depreciation. Until just a few years ago, the sale of depreciated property rarely resulted in substantial capital gains. But with the persistent inflation of recent years, older properties have appreciated in value, and the *recapture* requirement has become a more important tax consideration.

This requirement applies only at the time of sale, exchange, involuntary conversion, distribution by a corporation or partnership, or other disposition. Furthermore there must be a gain on the sale or exchange before this requirement is applicable. *Gain* means that the amount realized from the transfer of ownership must be in excess of the adjusted basis of property value.

Separate rules apply to a gain realized from a depreciation or cost recovery deduction taken on personal property (when used for business purposes) and that taken on real property. It should be noted that the 1981 Tax Act did not make any essential change in the recapture rules as it applies to personal property, but it did make significant changes with respect to real property recovery recapture.

Recapture of Gain on Personal Property (Section 1245 Property)

Personal property is governed by the simplest recapture rules. So we start there. Personal property in this context is the tax definition and thus may not be the same as a state law's definition of personal property. Personal property is movable property that is subject to depreciation, such as furniture or machinery. It can be either tangible or intangible property. Personal property under the tax code also includes such items as elevators and escalators, certified pollution control facilities, on-the-job training facilities, and child care facilities.

Treatment of Gain on Personal Property. The rule says that the portion of a personal property capital gain resulting from depreciation or cost recovery deductions during ownership term must be reported and taxed as ordinary income. The method used to determine these deductions does not affect the amount that is subject to recapture for personal property. In this category, *all* depreciation deductions are subject to recapture if a gain is made on a sale.

Consider, for example, personal property acquired for $6,000, assigned to a five-year class recovery period, and the taxpayer has used a straight-line recovery rate amounting to a deduction of $1,200 per year. At the end of three years the property is sold with the taxpayer having recovered deductions of $3,600. Following are the tax consequences for the property if sold at three different prices:

To figure adjusted basis of value:	
Initial basis	$6,000
Less: 3 yrs. cost recovery	3,600
Adjusted basis	$2,400
If sales price is	$2,000
Less: Adjusted basis	2,400
Loss	($400)

No recapture results since a loss was sustained

If sales price is	$4,000
Less: Adjusted basis	2,400
Gain subject to recapture	$1,600

The $1,600 gain must be reported as ordinary income, not as a capital gain.

If sales price is	$8,000
Less: Adjusted basis	2,400
Gain subject to taxation	$5,600

The gain in this instance *exceeds* the $3,600 cost recovered. Only the amount of cost recovered can be recaptured. Therefore, this gain is allocated:

Total gain	$5,600
Taxed as ordinary income	3,600
Taxed as capital gain	$2,000

Recapture of Gain on Real Property (Section 1250 Property)

The rules governing the recapture of gain upon disposition of real property have been changed under the 1981 Tax Act. Under prior law, real property gain was recaptured only to the extent that accelerated depreciation deductions exceeded straight-line deductions. With certain exceptions, the new law requires recapture of *all ACRS accelerated recovery deductions* as ordinary income, *including* the equivalent straight-line portion. More specifically, the recapture provisions are applied as follows:

- *15-year Nonresidential Real Property.* Recapture applies to *all gain* which must be treated as ordinary income to the extent of recovery under accelerated ACRS methods. Recapture is not limited to the excess of accelerated depreciation over the amount of straight-line depreciation. However, if the straight-line method is selected, *all gain is treated as capital gain.*
- *15-year Residential Rental Property.* Gain on a disposition is recaptured as ordinary income only to the extent ACRS deductions exceed the recovery that would have been allowed if the straight-line method had been used over a 15-year period. Therefore, if the straight-line method is elected, all gain is capital gain.
- *Low-Income Housing.* Recapture is being phased out for 15-year real property that is subsidized low-income housing.
- *Specialized Properties.* Theme park structures, single purpose agricultural and horticultural buildings, and facilities used for the storage of petroleum and its products are subject to taxation as ordinary income to the extent of all prior ACRS deductions.

Recapture applies only to properties used in business or for the production of income. Property used for personal purposes does not qualify for depreciation or cost recovery and, therefore, has no such deductions subject to recapture. However, gain upon the disposition of property used for personal purposes is subject to the capital gain tax. (See Chapter 18 for the special tax treatment accorded personal residential property.)

17

Tax Advantage Transactions

There are several types of transactions that offer special tax advantages for an investor. One is an exchange of like-kind property that offers a deferral of capital gains taxes; another is a change in the installment sales rules that allows taxes to be paid over the extended period of time that payments are received. Also, there is a new option to expense certain depreciable business assets (replacing the first-year bonus depreciation) and an expansion of tax credits to include rehabilitation of older buildings and qualifying historic structures. These are considered in this chapter.

TAX–DEFERRED EXCHANGE OF PROPERTY

The IRS allows some assets to be exchanged without requiring the immediate payment of a capital gain tax on the transaction. These rules extend beyond real estate: a bond may be converted into common stock; a life insurance policy may be exchanged for an endowment or an annuity; certain U.S. Treasury notes can be exchanged for other issues—all without a recognition of capital gain. A special section of the tax code (Section 1031) deals with certain types of property that can be exchanged for other like-kind property with a deferral of the tax on the capital gain. The deferral requires that the basis of the property given up must become the basis of the property acquired. Thus, any gain realized becomes taxable when the property is ultimately disposed of.

To illustrate the advantage that can accrue to the investor, consider a landowner called Smith. Smith owns a tract of land worth $75,000 which has an adjusted basis of value of $25,000. If Smith sells the land outright for $75,000, a capital gains tax is assessed against the $50,000 gain ($75,000 − $25,000 = $50,000). Now if Smith finds another property, say a rental house selling for $75,000, whose owner is willing to trade, a swap of the two properties can be accomplished with no taxes due. The method used to defer—not eliminate—the gains tax requires that Smith show a basis of value in the acquired property of $25,000—the same as applied to the property given up. When Smith sells the acquired property, any gain is computed from the $25,000 basis. If Smith had purchased the rental house outright after selling his own land, then the basis for the acquired property would be the purchase price of $75,000.

Obviously, the lower basis resulting from the exchange reduces the cost recovery deduction that can be taken. But the exchange procedure does defer the payment of any capital gains tax otherwise due in the year of sale. Of course, it is not realistic to believe that two properties can be exchanged on an exactly even basis because the equity of each owner is most likely different. To equalize the equities, the principals generally offer what is called *unlike* property, such as cash. Any unlike property *received* is subject to tax.

To Qualify for Tax-Deferred Treatment

1. The property given up and the property received must be held by the taxpayers for business or investment purposes. It cannot be property for personal use, such as a personal residence or a car. It cannot be stock in trade or property held for sale in an inventory. This qualification eliminates dealers in land or lots for tax-deferred treatment since their land is classed as "inventory"—not held for investment. The property can be most any kind of a capital asset used in the taxpayer's business for a productive purpose. It can be machinery, office equipment, cars, buildings, or land. It can be a leasehold for real estate providing the lease has 30 years or more remaining life.

2. The properties traded must be essentially like-kind, which depends on the nature of the property rather than its grade or quality. For the purpose of tax deferral, real estate carries a distinct advantage over other forms of property. Almost any type of real estate can be traded for other real estate and meet this qualification. An apart-

ment property, for example, might be traded for an unimproved tract of land as both are considered investment properties and, thus, *like-kind*. On the other hand, an exchange of investment real estate for a piece of machinery would not qualify since machinery is personal property.

3. If a part of the trade is *unlike property* (and this is most often the case), only the unlike portion is subject to capital gains tax in the year of the trade. Unlike property, such as cash, is usually necessary in an exchange to equalize the equities owned by each of the principals involved. It is the unlike property *received*—not paid out—that is subject to a capital gain tax. The gain (or loss) on the unlike property received is the difference between the adjusted basis and the fair market value of the unlike property.

4. A property exchange must occur between the principals in the transaction. Two-party exchanges are the most common, but three-party exchanges have been approved. If one of the parties must purchase additional property to satisfy a part of the property trade, care must be taken that title transfers first to the principal who is giving up the property. A transfer of the property directly to the recipient of the exchange can disqualify the transaction for tax-deferred treatment.

Tax Treatment for Unlike Property

In an exchange of property, it is the difference in equity ownership that requires some adjustment in the form of additional consideration. Two properties, each worth exactly $100,000 cannot be exchanged equally unless the equities are the same. For example, if Owner A has an equity of $65,000 in a $100,000 property and Owner B's equity is $45,000 in his $100,000 property, the two could not trade equally. Owner A would require additional consideration in the amount of $20,000 (the difference between his $65,000 ownership interest and the property to be acquired's equity of $45,000) to consummate the trade. Owner B would have to put up the additional $20,000 in the form of additional like property (say another piece of land), or it could be handled with unlike property. If like property is added, the tax can be deferred. The unlike property could be in the form of (1) cash, (2) property other than cash, such as shares of stock, which is called *boot*, or (3) net loan relief.

Cash

Requires no explanation but is always considered unlike property and subject to taxes.

Other property (boot)

Such property valued at its fair market worth at the time of the transaction becomes subject to capital gains tax. Further, if the party giving up the other property has realized a gain (the difference between the other property's adjusted basis and the fair market value at the time of the transaction), then an additional capital gains tax becomes due on the increase in value.

Net loan relief

When property with a mortgage debt is exchanged, the owner relinquishing the debt is relieved of paying that debt. This is true for property exchange tax treatment whether or not the liability for the mortgage debt is assumed. Relief of the debt is a form of unlike property and can result in a taxable gain. A special tax rule applies to debt relief in exchanges where *both* properties have mortgage debts. The rule is that the two mortgages are *netted out*, and the amount of unlike property received is the amount that the mortgage debt on the property given up exceeds the amount of the mortgage on the property received. Remember, gain is taxable only on the unlike property *received*—in this case it is the relief from a mortgage debt that is received.

EXAMPLE

Unlike Property Involved in Exchange

The following example illustrates how the receipt of unlike property is calculated. Consider the following transaction:

Owner A		Owner B
$70,000	Market value	$90,000
$45,000	Less: Mortgage	55,000
$25,000	Equity	$35,000

To equalize the equities in this transaction, Owner A would have to pay Owner B an additional $10,000, say, in cash. And since Owner B is exchanging a $55,000 mortgage for one of $45,000, Owner B also receives a net loan relief in the amount of $10,000. Following is a listing of how the tax consequences are figured:

Owner A:
  Pays $10,000 in cash
  Assumes $10,000 in new debt
    Owner A *receives* no unlike property.

Owner B:
Receives	$10,000 in cash
Receives loan relief of	$10,000
Owner B *receives*	$20,000 in unlike property.

Another Illustration of Nontaxable Exchange

The taxpayer exchanges real estate held for investment which has an ad-justed basis of $80,000 for other like-kind real estate. Say the real estate received has a fair market value of $100,000 and the taxpayer also received $10,000 in cash to equalize the equities. In this example, the total *realized* gain is $30,000 ($20,000 in an increase in property value plus $10,000 in cash). However, only the $10,000 cash received is *recognized* as a gain and becomes taxable in the year of the trade. The tax on the $20,000 gain from property value increase can be deferred until the property is sold.

Transaction Costs

All transaction costs—brokerage commissions, taxes, filing fees, escrow costs, and so forth—effectively reduce the proceeds of a sale and thus reduce the realized gain. The IRS has ruled that cash paid for transaction costs is the same as cash paid in the exchange. So, for the purpose of calculating the amount of unlike property received in an exchange, any transaction costs paid in cash reduce the amount of cash received. It follows that transaction costs would reduce the net amount of loan relief if these costs exceed the cash paid in an exchange.

Indicated Gain and Recognized Gain

The IRS identifies the actual gain that a taxpayer realizes in a property exchange as *indicated* gain (or in some cases it is called *realized* gain). This is not the gain subject to taxes in the year of the sale. It is the *recognized* gain that becomes taxable. The following example illustrates the difference in the two types of gain. The indicated gain is calculated from what the owner *gives up*—the difference between the adjusted basis and the fair market value, less transaction costs. The recognized gain is determined from what the parties *receive* in the transaction, with only the gain on unlike property becoming recognized and thus taxable in the year of the sale.

EXAMPLE

Computation of Indicated (Realized) and
Recognized (Taxable) Gains

In an exchange of property between Owner A and Owner B, the following conditions existed *before* the exchange:

Owner A		Owner B
$340,000	Property	$375,000
$220,000	Adjusted basis	$290,000
$190,000	Mortgage	$275,000
$150,000	Equities	$100,000

To equalize the equities:

> Owner B paid $50,000 cash to Owner A.

Costs of closing the transaction:

Owner A paid	$18,500
Owner B paid	$21,000

To calculate the indicated gain:

Owner A has given up:

Market value of property		$340,000
Less: Adjusted basis	$220,000	
Transaction costs	18,500	
		$238,500
Indicated Gain		$101,500

Owner B has given up:

Market value of property		$375,000
Less: Adjusted basis	$290,000	
Transaction costs	21,000	
		$311,000
Indicated Gain		$ 64,000

To calculate the recognized gain:

Owner A has received (in unlike property):

Cash	$50,000
Loan relief	-0-
Other unlike property (boot)	-0-
Less: Transaction costs paid	$18,500
Recognized Gain (Net unlike property received)	$31,500

Owner B has received (in unlike property):

Cash		-0-
Loan relief ($275,000 − $190,000)		$85,000
Other unlike property (boot)		-0-
Less: Cash paid	$50,000	
Transaction costs paid	$21,000	
		$71,000
Recognized Gain (Net unlike property received)		$14,000

Remember that (1) the *recognized gain* is the amount taxed as a capital gain, and (2) the recognized gain *is added to the basis* of the new property (so that it won't be taxed again when the new property is eventually sold).

To recap the gains for:

	Indicated Gain	Recognized Gain
Owner A	$101,500	$31,500
Owner B	$ 64,000	$14,000

INSTALLMENT SALES METHOD

The rules for reporting income from an installment sale were drastically altered, effective October 20, 1980. The old rules contained some very specific requirements, such as permitting no more than 30 percent of the total sales amount to be received in the year of sale, and requiring that at least two principal payments be made in separate tax years. If the taxpayer failed to qualify under the old rules, the transaction was disallowed for installment sale treatment and the capital gain tax on the entire transaction fell due in the year of sale.

The new rules are far more generous to the taxpayer, allowing payment of the tax only on the income collected each year, regardless of its amount. The taxpayer includes in his income only that portion of each payment that is profit. Further, the taxpayer no longer is required to decide whether or not the installment sale tax treatment is to be used—this is now the regular method. In fact, the shift in procedures has turned things around to such an extent that the taxpayer must now report to the IRS a decision to *not* apply the installment rules.

The new definition of an installment sale is a sale in which the taxpayer receives at least one payment after the year of sale. The installment method applies when the transaction results in a gain, whether or not the property sold is used for personal purposes or for business purposes. However, if the seller regularly sells personal or real property (such as building lots) from inventory as a dealer, the installment rules cannot be used.

Loss incurred on an installment sale of business assets cannot be spread over future years but must be deducted in the year of the sale. Also, as explained earlier under the capital gain tax rules, losses incurred on the sale of property held for personal use are simply not deductible under any rule.

Reporting Gain on the Installment Method

When property is sold on the installment basis, the income is determined by using a *gross profit percentage*. This percentage is the gain, or profit, realized and expressed as a percentage of the total *contract price*. In general, the gross profit percentage, once determined, remains unchanged and is applied to each installment payment as it is received. To facilitate understanding of these concepts, special definitions of the tax terminology follow:

1. *Selling price.* The entire cost of the property to the buyer, including cash, the fair market value of other property conveyed to the seller, and any debt the buyer pays or assumes. The selling price is not reduced by commissions or other selling expenses—this reduction is allowed against the gross profit.
2. *Gross profit.* The selling price, reduced by commissions and other selling expenses, less the adjusted basis of value for the property.
3. *Contract price.* The amount the seller receives, not reduced by selling expenses. This is the value of the equity—the selling price less any mortgage debt that the buyer assumes. If there is no debt, the selling price would be the same as the contract price.

EXAMPLE 1

If a property is sold at a contract price of $2,000 and the gross profit realized is $500, the gross profit percentage is 25 percent ($500 divided by $2,000). Whatever the installment payments are, 25 percent of each one (including the down payment) is gain and must be included in income for the tax year in which it is collected.

EXAMPLE 2

A property is sold for $25,000 (selling price) and has a mortgage of $15,000, which is assumed by the buyer. The contract price is $10,000 ($25,000 minus $15,000). Assume the basis for the property is $20,000 making the gross profit $5,000 ($25,000 minus $20,000—commissions are ignored in this example). To compute the gross profit percentage:

$$\frac{\text{Gross profit } \$5,000}{\text{Contract price } \$10,000} = .50 \text{ or } 50\%$$

The buyer agrees to pay $2,000 cash as a down payment and $2,000 plus 11 percent interest in each of the next four years. As each payment, plus the down payment, is collected, the seller must report as income $1,000 (gross profit percentage .50 times the payment received $2,000 equals $1,000). Interest received is reported each year as ordinary income.

EXAMPLE 3

A property is sold for $100,000 with an assumed mortgage of $45,000. The adjusted basis is $49,000, and sales costs are $5,000. The buyer pays $25,000 in cash and gives a second mortgage to the seller for $30,000 that is payable in six annual installments of $5,000 each plus 14% interest.

To calculate the gross profit on the sale:

Sales price		$100,000
Less: Adjusted basis	$49,000	
Sales costs	$ 5,000	
		$ 54,000
Gain		$46,000

To calculate the contract price (equity interest):

Sales price	$100,000
Less: Mortgage assumed by buyer, payable to 3rd party	$ 45,000
Contract price	$ 55,000

The gain of $46,000 represents 83.64 percent of $55,000 ($46,000 gain divided by $55,000 contract price = .8364). For each payment of principal received, the seller must report 83.64 percent as capital gain. Of the first $25,000 payment, therefore, $20,910 is gain; on each $5,000 annual payment, $4,182 is gain. The earned interest must be reported as ordinary income.

Tax on Installment Gains

The nature of the gain is determined at the time of the sale. If a portion of the gain qualifies for treatment as long-term capital gain, then a proportionate share of each installment is reported as a capital gain.

When depreciation recapture is involved, however, the proportions change. The tax rules require that a taxpayer who uses an installment method of reporting where part of the gain is subject to recapture must apply the first amounts of installments to recapture until the full amount of recapture has been paid. After the full recapture has been reported, the balance of the gain on each installment may be reported as capital gains.

Additional Rules for Installment Sales

The 1980 changes applicable to installment sales included a tightening of the rules for sales to related parties. A sale to a spouse, child, grandchild, parent, and certain related business organizations may be disallowed as an installment sale if the related party sells or otherwise disposes of the property before all payments have been made on the first sale. Special tax rules apply in these circumstances.

It is no longer necessary to have a complete deal agreed to prior to treating a sale under the installment rules. In the past, the rules permitted no contingencies. Since October 20, 1980, it is possible to leave such questions as the total sales price and terms of the sale open—dependent on later developments. With the new rules, the parties to the transaction have much greater freedom to negotiate a deal utilizing such contingencies as future profits, cost of living escalators, and others. The key factor is that whatever amount is paid on principal, the capital gain on the amount collected must be reported in the year received.

The IRS requires that adequate records be kept on the entire transaction when it is reported as an installment sale.

Unstated Interest.   A special rule applies to installment sale contracts if no provision is made for interest on future installments, or if the interest rate is too low. To be eligible under this rule, the contract must exceed $3,000 and at least one payment must be due more than one year after the date of sale. Under these conditions, the IRS can impute (meaning consider to exist) an interest rate and apply it to the calculations. The unstated interest amount reduces the original sales price of the property thus reducing the amount of gain. Most important, the imputed interest is taxable to the seller as ordinary income, rather than at the capital gain rates applicable to the installment sale.

OPTION TO EXPENSE CERTAIN DEPRECIABLE BUSINESS ASSETS

Under prior law, taxpayers were allowed an additional first year bonus depreciation on certain business assets. This deduction allowance has been repealed and replaced by a new expense deduction that is generally the same, but with increased annual limits on the amount of deduction.

Eligible for the expense allowance is tangible personal property purchased for use in a business, but *not* held for investment. Examples of qualifying property include machinery, office equipment, transportation equipment, refrigerators, individual air conditioning units, grocery counters, and more. Such property is eligible even if local law terms it a *fixture*.

The cost of a qualified capital investment can be expensed up to the aggregate dollar limitation allowed in any one tax year. The taxpayer must specify the property on which the expense allowance is claimed and the portion of the cost of each item so claimed. The expense deduction is taken *instead of* the ACRS deduction. The following limits apply to the aggregate deduction claimed in the tax year:

For Taxable Year Beginning	Limitation Amount*
1982	$ 5,000
1983	5,000
1984	7,500
1985	7,500
1986 and after	10,000

*Married, filing separately is one-half the amount.

The expense allowance can be claimed *only* in the first year of an asset's use. The expense deduction *reduces the basis of value* by the amount of the deduction claimed and, therefore, must be included in the amount of gain subject to recapture upon disposition of the property. If expensing is elected, *no investment tax credit* may be taken on the portion of the cost expensed.

Important consideration: The expensing of an asset's cost, instead of its recovery over three or five years, gives a much greater deduction in the first year, but at a cost of forfeiture of the investment tax credit. Remember, the tax credit is a direct reduction of the tax liability while the expense deduction is a reduction of the income subject to taxation. The taxpayer should weigh the respective benefits of each procedure to find the most advantageous cost benefits.

Application of Limitation. The dollar limitation each year applies to partnerships and to the partners. If an individual is involved in a partnership and a separate business, care must be taken to avoid a combined expense amount from exceeding the limits. The penalty could be a permanent disallowance of the expense deduction.

THE INVESTMENT TAX CREDIT

One of the most direct incentives for new investment is the Investment Tax Credit. It is a concept borrowed from several European countries and was first added to our tax law in 1962. Unlike accelerated capital recovery, the full impact of the investment credit is felt in the year of acquisition. The taxpayer is allowed to subtract the credit directly from gross tax liability.

No provision in the history of income tax law can compare with the investment credit for its record of being added to and removed from the law. Following its original passage in 1962, the credit was "suspended" in the fall of 1966, only to be reinstated in March of 1967. The Reform Act of 1969 repealed the credit, but the Revenue Act of 1971 reenacted it with only a few modifications. In every case, the investment credit was suspended to combat inflation and then reinstated to encourage investment. Confidence in the procedure was expressed in the Tax Reduction Act of 1975 which increased the rate for the credit. And in 1978, the Energy Tax Act added a tax credit for investments that conserve energy. The Economic Recovery Tax Act of 1981 continues the investment credit with specific applications to the new ACRS recovery property classes and makes an important addition: a new investment tax credit is allowed for rehabilitating qualified buildings.

The investment credit takes into consideration the useful life of an asset. If a single rate were used for all assets, industries whose primary investments are in assets with a short life would have a definite advantage. Frequent replacement would increase their investment credit. So the new law recognizes a difference and assigns a smaller tax credit to properties with shorter lives.

Regular Investment Tax Credit

The investment credit is claimed for qualified tangible personal property used for business purposes for the year it is placed in service. The 1981 Tax Act authorized the following tax credit rates for property placed in service after December 31, 1980:

ACRS 3-year property class	6%
ACRS 5-year property class	10%

In addition, a 10 percent investment credit is allowed for 15-year public utility property and certain kinds of specialized 10-year property.

At-Risk Limitation.   Tax credit for qualified investments is subject to an *at-risk* limitation, which formerly applied mainly to the deduction of losses. Essentially, the same rules apply to the deductibility of losses and to the allowance of an investment tax credit. The deductions are limited to the amount of investment capital that the taxpayer has at risk. Nonrecourse indebtedness—indebtedness with no personal liability to the investor—is not considered capital at risk. If the lender can look to the borrower for the balance due (instead of just the property pledged as collateral for the loan), then the capital is generally considered at risk for the purpose of these deductions. There is one major exception to this rule, insofar as the investment tax credit is concerned—even *nonrecourse* financing by a government agency, certain unrelated financial institutions, and qualifying pension trusts are considered at-risk capital and can qualify for the credit.

New Recapture Rules.   The investment tax credit does not reduce the basis of value, but it is subject to recapture (taxed as ordinary income instead of as capital gain upon disposition of the property). The method used to figure how much of the credit can be recaptured is to consider the credit as *earned* at the rate of 2 percent per year. For example, the tax credit for three-year property is 6 percent; for each year the property is held, 2 percent of the credit is earned. If the property is held for three years (or more) the full amount of the 6 percent credit is earned and no recovery is required. In the same manner, five-year property held for five years earns the full amount of the 10 percent investment tax credit (2 percent per year times 5 years equals 10 percent). This new procedure (1981 Tax Act) allows the credit to be earned over a shorter period of time than did the prior law, thus decreasing the importance of holding an asset longer to reduce the amount subject to recapture.

Investment Tax Credit for Rehabilitation

The 1981 Tax Act provides a new investment tax credit for rehabilitating qualified buildings and for rehabilitating qualified historic structures. Following are the credits allowed for rehabilitation costs (not the cost of the building):

For 30- to 39-year old nonresidential buildings	15%
For 40-year and over nonresidential buildings	20%

For structures certified
as historic by the Secre-
tary of the Interior—
residential or non-
residential   25%

The regular investment credit (see previous section) and the energy investment credit *do not apply* to any portion of the basis that qualifies for this rehabilitation credit. The costs of rehabilitation must be capitalized and must also be spent on real property with a 15-year recovery class. The new credit generally applies to expenditures made after 1981. Note that the prior law, which allowed a 60-month amortization of certain rehabilitation expenditures, has been repealed.

Rehabilitation Defined.   To qualify for the tax credit, there must be *substantial* rehabilitation of the building. For this purpose, substantial is defined as an amount of expenditures during the current tax year plus those made in the preceding year exceeding the greater of the adjusted basis of the property, or $5,000.

FIVE

The Personal Residence and Rental Houses

18

Tax Status of a Personal Residence

While a personal residence cannot be classified as investment property and thus be eligible for the tax advantages available to commercial or business property, the escalation in home values has created an investment situation. Since about the mid-70s, few homeowners have had to consider selling their house at anything less than they originally paid for it. Prior to that, and somewhat to the surprise of younger people, older houses declined in value as they aged. So, from the standpoint of realizing a gain, a house has proven to be an excellent investment.

In addition to providing living accommodations, most homeowners count on an increase in value to partially offset the much greater cost of owning a home as compared with some 10 years ago. Unfortunately, any measure of future escalation must be considered speculative. However, in those areas of the country where land restrictions have increased existing home values, the escalation of value is most likely to continue. In the South, Southwest, and West, strong demand should continue to exert upward pressures on building costs and thus continue to increase home values at least for the near future. In all areas there has been an increase in property prices resulting from the debasement in the value of currency. Stable and realistic monetary policies are within the power of the government, and price escalation from this cause may be on the decline.

The projection of future economic trends is beyond the scope of this discussion. Suffice it to say that escalation in value has continued for so long that it is now accepted as almost a permanent condition. Just keep in mind that money and credit are very important influences on this matter and are very much a matter of government policy—and this could change. In purchasing a house, count on inflation-induced escalation of value only with a careful eye on governmental policies.

The subject addressed in this chapter is the tax advantages of owning a home; that is, How does the government and the IRS view the taxpayer as a homeowner? Generally, he or she is viewed favorably and granted a number of tax concessions. Taxes and interest costs, for example, are deductible for the homeowner, but not for an apartment dweller. A capital gain on the sale of a home may be deferred, or if the homeowner is over 55 years of age, a $125,000 exclusion is permitted. While some economists consider these advantages too generous because they result in too great a total investment in what is essentially a nonproductive asset, the policy of encouraging homeownership as a worthy cause has long been a part of the government's goals.

THE PRINCIPAL RESIDENCE

In IRS terminology, a personal residence and a principal residence are synonomous, and the taxpayer is permitted only one. It is the place where he or she lives. The tax status cannot be assigned by the taxpayer; that is, the taxpayer cannot claim a vacation home as a principal residence. The portion of a multifamily residence that is owned and occupied by the taxpayer does qualify as a principal residence. The purchase of an accommodation in a retirement home does not qualify, except in certain cases where actual title to the property passes to the purchaser.

TAX DEDUCTIONS ALLOWED
FOR OWNING A HOME

Ownership of a home allows the taxpayer certain deductions from his or her personal income. The following four deductible expenses are discussed next: mortgage interest, property taxes, home energy conservation costs, and casualty losses.

Mortgage Interest

The interest portion of a mortgage payment made during the tax year is deductible. This information can be obtained from an amortization table, or better, from a statement provided by the mortgage lender.

Where the mortgage allows for graduated payments (as does FHA Section 245 of the National Housing Act), payments made in the early years are usually less than the amount of interest owed for the year. If the taxpayer reports on a cash basis (see Chapter 8 under "Methods of Accounting"), only the interest actually paid during that tax year is deductible. If the taxpayer uses the accrual method, the deduction is the interest that accrues during the tax year (that paid plus that deferred until later years). If the homeowner is purchasing under the Section 235, Mortgage Assistance Program, *no interest* costs are deductible.

Points paid by the borrower are also deductible. They are deductible in full in the year of payment provided the loan is to buy or to improve the personal residence. In some areas of the country, the terminology differs a bit, and a distinction is not made between the points charged solely for the use of money and those charged for services in connection with arranging the loan. Only points paid solely for the use of money are deductible.

Points paid by a *seller* as a loan placement fee are *not* deductible as interest. However, all points paid by the seller are deductible as a selling expense and thus reduce the realized selling price. (See Chapter 19.)

Prepayment penalties assessed for early payoff of a mortgage loan are deductible as interest.

Property Taxes

State and local ad valorem taxes on real property are deductible in the year of payment. This does not include taxes charged for local benefits and improvements that increase the value of the property (such as a paving assessment).

If real estate taxes include fees for trash and garbage pickup, this portion of the taxes is *not* deductible. If the taxpayer rents property and the landlord increases the rent in the form of a tax surcharge, this is *not* a deductible expense. While a homeowners' association may have the power to assess fees with the same legal force as that of a tax assessor, such fees are intended for the recreation, health, safety, and welfare of the residents and are *not* deductible.

Home Energy Conservation Costs

A relatively new deduction for homeowners is the residential energy credit.* The deduction is also allowed for the renter if he or she pays for the energy conservation improvement. The energy credits are available

---

*A tax *credit* reduces the tax due; a deduction reduces the *income* subject to tax.

in two forms, each with its own conditions and limits. These are as follows:

1. Costs for home energy conservation.
2. Costs for renewable energy sources.

The credit is based on the cost of items installed after April 19, 1977 and before January 1, 1986. Costs include that of installation. If the home is used for business, an allocation must be made between the business use and the residential use. Only the costs for the residential use qualify for the credit. One further point should be kept in mind: the basis of the house must be reduced by the amount of residential energy credit allowed.

Costs for home energy conservation

The credit permitted for home energy conservation is 15 percent of the first $2,000 spent for qualified items. The $2,000 limit is cumulative; that is, the full amount does not have to be used in one year but may be taken over a period of years. Also, the limit applies to each successive residence. For example, if the taxpayer, after having made energy conservation improvements to his home, relocates, he is allowed a new $2,000 limit for the new home even though both expenses occur in the same tax year. However, the deduction is allowed only for a principal residence. The energy-saving items that qualify must be new and must have at least a three-year life. Following are those items that qualify:

- Insulation designed to reduce heat loss or gain in the home or water heater.
- Storm or thermal windows or doors for the exterior of the home.
- Caulking or weather stripping of exterior doors or windows.
- Clock thermostats or other automatic energy-saving setback thermostats.
- Furnace modifications designed to increase fuel efficiency, including replacement burners, modified flue openings, and ignition systems that replace a gas pilot light.
- Meters that display the cost of energy use.

Among the items that do not qualify for credit are heat pumps, fluorescent lights, wood- or peat-burning stoves, replacement boilers and furnaces, and hydrogen-fueled equipment.

Costs for renewable energy sources

In addition to the credit allowed for home energy conservation, the tax-payer may take credit for amounts spent on solar, wind-powered, or geothermal equipment installed in the home. The credit allowed is 40 percent of the first $10,000 (or a maximum credit of $4,000).* As with the home energy conservation credit, the costs may be spread over several years, and a new limit is available for each principle residence in which the taxpayer lives.

Unlike the energy conservation credit, the renewable energy sources credit is allowed for both new construction and existing homes. It does not matter when the home was constructed, as long as the re-newable energy source was installed after April 19, 1977. If the installation is made during construction, or a reconstruction of the house, the credit is allowed for the tax year in which the home is first lived in as a principal residence. This does not have to be the year the equipment was installed.

To qualify as a renewable energy source, the equipment must be new and have an expected life of at least five years. The cost includes labor needed for on-site preparation, assembly, or installation of the equipment. Renewable energy source equipment that qualifies for this deduction includes the following:

- *Solar energy* equipment for heating or cooling the home or providing hot water for use within the home.
- *Wind energy* equipment for generating electricity or other forms of energy for personal or home use.
- *Geothermal* energy equipment.

Casualty Losses

Losses due to theft or casualty to property used for personal or business purposes are deductible on the federal income tax return. The IRS defines a casualty loss as the complete or partial destruction or loss of property from an identifiable event that is damaging to property and is sudden, unexpected, or unusual in nature. Casualty losses include the following:

1. Damage from a hurricane, tornado, flood, storm, fire, or accident.
2. Mine cave-in damage to the property.

---

*Revised allowance effective 1980.

3. Sonic boom damage from jet aircraft, such as broken windows.
4. Vandalism caused by agencies beyond your control if the loss is sudden and destructive.
5. Damage to trees and shrubs may result in a casualty loss deduction if resulting from an accident.

Casualty losses do *not* include the following:

1. Breakage of china or glassware through normal handling or any damage by a family pet.
2. Loss of trees, shrubs, or other plants on residential property if caused by disease, fungus, or insects.
3. Damage caused by termites or moths.
4. Progressive deterioration from a steadily operating cause such as rust or rot.
5. Prolonged drought that results in progressive deterioration of property.
6. General decline in market value caused by being in or near an area that suffered a casualty. There must be actual physical damage to the property, not just the potential for damage.
7. Expenses incident to the casualty, such as the care of personal injuries or the cost of temporary quarters.

Proof of Loss.   The taxpayer must keep records of when the loss occurred and show some proof that the damage was the result of a casualty. Further information must be available as to the value of the property before and after the casualty. The amount of insurance recovery is needed plus any restoration or cleanup furnished without cost by disaster relief agencies. Photographs taken before and after the casualty are very helpful in establishing the condition of the property.

Amount of Loss.   The amount of a casualty loss deduction is generally the lesser of: (1) the decrease in the fair market value of the property as a result of the casualty; or (2) the adjusted basis in the property. The amount of the loss is reduced by the amount of any insurance recovery. Also, for personal use property there is a $100 deductible from the loss amount.

How to Determine the Decrease in Value Resulting from Casualty.   The best measure of the decrease in property value that results from a casualty is the cost of cleaning up, repairing, or replacing the damaged property. The taxpayer, however, should be aware of the following stipulations:

1. The repairs must be necessary to restore the property.
2. The amount spent for repairs must not be excessive.

3. The replacement or repairs can do no more than take care of the damage suffered.
4. The value of the property after the repairs must not, as a result of the repairs, exceed the value of the property before the repairs.

Effect on Adjusted Basis of Value.   The amount of a casualty loss that is deductible from current year income (the loss less any recovery) is also deducted from the basis of value for the property.

In figuring a loss for real property used for personal purposes, all improvements, such as buildings and ornamental trees, are considered together. The amount of the loss is the lesser of the decrease in fair market value of the *entire* property or its adjusted basis. If personal property is stolen, damaged or destroyed, the loss must be figured separately for each item. If the loss is on investment or business property, each item must be figured separately and the $100 reduction rule does not apply.

Theft Losses

For IRS purposes, a theft is the unlawful taking of money or property by another with the intent of depriving the taxpayer of it. Theft includes, but is not limited to larceny, robbery, embezzlement, extortion, kidnapping for ransom, threats and blackmail. However, the mere disappearance of money or property from your person or home is not considered a theft.

Amount of Loss.   The taxpayer must be able to prove the theft occurred and the amount of loss sustained. As in a casualty loss, the theft loss on property used for personal purposes is subject to a $100 deductible before a tax deduction can be claimed.

USING THE HOME AS A WORKPLACE

Tax laws allow the use of a home as a workplace and permit appropriate deductions for the portion so used.* There are, of course, restrictions. However, the former limitations that required a home-office to be *both* the principal place of business and the primary business activity of the taxpayer were modified by a new law in late 1981. The new law allows expense deductions when the in-home office is a *principal place of business* even if the business is secondary to the taxpayer and not his or her main source of earned income. Thus, for example, a full-time factory employee who also free-lances from an in-home office or workshop can often deduct its full cost.*

---

*See IRS Publication 587 "Business Use of Your Home."

The new law is based on the idea that if an office at home is used to generate sideline income, it is the principal place of business for that income. While not so defined in the law, it appears that a floor space formula may be used to determine the allowable tax deductions. This would mean that if 10 percent of a house is used as an office, then one-tenth of the total cost of maintaining the home can be deducted as a business expense. This includes a proportionate share of the depreciation. Any depreciation taken as an expense reduces the basis of value for the home. The deduction is retroactive to the 1978 tax year.

If the taxpayer uses a portion of the home in connection with service as an employee, then the use must be for the convenience of the employer, not just helpful to the job. Deductions of expenses are not allowed if the home is used in connection with a profit-seeking activity that does not qualify as a trade or business. For example, the taxpayer cannot deduct expenses for the use of the home to read financial publications and reports to guide personal investment activities as this is not classed as a trade or business. If a part of the home is used for storage of goods that the taxpayer sells at retail or wholesale, the expenses are deductible.

Limit on Deductions.   If the use of the home for business purposes does qualify for deduction of expenses, the expenses deducted *cannot exceed* the gross income derived from the business use of the home.

19

Sale of a Personal Residence

Tax laws have long required a gain from the disposition of assets—whether business or personal—to be reported and made subject to the capital gains taxes. What has changed in the past few years is that many assets that formerly declined in value with age are now increasing in value because of inflation. As a result, more transactions are subject to capital gain taxation. Foremost among such examples is the single-family residence. Congress has enacted some special legislation that now grants the homeowner relief from immediate taxation when he or she moves, plus an exemption from taxation if the home seller is age 55 or older. The special legislation applies only to the sale of a personal residence, which is quite different from a house converted to rental property.

FIGURING THE GAIN

A gain from the sale of a personal residence (more fully defined in Chapter 18) is calculated in the same way as any other capital gain. It is the difference between the adjusted basis of property value and the realized selling price. There are two essential differences in the tax treatment of gain from sale of a personal residence and from sale of property used for business purposes. One is that *no depreciation or cost recovery* is permitted for a personal residence. The other is that a homeowner may *not* deduct any loss incurred in the sale of a personal residence from taxable income.

Keeping Records.   It is most important that the homeowner maintain records of all transactions that affect the value of the home. In the past this has not been very important as seldom did homes sell for more than their acquisition cost, and capital gain was not a matter of any consequence. Now it is—and the IRS requires their Form 2119, "Sale or Exchange of a Principal Residence," be submitted with the taxpayer's income tax form in the year of the sale whenever a gain is made.

Adjusted Basis of the Home

The first step in keeping records is to enter the initial basis of value for the newly acquired home. The basis is determined by the method of acquisition. (See Chapter 15 "Capital Gain or Loss.") Usually this is by purchase, and the cost becomes the basis. Adjustments to the basis may increase or decrease the value. Improvements and additions will add to the basis. An improvement is something that prolongs the life of the property or adds value. It should not be confused with a repair which is defined as something that maintains the home in good condition but does not add to the value or prolong its life.

Decreases in the basis result from losses such as fire or other casualty, and from any payments received from the sale of an easement or from a right-of-way that had to be given up. Depreciation, or cost recovery, is not a permissible deduction for a personal residence. The denial of depreciation as a deduction offers an interesting possibility: improvements may be added to the basis, but there is no provision for deducting them when normal deterioration occurs. If, for example, a fence that deteriorates from age and rot is replaced with a new fence, it can be added to the basis of value, but there is no provision that requires that the value of the old fence be deducted. Remember, all additions to the basis *reduce* the amount of taxable gain at time of disposition.

Realized Selling Price

Since the capital gain is the *difference* between the adjusted basis of value and the amount *realized* from the sale of the property, the next step is to calculate the realized selling price. The calculation starts with the total consideration received from the sale.

Total consideration received

This includes cash, notes, mortgages, and the fair market value of any real or personal property received in the transaction. If the taxpayer is moved by his employer, any payment from the employer in excess of fair market value or any reimbursement for a decline in property value is *not* included in the selling price for the calculation of capital gain. Any such money received from an employer must be reported as ordinary income for services rendered. The sales price for any personal property is not included in the total consideration received.

Deduct selling expenses

The expenses that the homeowner can deduct from the sales price in calculating the realized selling price are as follows:

1. Sales commission.
2. Advertising paid for by the seller.
3. Legal fees paid by the seller in the transaction.
4. Loan placement fees or discount points paid by the seller.

Deduct fixing-up expenses

Fixing-up expenses are deductible only in the calculation of the gain realized from the sale, but not in the computation of the actual profit on the sale of the old home. To define fixing-up expenses, the IRS lists decorating and repair costs incurred solely to assist in the sale of the property. They cannot be capital expenses or improvements. The work must be performed within 90 days before the sales contract is signed and must be paid for within 30 days after the sale. The deduction is only allowed for the calculation of the gain on which tax is deferred. This limits its use to transactions where a replacement house is acquired or the taxpayer is able to elect the 55-or-older exclusion. It is a tricky sort of deduction and is explained further in the following example.

EXAMPLE

Fixing-up Expense Deduction

The old home being sold has a basis of $25,000 and is sold for $41,400 with selling expenses of $1,800. Improvements were made in the house by adding new Venetian blinds and a water heater costing $500. Fixing-up expenses of $800 were incurred for inside and outside painting and wallpapering. Within the required time a replacement house is acquired at a cost of $37,800. Following is the way in which the report of gain postponed, gain not postponed, and the basis for the replacement home are calculated:

To compute gain:		
1. Selling price of old home	$41,400	
2. Less: Selling expenses	1,800	
3. Amount realized		$39,600
4. Basis of old home	$25,000	
5. Plus: Improvements (blinds and heater)	500	
6. Adjusted basis of old home		25,500
7. Gain on old home (3 minus 6)		$14,100
To compute gain not postponed:		
8. Amount realized on old home	$39,600	
9. Less: Fixing-up expenses (painting and wallpapering)	800	
10. Adjusted sales price		$38,800
11. Cost of new home		37,800
12. Gain not postponed (10 minus 11)		$ 1,000
To compute gain postponed:		
13. Gain postponed (7 minus 12)		$13,100
To compute new basis for replacement home:		
14. Cost of new home		$37,800
15. Less: Gain postponed (Item 13)		13,100
16. Basis of new home		$24,700

DEFERRAL OF CAPITAL GAINS TAX ON SALE OF PERSONAL RESIDENCE

Replacing an existing home today generally requires a larger expenditure than was originally necessary to acquire it. In past years, when capital gains taxes were assessed on every gain realized in the sale of a personal residence, it was very difficult for the homeowner to maintain his or her standard of living. Congress recognized this problem and introduced several new measures to give relief to homeowners on capital gains taxes. One procedure allows a deferment—not an exemption—of the capital gains tax on the sale of a personal residence provided a replacement property is acquired within a specified period of time. The other procedure is an exclusion from taxation of up to $125,000 in capital gains if the home seller is 55 or older.

The method used to defer taxation when an existing home is replaced with another is to reduce the basis of the newly acquired property by the exact amount of the gain that is deferred. In this way, when the newly acquired home is eventually sold, the gain that may result then will reflect the gain from the first sale; unless, of course, the home seller elects to purchase another house and rollover the gain once more. There is no limit to the number of rollovers permitted, but it cannot be more often than once every 18 months, unless the relocation is required in order to commence work at a new principal place of employment.

Time Limits to Qualify

The tax code specifies deadlines for the purchase and occupancy of a new home in order to qualify for postponement of the capital gains tax on the sale of the old house. These deadlines vary and are based on the following:

1. Whether the new home is already built or is to be constructed.
2. Whether the taxpayer is eligible for additional time, as a result of being a member of the Armed Forces.

Already Built.   The time limits within which a homeowner must purchase and occupy a house in order to qualify for a deferment of the capital gain tax was increased from 18 to 24 months after the effective date of July 21, 1981. Now, the homeowner has a 48-month period beginning 24 months before the sale of the old home and ending 24 months after the sale within which time period a replacement house must be acquired to qualify for a tax deferral.

To Be Constructed.   Under the new rules (effective July 21, 1981) the taxpayer is allowed the same time period for replacement as with an "already built" home; that is, construction must commence within 24 months before the sale of the old home and completed and occupied within 24 months after the sale of the old home. The IRS rules carry some limitations on the meaning of this allowance. To begin construction is defined as "to obtain a building site, construction loan, approval of plans, and a building permit". Any construction costs incurred *prior* to 24 months before the sale of the old house cannot be included in the acquisition cost for basis of value calculation on the replacement house. Nor can construction costs incurred *after* 24 months after the sale of the old house be included.

Occupancy Test.   Both newly constructed houses and those already built must be *occupied* not later than 24 months after the sale of the old residence. Occupancy means to physically live in the replacement house as the principal residence within the time period allowed, not just to move in furniture or other personal belongings.

Armed Forces Eligibility.   If the home buyer is on active duty pursuant to a call for (1) an indefinite period of duty or (2) for more than 90 days, the allowable replacement period after the sale of the old home is suspended. The suspension applies only if service begins before the end of the normal 2-year replacement period. This time plus any period of suspension cannot last for more than 4 years after sale of the old house.

Purchase Price of Replacement Residence

To determine the amount of gain that is subject to tax and the amount of gain that is eligible for tax deferment, it is necessary to calculate the purchase price of the replacement residence in accordance with the tax rules. The purchase price includes the following items of cost, which are confined to a 48-month period for an existing replacement house (24 months before sale and 24 months after sale). The same time limits apply to a newly built replacement house.

1. Cost of acquiring the residence.
2. Cost of constructing the residence.
3. Cost of reconstructing an older property.
4. Cost of long-term improvements or additions.

In addition to these basic costs, any fees or other expenses paid to acquire the replacement residence are considered part of the purchase price. Essentially, these fees and expenses are those cost items that are not otherwise deductible in the year of the sale.

EXAMPLE

The deferral of a gain is permitted whether the replacement residence costs more or less than the selling price of the old residence. If the replacement residence costs more than the amount realized from the sale of the old home, the entire amount of taxable gain can be deferred. However, if the replacement house costs less than the amount realized from the sale of the old home, the gain that can be deferred is limited to the amount that is reinvested. To illustrate the procedure, examples of IRS Form 2119 follow, first for a more expensive replacement home, then for a less expensive one.

Form **2119**	**Sale or Exchange of Principal Residence**	OMB No. 1545-0072
Department of the Treasury Internal Revenue Service (O)	▶ See instructions on back. ▶ Attach to Form 1040 for year of sale (see instruction C).	**1981** 24

Note: *Do not include expenses you are deducting as moving expenses.*

Name(s) as shown on Form 1040   FRANK + MARY JONES   Your social security number 444 02 6854

		Yes	No
1 (a)	Date former residence sold ▶ MAY 5, 1981		
(b)	Enter the face amount of any mortgage, note (for example second trust), or other financial instrument on which you will receive periodic payments of principal or interest from this sale ▶ 18,000		
(c)	Have you ever postponed any gain on the sale or exchange of a principal residence?		✓
(d)	If you were on active duty in the U.S. Armed Forces or outside of the U.S. after the date of sale of former residence, enter dates. From _____ to _____		
2 (a)	Date you bought new residence. (If none bought, so state). ▶ MAY 20, 1981		
(b)	If you constructed new residence, date construction began ▶ _____ date occupied ▶ _____		
(c)	Did you use both the old and new properties as your principal residence?	✓	
(d)	Are any rooms in either residence rented out or used for business for which a deduction is allowed?		✓
	(If "Yes" do not include gain on the rented or business portion in line 7; instead include in income on Form 4797.)		

Part I   Computation of Gain and Adjusted Sales Price

3	Selling price of residence. (Do not include selling price of personal property items.)	3	72,000
4	Commissions and other expenses of sale not deducted as moving expenses	4	6,000
5	Amount realized (subtract line 4 from line 3)	5	66,000
6	Basis of residence sold 6	41,000	
7	Gain on sale (subtract line 6 from line 5). (If line 6 is more than line 5, enter zero and do not complete the rest of form.) If you bought another principal residence during the allowed replacement period or you elect the one time exclusion in Part III, continue with this form. Otherwise, enter the gain on Schedule D (Form 1040), line 2a or 9a.	7	25,000
	If you haven't replaced your residence, do you plan to do so within the replacement period? ☐ Yes ☐ No		
	(If "Yes" see instruction C.)		
8	Fixing-up expenses (see instructions for time limitations.)	8	3,000
9	Adjusted sales price (subtract line 8 from line 5)	9	63,000

Part II   Computation of Gain to be Postponed and Adjusted Basis of New Residence

10	Cost of new residence	10	82,300
11	Taxable gain this year (Subtract line 10 from line 9. Do not enter more than line 7.) If line 10 is more than line 9, enter zero. Enter any taxable gain on Schedule D (Form 1040), line 2a or 9a. If you were 55 or over on the date of sale, see Part III	11	—0—
12	Gain to be postponed (subtract line 11 from line 7)	12	25,000
13	Adjusted basis of new residence (subtract line 12 from line 10)	13	57,300

Part III   Computation of Exclusion, Gain to be Reported, and Adjusted Basis of New Residence

		Yes	No
14 (a)	Were you 55 or over on date of sale?		
(b)	Was your spouse 55 or over on date of sale?		
	(If you answered "No" to 14(a) and 14(b), do not complete the rest of form.)		
(c)	If you answered "Yes" to 14(a) or 14(b) did you own and use the property sold as your principal residence for a total of at least 3 years (except for short temporary absences) of the 5-year period before the sale?		
	(If you are 65 or over and 1(a) is before 7/26/81, see instruction D.)		
(d)	If you answered "Yes" to 14(c), do you elect to take the once in a lifetime exclusion of the gain on the sale? . .		
	(If "Yes," check yes box and complete the rest of Part III. If "No," return to Part II, line 12 above.)		
(e)	At time of sale, was the residence owned by: ☐ you, ☐ your spouse, ☐ both of you?		
(f)	Social security number of spouse, at time of sale, if different from number on Form 1040 ▶...............................		
	(Enter "none" if you were not married at time of sale.)		

15 (a)	If line 1(a) is before 7/21/81, enter the smaller of line 7 or $100,000 ($50,000, if married filing separate return) .	15(a)	
(b)	If line 1(a) is after 7/20/81, enter the smaller of line 7 or $125,000 ($62,500, if married filing separate return) . . .	15(b)	
16	Part of gain included (subtract line 15a or 15b from line 7)	16	
17	Cost of new residence. If you did not buy a new principal residence, enter "None." Then enter the gain from line 16 on Schedule D (Form 1040), line 9a, and do not complete the rest of Form 2119 . . .	17	
18	Gain taxable this year. (Subtract the sum of lines 15 and 17 from line 9. The result cannot be more than line 16.) If line 17 plus line 15 is more than line 9, enter zero. Enter any taxable gain on Schedule D (Form 1040), line 9a	18	
19	Gain to be postponed (subtract line 18 from line 16)	19	
20	Adjusted basis of new residence (subtract line 19 from line 17)	20	

For Paperwork Reduction Act Notice, see back of form.   Form **2119** (1981)

IRS Form: Buying up.

Form **2119**	**Sale or Exchange of Principal Residence**	OMB No. 1545–0072
Department of the Treasury Internal Revenue Service (O)	▶ See instructions on back. ▶ Attach to Form 1040 for year of sale (see instruction C).	**1981**

Note: *Do not include expenses you are deducting as moving expenses.*

Name(s) as shown on Form 1040 RICHARD & HELEN VALDEZ   Your social security number 384 77 2041

		Yes	No
1 (a) Date former residence sold ▶ JULY 8, 1981			
(b) Enter the face amount of any mortgage, note (for example second trust), or other financial instrument on which you will receive periodic payments of principal or interest from this sale ▶ 15,000			
(c) Have you ever postponed any gain on the sale or exchange of a principal residence?			✓
(d) If you were on active duty in the U.S. Armed Forces or outside of the U.S. after the date of sale of former residence, enter dates. From _____ to _____			
2 (a) Date you bought new residence. (If none bought, so state). ▶ JULY 14, 1981			
(b) If you constructed new residence, date construction began ▶ _____ date occupied ▶ _____			
(c) Did you use both the old and new properties as your principal residence?		✓	
(d) Are any rooms in either residence rented out or used for business for which a deduction is allowed? . . . . (If "Yes" do not include gain on the rented or business portion in line 7; instead include in income on Form 4797.)			✓

Part I Computation of Gain and Adjusted Sales Price

3 Selling price of residence. (Do not include selling price of personal property items.)	3	72,000
4 Commissions and other expenses of sale not deducted as moving expenses	4	6,000
5 Amount realized (subtract line 4 from line 3)	5	66,000
6 Basis of residence sold	6 41,000		
7 Gain on sale (subtract line 6 from line 5). (If line 6 is more than line 5, enter zero and do not complete the rest of form.) If you bought another principal residence during the allowed replacement period or you elect the one time exclusion in Part III, continue with this form. Otherwise, enter the gain on Schedule D (Form 1040), line 2a or 9a.	7 25,000		

If you haven't replaced your residence, do you plan to do so within the replacement period? ☒ Yes ☐ No

(If "Yes" see instruction C.)

8 Fixing-up expenses (see instructions for time limitations.)	8	3,000
9 Adjusted sales price (subtract line 8 from line 5)	9	63,000

Part II Computation of Gain to be Postponed and Adjusted Basis of New Residence

10 Cost of new residence	10	51,000
11 Gain taxable this year (Subtract line 10 from line 9. Do not enter more than line 7.) If line 10 is more than line 9, enter zero. Enter any taxable gain on Schedule D (Form 1040), line 2a or 9a. If you were 55 or over on the date of sale, see Part III.	11	12,000
12 Gain to be postponed (subtract line 11 from line 7)	12	13,000
13 Adjusted basis of new residence (subtract line 12 from line 10)	13	38,000

Part III Computation of Exclusion, Gain to be Reported, and Adjusted Basis of New Residence

		Yes	No
14 (a) Were you 55 or over on date of sale?			
(b) Was your spouse 55 or over on date of sale? . . . . (If you answered "No" to 14(a) and 14(b), do not complete the rest of form.)			
(c) If you answered "Yes" to 14(a) or 14(b) did you own and use the property sold as your principal residence for a total of at least 3 years (except for short temporary absences) of the 5-year period before the sale? . . . . (If you are 65 or over and 1(a) is before 7/26/81, see instruction D.)			
(d) If you answered "Yes" to 14(c), do you elect to take the once in a lifetime exclusion of the gain on the sale? . . (If "Yes," check yes box and complete the rest of Part III. If "No," return to Part II, line 12 above.)			

(e) At time of sale, was the residence owned by: ☐ you,   ☐ your spouse,   ☐ both of you?

(f) Social security number of spouse, at time of sale, if different from number on Form 1040 ▶ _____
(Enter "none" if you were not married at time of sale.)

15 (a) If line 1(a) is before 7/21/81, enter the smaller of line 7 or $100,000 ($50,000, if married filing separate return) . .	15(a)		
(b) If line 1(a) is after 7/20/81, enter the smaller of line 7 or $125,000 ($62,500, if married filing separate return) . . .	15(b)		
16 Part of gain included (subtract line 15a or 15b from line 7)	16		
17 Cost of new residence. If you did not buy a new principal residence, enter "None." Then enter the gain from line 16 on Schedule D (Form 1040), line 9a, and do not complete the rest of Form 2119	17		
18 Gain taxable this year. (Subtract the sum of lines 15 and 17 from line 9. The result cannot be more than line 16.) If line 17 plus line 15 is more than line 9, enter zero. Enter any taxable gain on Schedule D (Form 1040), line 9a	18		
19 Gain to be postponed (subtract line 18 from line 16)	19		
20 Adjusted basis of new residence (subtract line 19 from line 17)	20		

For Paperwork Reduction Act Notice, see back of form.   Form **2119** (1981)

IRS Form: Buying Down

Age 55-or-Older Exclusion

Prior IRS rules permitted a taxpayer aged 65 or over to exclude from taxable income any gain on the sale of a principal residence when the adjusted *sales price* of the old residence was $35,000 or less. If the sales price exceeded $35,000, a proportionate part of the gain could be excluded. This rule was dropped in favor of an expanded exclusion which became effective in 1981 permitting a taxpayer, age 55 or older, to exclude from taxable income up to $125,000 in *capital gain* on the sale of a principal residence. There is no longer any limit on the sales price of the house eligible for qualification.

The election to take the exclusion offered under this rule is allowed only once in a lifetime—and the rule allows married couples only one such election. That is, if either spouse has previously exercised this option, as a single person or during a prior marriage, the other spouse is denied the use of this rule. However, there is no *recapture* if a couple is married after each has independently taken advantage of the tax-free gain.

There are several provisions in the age 55-or-older exclusion which should be noted:

1. The house must have been owned and occupied as a principal residence for three out of the five years preceding the sale in order to qualify.
2. If either the husband or wife is 55 or older, the exclusion may be claimed.
3. The right is for the exclusion of *one gain* up to the amount of $125,000. There is no right to use a portion of the gain for one sale and carry over the balance for a later sale. (If a gain is small, it might be beneficial to use the rollover rule until a larger gain is available.)
4. Any election to exclude gain under the prior "65-or-older" rule is disregarded. If the homeowner used this benefit previously, he is still eligible for the new 55-or-older exclusion.

EXAMPLE

IRS Form 2119, Sale or Exchange of Principal Residence, is used to report the 55-or-older exclusion. A completed form, found on page 188, illustrates the proper reporting of the necessary information.

Form **2119**

Department of the Treasury
Internal Revenue Service (O)

Sale or Exchange of Principal Residence

▶ See instructions on back.
▶ Attach to Form 1040 for year of sale (see instruction C).

1981
24

Note: Do not include expenses you are deducting as moving expenses.

Name(s) as shown on Form 1040 DONALD ADAMS

Your social security number 286 00 6914

		Yes	No
1 (a) Date former residence sold ▶ September 20, 1981			
(b) Enter the face amount of any mortgage, note (for example second trust), or other financial instrument on which you will receive periodic payments of principal or interest from this sale ▶ 38,000			
(c) Have you ever postponed any gain on the sale or exchange of a principal residence?			✔
(d) If you were on active duty in the U.S. Armed Forces or outside of the U.S. after the date of sale of former residence, enter dates. From to			
2 (a) Date you bought new residence. (If none bought, so state). ▶ N/A			
(b) If you constructed new residence, date construction began ▶ N/A date occupied ▶			
(c) Did you use both the old and new properties as your principal residence?		✔	
(d) Are any rooms in either residence rented out or used for business for which a deduction is allowed?			✔
(If "Yes" do not include gain on the rented or business portion in line 7; instead include in income on Form 4797.)			

Part I Computation of Gain and Adjusted Sales Price

3 Selling price of residence. (Do not include selling price of personal property items.)	**3**	130,000
4 Commissions and other expenses of sale not deducted as moving expenses	**4**	10,000
5 Amount realized (subtract line 4 from line 3)	**5**	120,000
6 Basis of residence sold	**6** 50,000	
7 Gain on sale (subtract line 6 from line 5). (If line 6 is more than line 5, enter zero and do not complete the rest of form.) If you bought another principal residence during the allowed replacement period or you elect the one time exclusion in Part III, continue with this form. Otherwise, enter the gain on Schedule D (Form 1040), line 2a or 9a.	**7** 70,000	
If you haven't replaced your residence, do you plan to do so within the replacement period? ☐ Yes ☐ No		
(If "Yes" see instruction C.)		
8 Fixing-up expenses (see instructions for time limitations.)	**8**	NONE
9 Adjusted sales price (subtract line 8 from line 5)	**9**	120,000

Part II Computation of Gain to be Postponed and Adjusted Basis of New Residence

10 Cost of new residence	**10**	
11 Gain taxable this year (Subtract line 10 from line 9. Do not enter more than line 7.) If line 10 is more than line 9, enter zero. Enter any taxable gain on Schedule D (Form 1040), line 2a or 9a. If you were 55 or over on the date of sale, see Part III	**11**	
12 Gain to be postponed (subtract line 11 from line 7)	**12**	
13 Adjusted basis of new residence (subtract line 12 from line 10)	**13**	

Part III Computation of Exclusion, Gain to be Reported, and Adjusted Basis of New Residence

		Yes	No
14 (a) Were you 55 or over on date of sale?		✔	
(b) Was your spouse 55 or over on date of sale?		✔	
(If you answered "No" to 14(a) and 14(b), do not complete the rest of form.)			
(c) If you answered "Yes" to 14(a) or 14(b) did you own and use the property sold as your principal residence for a total of at least 3 years (except for short temporary absences) of the 5-year period before the sale?		✔	
(If you are 65 or over and 1(a) is before 7/26/81, see instruction D.)			
(d) If you answered "Yes" to 14(c), do you elect to take the once in a lifetime exclusion of the gain on the sale?		✔	
(If "Yes," check yes box and complete the rest of Part III. If "No," return to Part II, line 12 above.)			
(e) At time of sale, was the residence owned by: ☐ you, ☐ your spouse, ☑ both of you?			
(f) Social security number of spouse, at time of sale, if different from number on Form 1040 ▶			
(Enter "none" if you were not married at time of sale.)			

15 (a) If line 1(a) is before 7/21/81, enter the smaller of line 7 or $100,000 ($50,000, if married filing separate return)	**15(a)**	
(b) If line 1(a) is after 7/20/81, enter the smaller of line 7 or $125,000 ($62,500, if married filing separate return)	**15(b)**	70,000
16 Part of gain included (subtract line 15a or 15b from line 7)	**16**	NONE
17 Cost of new residence. If you did not buy a new principal residence, enter "None." Then enter the gain from line 16 on Schedule D (Form 1040), line 9a, and do not complete the rest of Form 2119	**17**	NONE
18 Gain taxable this year. (Subtract the sum of lines 15 and 17 from line 9. The result cannot be more than line 16.) If line 17 plus line 15 is more than line 9, enter zero. Enter any taxable gain on Schedule D (Form 1040), line 9a	**18**	
19 Gain to be postponed (subtract line 18 from line 16)	**19**	
20 Adjusted basis of new residence (subtract line 19 from line 17)	**20**	

For Paperwork Reduction Act Notice, see back of form.

Form **2119** (1981)

188

Rental of Residential Property

In this chapter, residential property rentals mean one to four family units rather than large apartment projects. These smaller properties have become increasingly popular as good investments and until about 1980 had increased in value at a greater rate than inflation.

If such a property is acquired for the specific purpose of renting it on a full-time basis, the tax questions are reduced to those that concern any type of commercial venture. All operating expenses plus depreciation (cost recovery) are deductible from gross income to determine taxable income (or loss). In 1981, new legislation modified a previous IRS rule that disallowed any deductions if a residence was rented to a family member even at a fair market price. The new law permits full deductions for operating expenses and depreciation provided the residence is used by the family member as a principal residence and is let at fair market rates. Further, the deduction allowance is retroactive to 1976, and a refund can be claimed by filing an amended tax return.

It is when a personal residence is used as a *part-time* rental unit that tax procedures differ. Three separate tax treatments apply to three different categories of usage. Only Category 3 allows a full deduction for operating costs and depreciation. The other two categories apply restrictions to the amount of deductions. Later in the chapter each of these three categories is explained more fully.

RESIDENCE CONVERTED TO RENTAL USE

If a taxpayer's personal residence is converted (in whole or in part) for use in the taxpayer's business or for the production of rental income, it is necessary to determine the basis from which the property may be depreciated. This basis is the *lesser* of: (1) the fair market value of the property on the date of conversion; or (2) the adjusted basis of the property. The income and expenses of rental property are subject to IRS rules, which are examined next.

Rental Income

Regular Payments.   The money received for the normal use of rental property is income and must be reported in the year it is received.

Advance Rent.   Advance rentals must be included as regular income in the year they are received, regardless of the time period covered and the accounting method used by the taxpayer.

Payment for Lease Cancellation.   Such a payment must be treated as rental income in the year it is received, regardless of the taxpayer's accounting method.

Expenses Paid by Tenant.   If a tenant pays any of his landlord's expenses, these payments are rental income to the landlord and must be reported. However, the landlord may claim those expenses that are normally deductible.

Depreciation or Cost Recovery Deductions.   After determining the basis of value of the building and of any personal property used for rental purposes, it is necessary to assign each item to a recovery period class. (See Chapter 16.)

Repairs and Maintenance.   Any repairs to maintain the buildings and equipment or other rental property in an efficient condition are considered operating expenses and are deductible. Anything that adds to the value of the property or prolongs its useful life is considered an improvement, which is capitalized and then depreciated over its useful life.

Handicap Exception.   The taxpayer may elect to deduct up to $25,000 each year for an improvement or alteration (such as a ramp) that assists a handicapped or elderly person's access to the building. This rule applies to all kinds of rental property, not just to residential units.

Other Expenses.   All normal operating expenses for the property are deductible. These include advertising, trash collection, maintenance services, employees' wages, utilities, fire and liability insurance, taxes, interest, and commissions paid to rent the property or to collect the rents.

The 1978 Tax Code provides an exception to the limitations imposed on the amount of deductible rental expenses for the taxable year during which a personal residence is converted to a rental property.

PART–TIME RENTAL UNITS

If a dwelling unit is used part-time for rental purposes and part-time as a personal residence, it is necessary to allocate expenses between the rental use and the personal use. Special tax rules apply to this allocation. The rules apply to any type of dwelling unit so used, but they are most commonly used for vacation homes. If the taxpayer owns a partial interest in such property, he may deduct only his proportionate share of the ownership expenses, even if he paid more than his proportionate share.

Tax Definition of Dwelling Unit.   For tax purposes, a *dwelling unit* may be a house, apartment, condominium, mobile home, boat, or other similar property. The term does not include hotels, motels, and inns that are operated as businesses.

Tax Definition of Personal Use.   *Personal use* occurs any day or part of a day when a dwelling unit is used by:

1. The taxpayer.
2. A member of the taxpayer's family, unless a fair market rental is paid; then its usage is classified as a rental day (per modification in 1981).
3. Any other person with an interest in the property.
4. Anyone under a reciprocal arrangement which enables the taxpayer to use some other dwelling unit.
5. Anyone at less than a fair rental.

Allocation of Expenses

Expenses must be allocated between personal use and rental use. However, the allocation method and the deductible expenses vary with the number of days of personal use during the year. There are three categories of use, each of which is governed by its own tax rules:

1. Used primarily as a personal residence and rented for less than 15 days during the year.

2. Used as a personal residence for more than the greater of (a) 14 days or (b) 10 percent of the number of days during the tax year when the property was rented for a fair price.
3. Used as a personal residence, but for *not* more than the greater of (a) 14 days or (b) 10 percent of the number of days it was rented at a fair price.

A 1981 modification of an older rule allows the owner to ignore repair days in counting the 14-day time limit. *Repair days* are those when an owner occupies the vacation house for repair and maintenance.

Category 1—Rented less than 15 days

A personal residence rented for less than 15 days during the year is excluded from the rule permitting deduction of expenses (other than interest, taxes, and casualty losses). Any rent received under this category is *not included* in personal gross income. The normal deductions permitted for a personal residence—interest, taxes, and casualty losses—are deductible only if the taxpayer itemizes deductions (Schedule A, Form 1040).

Category 2—Part rental, part personal use

If the dwelling unit is used both as a residence and for rental purposes, expenses must be allocated between the two. The allocation is based on the number of days that the property is used during the year, not on the 365-day year. The number of "days used" includes those for both rental and personal purposes, but not those days on which the unit was held out for rent. To count as a rental day, the unit must be rented at a fair price. For example, if the taxpayer owns a beach cabin that has been rented for 120 days during the tax year and used for personal puposes for 30 days, the total "days used" would be 150. To allocate:

For rental: $\dfrac{120}{150}$ = .80 or 80% of expenses

For personal use: $\dfrac{30}{150}$ = .20 or 20% of expenses

Limits on Allocation of Expenses. Under this category, the amount of deducted expenses may not exceed the unit's gross rental income. For tax reporting purposes, the taxpayer must first deduct from gross rental income that portion of total expense for interest, taxes, and casualty losses that is allocated to rental use. Next, the taxpayer deducts the portion of operating expenses allocated to rental use. Finally, the allocated portion of depreciation is deducted. In no case, however, can the deductions exceed gross rental income from the property. The following example will illustrate the steps in allocating deductions:

EXAMPLE

Start with the following expenses for the beach cabin for a year:

Interest	$1,400
Taxes	$1,000
Utilities	$ 750
Maintenance	$ 300
Depreciation	$1,200

As calculated on page 192, the cabin was used for rental purposes 80 percent of the time it was in use, and 20 percent for personal purposes. Assuming that gross rental income is $3,300 the results are as follows:

Gross rental income		$3,300
Interest (80% of $1,400)	1,120	
Taxes (80% of $1,000)	800	
Less: Interest and taxes		$1,920
Rental income exceeding interest and taxes		$1,380
Utilities (80% of $750)	600	
Maintenance (80% of $300)	240	
Less: Utilities and maintenance		$ 840
Rental income exceeding interest, taxes, and operating expenses		$ 540
Less: Depreciation (limited in this example to the lesser of 80% of $1,200 [$960] or the remainder of the gross rental income not already deducted [$540])		$ 540
Net rental income		-0-

Rental income and expenses should be reported on Schedule E (Form 1040). Interest and taxes allocated to personal use (20 percent of each, in this example) are deductible on Schedule A (Form 1040), *provided* the taxpayer itemizes deductions (rather than taking the standard deduction).

Category 3—Personal use, less than 15 days

If a dwelling unit is used primarily for rental with the expectation of making a profit, it is not considered the taxpayer's personal residence. To qualify in this category, use as a personal residence during the year must not exceed the greater of (a) 14 days or (b) 10 percent of the number of days it was rented at a fair price. The tax benefits of this category are significant—the taxpayer's permissible deductions are not limited by the gross rental income from the property. It is still necessary to calculate the total days of use and to allocate expenses between rental use and personal use, as in Category 2.

Income and expenses allocable to rental use are reported on Schedule E (Form 1040). The taxpayer may deduct the allocable "personal use" portion of interest, taxes and casualty losses on Schedule A (Form 1040).

Disposition of Rental Property

If rental property is sold or otherwise disposed of, any depreciation that was taken under the rules outlined in this chapter must be deducted from the basis of property value for the calculation of the capital gain.

SIX

The Law Pertaining to Real Property

21

Ownership Rights to Real Property

Land is everlasting and that makes it different from everything else that can be owned. Land can be used for many purposes. The laws concerning landownership have developed in ways that recognize the many uses of land and the changing needs of the population. Landownership consists of legal rights, which can be limited in nature and duration. When a person owns all of the rights to a tract of land with no time limitation, the ownership is termed *fee simple*. As the number of ownership rights diminishes, so does the quality of ownership. These are the major rights to land.

1. *Possession*—the right to occupy the land.
2. *Use*—the right to work the land, which includes what may be grown, what minerals may be recovered.
3. *Enjoyment*—the use and occupancy of the land free of harassment or interference.
4. *Disposition*—the right to sell, lease, give away, or otherwise dispose of the land.

How these rights are held differentiates the various interests, or *estates*, that can be owned.

In modern law the right of disposition, which includes the right to sell or mortgage the property, necessarily includes the right to determine the duration of the ownership term. It is this crucial right of disposition—more than mere possession or use, which can be obtained under a lease—that provides the best test of ownership.

Land rights and ownership methods are embodied in the laws of each state, and there are differences which stem from the origin of the region. The Eastern and Midwestern states normally follow English common law. The Southwestern states incorporate Spanish law, with its emphasis on community property rights. Louisiana is unique, with property rights based on French civil law.

This chapter is intended to provide the real estate investor with an overview of real property law and its terminology. By understanding the major rights that are involved in landownership and the complex nature of the law, the investor can readily recognize the need for competent legal counsel when landownership rights are being determined. With a basic knowledge of the subject and its terminology, the investor can better understand the advice that a competent attorney will provide.

CLASSIFICATION OF ESTATES

The laws of real property concern the many aspects of landownership, its use and its conveyance. Its subjects include estates, ownership, leaseholds, contracts, mortgages, deeds, land titles, recording, and more. This chapter concentrates on two of these subjects—estates and landownership. And it outlines property rights as they relate to (1) the interest in land and (2) how the land is owned.

Historical Background

Today, every person in most free societies has the right to acquire an interest in land. We tend to overlook the fact that this was not always true. But much of our modern real property law can be directly traced to its origins in medieval Europe, where property rights were substantially less than universal.

Under the feudal system of the early Middle Ages, landownership represented far more power than it does today. Landholding provided a basis for government, as well as for military protection. It was used to determine both the social and economic status of the landowner. Land was parcelled out by the king to various lords who might pass on a portion of their land to lesser lords in exchange for some form of service. Actual possession or use of the land was usually left to the lower classes who worked the land for a share of its produce. This right to work the land was essentially a lease and did not grant any continuing interest in the land or the right to dispose of it. Upon the death of a tenant, all rights returned to the landlord. Thus, landownership was primarily an ownership of *present interest*. Not until after the Norman conquest of England did the concepts of landownership, which are the foundation of modern law, begin. About this same time, certain other rights to land began to be more clearly defined. For example, freehold estates became distinguished from nonfreehold estates. *Freehold* came to mean the more extensive rights of ownership, while *nonfreehold* was considered to be the "lease for years." Medieval law was essentially the law of freehold estates (since the rights of tenants in nonfreehold estates were not a matter of great concern). Also, what we now identify as *future interests*, which are principally the reversions and remainders stemming from life estates, began when the varieties of freehold estates came to be differentiated.

Outline of Major Classes of Estates

The law—and subsequent court rulings—have identified a number of qualifications to the precise nature of land interests, which makes understanding difficult for the person who is not a student of the law. Further confusion results from the fact that the word *estate* has other real estate meanings, being both a large property with an elaborate house and the property of a deceased person. For the purpose of this text, the word *estate* means the degree or quantity of interest that a person has in land, the nature of the right, its duration, and its relation to the rights of others.

There is also a distinction in the law between an heir and anyone else to whom a grantor conveys property upon his death. An *heir* is the legally designated person who would be entitled to receive the deceased person's property in the absence of a will. If a grantor conveys property by will to someone other than an heir, that person is known as a *devisee*.

In legal terminology, the word *fee* is often used interchangeably with the term *fee simple*, which is the highest form of an interest in land and includes the right of disposition.

Following is an outline of the major classes of estates, followed by an explanation of each.

A. Present Possessory Freehold Estates of Potentially Infinite Duration
   1. Fee Simple Absolute
   2. Fee Simple Conditional
   3. Fee Simple Estates of Potentially Limited Duration
      a. Fee Simple Determinable
      b. Fee Simple Subject to Condition Subsequent
      c. Fee Simple Subject to an Executory Limitation

B. Present Possessory Freehold Estates of Limited Duration (Life Estates)
  1. Conventional Life Estates
      a. Life Estate for Grantee's Life
      b. Life Estate Limited by Life of Someone Other than Grantee
  2. Legal Life Estates
      a. Dower
      b. Curtesy
      c. Homestead Protection
C. Future Interests
  1. Reversion
  2. Remainder
  3. Executory Interests
D. Nonfreehold Estates (Leasholds)
  1. Tenancy for Years
  2. Tenancy from Period to Period
  3. Tenancy at Will
  4. Tenancy at Sufferance
E. Land Interests Not Deemed Estates
  1. Easements
  2. Licenses
  3. Profit
  4. Covenants

Present Possessory Freehold Estates of Potentially Infinite Duration

The legal expression *present possessory* can be defined as "to own now." *Possessory* is to possess or to own. And *present* means "now," not after someone has passed away or made a gift of the property. The modern definition of *freehold* is almost the same as the medieval definition—that is, "ownership of land." *Infinite duration* means that the property is inheritable by the heirs and devisees of the owner. It is not subject to *defeasance*, meaning that inheritance cannot be defeated by any limiting condition in the title to the property.

Fee Simple Absolute.   This is the highest and most extensive estate in common law. It is inheritable and not limited to a particular class of heirs. Termination of the estate can be accomplished only if the owner dies without a will (*intestate*) and without heirs. If these two circumstances occur, the property passes to the state *by escheat.*

Fee Simple Conditional.   If the owner places a limit on which heirs are entitled to inherit the property, he may create a conditional estate. In early common law, the grantor might convey land "to grantee and the heirs of his body." This wording was interpreted to mean that the conveyance was conditional on the grantee's having a child; that is, if no children came to the grantee, then the estate became a life estate for the grantee. Such an estate would terminate with the death of the grantee, and the estate would then revert to the original grantor and/or his other heirs. This interpretation of the conditions of inheritance was modified in 1285 to provide a life estate for the grantee and a *fee* for his heirs. Later judicial rulings limited the fee so conveyed to a life estate. If the lineal, directly descended heirs failed to produce children, the estate, as before, reverted to the original grantor and his heirs. The result of these rulings is the *fee tail*, which is a form of estate controlled by the grantor after his death through restrictions on the class of potential transferees.

Fee Simple Estates of Potentially Limited Duration.   When the owner, or grantor, wants to control the *use* of land after his death, the wording used to convey the property expresses the intended limitation. How the conveyance is worded determines the type of estate that is granted. This method of limitation was not available under early common law, but came into existence after passage of the *Statute of Uses* in 1536. Under modern law, there are three forms of controlling land use by words of conveyance.

- *Fee simple determinable.* The words of conveyance to the grantee can read, for example, "so long as the premises are used for a public park," or "until premises are no longer used for a public park," or "while premises are used for a public park." The conveyance may be silent as to disposition of the property if the limiting conditions are no longer met. The law holds that, in such a case, the possibility exists that the property would revert to that grantor or his heirs.

- *Fee simple subject to condition subsequent.* The words of conveyance to grantee contain a disposition clause in the event the limiting conditions are not met. These words could be "but if the property is not used for a public park, grantor may re-enter." Modern law requires court action as a prerequisite to enforcement of the grantor's right to re-enter the property.

- *Fee simple subject to executory limitation.* This form of estate is similar to "fee simple subject to condition subsequent." The distinguishing feature is that the executory limitation causes a transfer of the interest to a third party named in the instrument of conveyance, rather than a return of the interest to the grantor. The conveyance wording might be "to grantee, but if not used for a public park, then to [a third party (not the grantor)]."

It should be noted that all three of these forms of conveyance—fee simple determinable, fee simple subject to condition subsequent, and fee simple subject to executory limitation—create a present possessory interest in the grantee, plus a future interest for the grantor in the event that the expressed condition causes a termination of the limited fee simple estate.

Present Possessory Freehold Estates of Limited Duration (Life Estates)

A life estate is limited to the lifetime(s) of one or more persons. Because of its limited duration, some legal definitions class this form as a "less than freehold" interest. There are two forms of life estates: (1) the conventional form, created by an express act of the parties, and (2) the legal form, created by operation of the law.

Conventional Life Estates.   The purpose of granting a life estate is to provide for the financial well-being of the grantee during his life, but to deny him the right to pass on the property to his heirs or others. The limitation can be based either on the life of the grantee or on the life of someone else.

- *Life estate for grantee's life.* When the intention of the grantor is to limit the benefit from an estate to the grantee's life, the conveyance might be "to grantee for his life." The recipient might be, for example, an uncle faced with heavy family medical expenses. Upon his death, the property would revert to the grantor.
- *Life estate limited by someone other than the grantee.* In this form of estate, the conveyance would read "to grantee for the life of [a third party]." The purpose might be to provide the benefit of an income property to a brother needing assistance until the death of a parent whose estate would pass in part to the brother.

Legal Life Estates.   This form of estate is created by statute (not common law). The thrust of these state laws is to protect the interests of parties to a marriage. English common law considered property acquired during marriage as belonging to the husband only. As a measure of balance, these statutes grant the wife ownership of one-third (one-half in some states) of the family's property *upon the death of the husband*. This estate owned by the wife is termed *dower right*.

- *Dower*. To be eligible for dower rights, a wife must meet three legal requirements. These are (1) a valid marriage, (2) possession of property by the husband during marriage, and (3) the death of the husband. In those states that still recognize a wife's dower rights, a purchaser of property must obtain the wife's written consent to the sale, either through signing the deed with her husband or through a separate *quit claim deed*. Failure to obtain the wife's consent to the sale of property leaves her dower rights intact, and they may be asserted upon the husband's death at a much later date. This is one more reason for a purchaser of real property both to require a title search by a qualified attorney and to insure the title.
- *Curtesy*. In some states a husband holds benefits in his deceased wife's property—called curtesy—that are similar to dower rights. These rights are not so clear as dower and may be defeated by the wife in her will. In some states the law requires that a child be born of the marriage before a husband may qualify for curtesy.

Both dower and curtesy rights developed from a concept of male dominance in marriage that is contrary to the modern concept of equal rights for men and women. The current trend favors a more equitable system of husband-wife property ownership, as under community property laws. The third form of legal life estate—homestead protection—is associated with marriage but provides almost equal protection for husband and wife.

- *Homestead protection*. All states except six* have some form of homestead protection that amounts to a life estate in the family residence. These laws are directed toward providing legal protection for a husband and wife against the forced sale of the family home as a result of debts or judgments. The laws further restrict the rights of a husband or wife to act without the other when conveying their homestead or offering it as collateral for a loan. Depending on the state, the law may require that the homestead right be indicated by a written declaration recorded in the public records. This is unlike dower and curtesy rights, which are *automatic*—not recorded—in the states that recognize them.

---

*Connecticut, Delaware, Hawaii, Maryland, Pennsylvania, and Rhode Island (plus the District of Columbia).

Future Interests

A future interest is a right to real property that allows possession at some future time. The term itself is somewhat imprecise, since the interest must also have a present existence. There are three general classes of future interests: reversion, remainder, and executory interest.

Reversion.   If a grantor conveys an interest in property to someone for that person's life (a life estate) and makes no disposition of the property upon the death of the grantee, the law presumes that the grantor intended that the interest would come back to himself (revert) or to his estate. The grantor can, of course, be more specific, stipulating in the conveyance that the property reverts to him upon the death of the grantee.

Remainder.   Remainder is like reversion, except that it favors a third party, rather than the grantor. The remainder is created when a grantor conveys a life estate to someone, specifying that upon the person's death the interest passes to a third party. For example, a man might convey an interest in real property to his wife for the rest of her life and specify that upon her death the interest is to be divided equally among the surviving children. The children own a future interest in the property and are called *remaindermen*. Since remaindermen do hold an interest in the property, they have a right to require both maintenance of the premises and payment of taxes, property assessments, and any interest on debt secured by the property.

Executory Interests.   Executory interests are future interests very similar to a remainder, except that possession is not taken immediately upon the death of the person holding the life estate. These future interests follow limited interests held by others. There are two types:

- *Springing executory interests.* The interest comes after a reversion of limited duration. A typical conveyance would read "to life tenant for life tenant's life; then, one year after the life tenant's death, to [a third party] and his heirs." For the year following the death of the life tenant, the interest would revert to the grantor (or his estate). At the end of that year, the fee simple interest would automatically pass to the third party named in the conveyance.
- *Shifting executory interests.* The future interest comes after a limited interest in persons other than the grantor. An example of the conveyance that might be used is "to life tenant for life tenant's life; but if life tenant marries outside the faith, then to [a third party] and his

heirs." A marriage "outside the faith" would automatically divest the life tenant of the life estate and simultaneously vest a fee simple estate in the third party.

Nonfreehold Estates (Leaseholds)

As developed under common law, the type of estate that conveys possession and use to the grantee—but retains ownership (with the right of disposition) in the grantor—is called a *leasehold estate*. It is not a freehold estate because it is not ownership of the land. The types of lease are not always clearly defined, and state laws provide some variations in interpretation. However, the following classification explains the basic kinds of tenancy under a leasehold estate.

The Tenancy for Years.   This estate is defined as any leasehold with a term that must end on or before a specified date. Most states limit the number of years for which a leasehold may be created. In California, for example, the maximum term is 15 years for farm property and 99 years for urban property.

The Tenancy from Period to Period.   Also called a *periodic tenancy*, the duration of the lease is expressed as "from [time period] to [time period]." The permissible periods may be from a day to a year in length. A term longer than one year would fall under the "for years" classification. The periodic tenancy is the leasehold found in a month-to-month apartment lease. Terminating a period-to-period lease requires some form of notification. The rule varies from state to state—generally the notification requirement is the length of the period, but no more than six months.

The Tenancy at Will.   This type of leasehold estate lasts as long as both landlord and tenant wish it to last. Either party may terminate this lease at any time. Usually, however, the terminating party must satisfy a notification requirement.

The Tenancy at Sufferance.   This estate describes the continued occupancy of a tenant who fails to vacate the premises at the expiration of his lease. This tenancy is without right and without the landlord's consent. However, if the landlord fails to take the necessary steps to evict the tenant, continued occupancy can be interpreted as a periodic estate. Even under tenancy at sufferance, some states require a termination notice.

Land Interests Not Deemed Estates

Some *relationships* regarding land can be created between a landowner and others which fall short of being *interests* in the land. Prime examples include easements, licenses, profit, and covenants.

Easements.   An easement is a right to *use* a piece of land, but carries no other rights of ownership. Under the law, the right of use is not the same as the right of possession.

Licenses.   A license is similar to an easement, in that it grants the right to use a portion of the land. But it differs from an easement in that it is revocable. For example, the license of a guest to use an owner's home may be revoked at any time by the owner.

Profit.   The right to sever and remove certain things attached to the land, such as ore or live timber, is called in the law a *profit.*

Covenants.   These are the steps an owner takes to restrict the use of land under his control. A covenant can benefit the noncovenanting party, but does not entitle him to personal use.

CLASSIFICATION OF PROPERTY OWNERSHIP

Ownership of land may be held by individuals in a number of ways. When two or more individuals hold a property, the manner in which they hold it determines whether or not each individual owner may dispose of his interest separately, and whether or not there is a right of survivorship. Following are the categories of ownership.

Sole Ownership

Property held by one person is called an *estate in severalty.* Don't let the legal terminology confuse you; think of *severalty* as "severed" ownership. Both single and married persons can be sole owners of property. However, state requirements concerning community property, dower, and curtesy rights must be considered when a married person is a sole owner.

Tenants in Common

When two or more persons hold undivided shares in a single property, they may do so as *tenants in common.** No owner can claim a specific portion of the property, as each has a right to possession of the entire prop-

---

*Recognized by all states except Louisiana.

erty. Interests need not all be the same size. Each owner can sell, mort-gage, or otherwise dispose of his individual interest. There is no right of survivorship in this form of ownership, which means that each in-dividual's share passes to his heirs or devisees as part of his estate. The share does not pass automatically to any of the other owners holding shares as tenants in common.

Joint Tenancy

A joint tenancy* of two or more persons is distinguished by the following features:

1. Each owner has an undivided interest, with the right of possession to the entire property.
2. All joint tenants' ownerships must be acquired simultaneously. New joint tenants cannot be added later without creating a new joint tenancy.
3. There is only one title to the property, and each owner has a share in it. If a share is sold, the new owner must join with the remaining joint tenants to create a new joint tenancy, or else the new share owner becomes a tenant in common.
4. The interest of each joint tenant is considered equal, regardless of how much each has contributed. If there are two joint tenants, each would own one-half; if three, each would own one-third. If shares are claimed disproportionately, the law considers the owners to be tenants in common.
5. The major distinction between joint tenants and tenants in com-mon is that joint tenancy includes the *right of survivorship*; that is, when a joint tenant dies, his interest passes automatically and im-mediately to the remaining joint tenants. The deceased person's in-terest never becomes a part of his probate estate.

Tenancy by the Entirety

This form of ownership is available *only* for property owned by a *husband and wife*. It is similar to a joint tenancy in that it carries the right of sur-vivorship. (The surviving spouse becomes the sole owner.) It is different from a joint tenancy in that—while they both live—neither husband nor wife can dispose of any interest in the property without the consent of the other. Many states do not recognize this form of ownership, while others restrict its use.

---

*Recognized by all states except Alaska, Georgia, Louisiana, Ohio, and Oregon.

Community Property

In the southwestern United States, Spanish law provided a basis for *community property** ownership, which is *limited to married persons*. There is some variation among the several state laws, but they are all based on the concept that a husband and wife contribute equally to a marriage and should therefore share equally any property purchased during the marriage. In contrast, English law is based on the concept that a husband and wife merge upon marriage.

Under community property ownership, both spouses must sign any conveyance or mortgage on the property. Each spouse has the right to devise his or her one-half interest to whomever he or she pleases. An interest need not go to the surviving spouse. If there is no will, however, the surviving spouse retains certain rights, which vary among the community property states.

Under community property law, both husband and wife may own *separate property*; that is, property that is excluded from the community property estate. Separate property includes:

1. Property owned by either husband or wife *before* marriage, the "separate" nature of which is retained after marriage.
2. Property acquired by either husband or wife after marriage through gift, devise, or inheritance.
3. Property purchased with funds which have been maintained as separate funds after marriage.

Separate property can be conveyed or mortgaged without the signature of the owner's spouse.

Because both parties to a marriage retain equal ownership rights to property accumulated during the marriage, community property states recognize neither dower nor curtesy rights.

---

*Recognized in Arizona, California, Idaho, Louisiana, Nevada, New Mexico, Texas, and Washington. Replaces tenancy by the entirety.

22

Restrictions on Real Property Rights

Restrictions on an owner's right to use his land stem from a number of sources. State and local governments exercise restraints on land use to protect the health and safety of the general population, government agencies can influence land use through the power of their various programs, and landowners can place limitations on the use of land through deed restrictions. Also, there are practical limitations on land use brought about by lack of sufficient services and utilities. This chapter will consider these restraints and some of the effects they create.

There has been an interesting evolution of government land use regulations, from its beginning during the nineteenth century's westward migration of settlers, to the police powers exercised by local governments as communities developed, to the present-day concern for adequate safeguards for the living environment. The concept of private property as the basis for personal liberty continues to change as greater emphasis is placed on the needs of society as a whole.

HISTORY OF THE LAND USE LAWS

As the new country began to grow, private ownership of land represented only a small portion of available land wealth; most was held by state and federal governments. Public lands were offered free to any settler willing to work the land. The great debates of this nineteenth century expansion concerned the proper objectives for the government in the disposition of the vast land areas under its control. Should the purpose be to encourage settlement, as Thomas Jefferson so eloquently argued? Or should the objective be to generate revenue for the federal government, as Alexander Hamilton had contended?

As the population moved westward, small towns grew where the need arose—where preparations had to be made to ford a river, where protection could be found from marauding tribes, where mountain passes could cause delays. The small towns grew partly by plan and partly to accommodate existing access trails. Rich farm and ranch land was purchased or homesteaded. By the middle of the nineteenth century, railroads were creating their own towns—where the tracks stopped, where junctions developed, or where difficult crossings required a support depot. Always it was individuals who found the most expeditious way to overcome the problem at hand.

By the latter part of the nineteenth century, settlers in the growing western states and territories realized that the unstructured growth of their towns must give way to planned development. Urban planning in the large eastern cities had focused on orderly street patterns with some landscaped park areas for beautification. Among the first of these attractive plans was William Penn's design for Philadelphia initiated in 1682, followed by Annapolis, Williamsburg, and Savannah. In 1791, Pierre L'Enfant was chosen to develop a master plan for the nation's new capital city in the District of Columbia. However, as the nation's growth accelerated, planning for beauty and open spaces within the cities became a less important goal than supporting a vibrant economic growth. The new planning centered on the more practical need for water supplies, sewage systems, and paved streets. It soon became apparent that the layout of streets and location of utility systems could be more easily accomplished if the planners also directed the usage of the land to be served. And steps were taken to include municipal zoning as an essential part of the city's planned growth.

The initial municipal effort to control the use of private land brought forth zoning laws. *Zoning* designates the use that may be made of each tract of land within a municipal jurisdiction and has a major impact on property values. The same police power that allows the city to zone the land provides authority to establish and enforce building codes, subdivision controls, and overall community planning. With these regulatory powers, the cities were better able to provide the individual landowner with adequate water supplies, sewage disposal systems, streets, schools, and parks.

ZONING

The police power of each state gives it the authority to protect the health, safety, and general welfare of its citizens. It is this authority that gives a state the right to restrict the use of privately-owned land. Through zoning laws, a community can (1) designate which tracts of land may be used for residential, commercial, industrial, or agricultural purposes, and (2) enforce these restrictions.

The first zoning law was New York City's, passed in 1916. (Today zoning is used in almost every town and major city in the country, a major exception being Houston, Texas.) The Advisory Committee on Zoning, set up under the then Secretary of Commerce Herbert Hoover, released the "Zoning Act" in 1922. And in 1926, the U.S. Department of Commerce published the Standard State Zoning Enabling Act, which set guidelines under which states were allowed to grant existing local governments the police powers needed to regulate the use of privately owned land. Implementation of the Act often resulted in disputes between the cities and the states. Urban groups had become suspicious of legislation enacted by rural-dominated legislatures. In a rather short period of time, nearly all communities adopted zoning plans that essentially confined land use to the status quo. Neighborhoods were simply zoned to their present use, with minimal allowance for any future growth.

Proponents of the zoning concept hoped that these laws could influence growth patterns. However, no method of controlling growth was incorporated in early zoning laws. No mechanisms were established to influence or control growth in the unincorporated areas surrounding the cities, even though these areas might later be annexed. And no provision was made to cover the relationship of one city to neighboring municipalities. The regional concept of growth did not evolve until later.

How Zoning Operates

A municipal zoning law is under the control of a regulatory body, usually a zoning commission. This commission develops the plans and establishes the procedures for implementing zoning legislation. A city is divided into districts, with a designation for each district indicating the type of building that may be erected (or how the land may otherwise be used). The rules and designations vary considerably. Generally, the basic designations are residential, commercial, industrial, and agriculture. Then the breakdown becomes more specific—one area may be zoned for single-family residences, with another for duplex to fourplex residences.

Similar subdesignations may be made in all designated areas. The rules may even go further than listing the *general* type of building that may be constructed. They may set a minimum and/or maximum size, height, living area, set-back from the property lines, and size of the lot itself. All communities with zoning laws have plans, available to the public, that identify the zones and the building requirements that apply to each tract of land.

Zoning laws may, of course, be changed. An ordinance may be amended to recognize a changing growth pattern or to accommodate a new development. Or a property owner may seek a *variance* from a zoning requirement that causes undue hardship. Applications for variances usually require substantial evidence of the need for the variance, some proof that it will not change the basic character of the existing zone, and a public notice of the request. While the initial zoning pattern seldom creates any land value that was not already inherent in the property, variance requests are often associated with efforts to increase land value. It is in this area that political pressures can undermine the benefits attributed to zoning laws.

Under zoning laws, a landowner must obtain a building permit from the community government (township, city, or county) before commencing construction of any building. Before the permit can be issued, building plans must be submitted to show that they conform with the zoning regulations. If a building is constructed without a permit, it is subject to demolition. If a building exists before the zoning ordinance becomes effective for that tract of land, it is generally accepted under a *grandfather clause* as a nonconforming use of the land. However, a "grandfathered" building cannot be enlarged or remodeled to extend its life; when it is demolished, any new building on the site must conform to the law.

A City Without Zoning

In spite of the almost universal (over 98 percent) adoption of zoning regulations by American cities of over 10,000 residents, these laws are still subject to serious questions. Many feel that they have misdirected growth patterns and that political manipulation of zoning causes undue delays and favoritism. Opponents of zoning regulations often point to Houston, a major city that has grown naturally without any zoning restrictions. There is little question that Houston has grown in an orderly and effective pattern. So far, no overwhelming civic problems have been created by that growth. (There is, of course, no valid method of comparing present growth with "what might have been" had zoning restrictions been instituted.)

The important lesson of Houston is that the expansion of a city must follow economic patterns—with or without a zoning authority. Location of commercial zones is clearly dictated by street and freeway patterns, which are the key to accessibility. Industrial zones, on the other hand, are dictated by the availability of relatively cheap land and good access to materials and transportation systems. These forces are all primarily economic. And while the direction of economic growth can be assisted by intelligent planning, economic need is rarely created by laws alone.

What is sometimes overlooked in a study of Houston's zoning-free growth is that the city does have a very active planning commission. The planning commission controls street patterns and utility systems within the city and for five miles beyond city limits. The availability of these facilities—or the lack of them—effectively tells a landowner what use he may make of the land. If the city does not have an immediate plan to furnish sewer and water services to a particular tract of land, its owner may construct his own streets and utility system. However, any such construction within five miles of the city limits must comply with city requirements, since the area may eventually be annexed into the city. This conformance requirement has proven to be an effective procedure.

BUILDING CODES

Both state and local governments have enacted building codes that are intended to protect the public against low-quality—and possibly dangerous—construction practices. The result has been a hodgepodge of requirements that often perpetuate outmoded and costly construction practices. In metropolitan Chicago, for example, there are between 30 and 40 separate codes (depending on what one calls a "code"). Attempts have been made to standardize requirements and encourage lower-cost modular housing, but these efforts have met with considerable resistance.

In spite of the problems involved, building codes serve a useful purpose in providing minimum standards for structural loads, ventilation, electrical installations, plumbing, and fire protection. Building plans must meet all code requirements before a building permit can be issued. The city building department generally inspects the building during construction to assure compliance with the laws. Upon the building's completion, the department must issue a certificate of acceptance before the building can be occupied.

Building code requirements do not end when construction is complete; they continue during its use. The methods of enforcement vary with the community, but generally the fire and health departments inspect buildings and cite any code violations.

SUBDIVISION REQUIREMENTS

In earlier times, a landowner could subdivide his land into lots with little concern for government restrictions, particularly if the land lay just outside community limits. Recently, however, local governments have used their police powers to enforce subdivision requirements. Flood control districts have been created and given authority to set minimum requirements in land development. The FHA and the VA have set minimum standards for the subdivisions in which they will agree to underwrite homes. And the Office of Interstate Land Sales Registration, part of the Department of Housing and Urban Development, has certain disclosure requirements (not minimum standards) for larger land developments.

Essentially the requirements for a subdivision concern the design, location, and quality of the streets; the adequacy of water and sewage systems; the location of fire hydrants and street lighting; and the size of the lots themselves. Depending on the size of the subdivision, the developer may be required to commit a portion of the land for schools and public areas. Once all requirements have been met, the community gives its approval for construction. In general, government approval concerns only the physical aspects of the development, not its economic value for the investor.

PLANNING

Although the implementation of zoning laws required a certain amount of community planning, early zoning's emphasis on the status quo gave little encouragement to the concept of urban or regional planning. As zoning laws began to create a mix of land use districts—some of which were desirable, and some of which were not—communities realized the need for better plans for growth and land use. But these efforts largely failed, because communities could not control the land outside of their boundaries. Probably the strongest encouragement to overcome this problem came from the federal government, which has authorized planning assistance in each of the National Housing Acts passed since 1954. The program became known as the *701 program.*

The 701 Program

In Section 701 of the Housing Act of 1954, Congress authorized the first program of Urban Planning Assistance. Its intent was to encourage land use planning—through surveys and land use studies—by providing federal funds to urban communities and to state, metropolitan, and regional planning agencies. As these programs multiplied, the goals were broadened to include human resources planning, fiscal planning, and the preparation of regulatory and administrative measures to implement the plans.

While the initial aim of the 701 Program has been diluted by an expansion of its goals and by increased emphasis on housing requirements, the program has been important to land use planning. One lasting contribution of the program has been its assistance in the training and development of the urban planning profession.

LAND USE RESTRICTIONS

As discussed in Chapter 21, the use of land can be restricted by the wording with which the land is conveyed. When land is conveyed with a restrictive condition (for example, "to grantee so long as the premises are used for a public park"), the right of ownership can be forfeited through failure to comply. A more common method of limiting the right to use land is the *deed restriction,* which does not carry the potential penalty inherent in the limited conveyance of rights. A lease agreement may also contain clauses that limit the tenant's use of the land.

The purpose of a deed restriction is to protect future property value for both the grantee and the neighborhood. Building lot developers, for example, often set usage standards when a lot is sold. The deed to a lot, for example, may contain a restrictive covenant that sets a minimum size of 1,500 square feet for the house to be built, requires that it be constructed with a brick or stone facade on the front and sides, and requires a wood shingle roof. The deed restrictions may dictate landscaping and building design, number of stories, set-back, and minimum cost. As long as the requirements are reasonable and are generally for the betterment of the neighborhood, they can be enforced. (The theory is that if a buyer agrees to restrictions, he is bound by them.) Enforcement is usually accomplished by a damaged party seeking an injunction, which is a court order that forbids a certain act.

Limitations by Private Agreements

Land use cannot be unduly restricted by private agreement. It is not permissible to limit future ownership in a manner that may cause discrimination due to sex, race, national origin, color, or creed. Furthermore, no private agreement can place an unreasonable restraint upon the disposition of the property that would prohibit any alienation (that is, a sale or other means of disposition) by the grantee. A reasonable restraint on disposition would be to require that the owner offer the property initially to a narrowly defined group for a limited time before offering it to persons outside the group.

Termination of Restrictions

Deed restrictions generally include a time limitation of 25 to 35 years—the character of a neighborhood usually changes during that time, leaving the original restriction irrelevant. There are other methods by which deed restrictions may be terminated. One way is by a failure to enforce the requirements. If a developer has sold all the lots, it is sometimes difficult to find a neighbor willing to sue for enforcement when damages may be ill defined. Other methods of termination include (1) by agreement among the parties involved (which may include a neighborhood association), (2) by a new zoning requirement which would take precedence, (3) by condemnation of the property for a public use, or (4) by other legislative action.

EMINENT DOMAIN

Under the state's right of *eminent domain*, the government can take private property for a public purpose or control its use. This action can be taken against the owner's wishes through *condemnation* proceedings. Unlike the exercise of state police powers, the right of eminent domain requires that the landowner receive fair compensation for his land. Normally the public authority negotiates with the property owner to determine an acceptable price for the property. If an agreement cannot be reached, the price is determined by court proceedings, with acceptance mandatory upon the landowner. It is through this procedure that the government retains the ultimate right to acquire land for streets, freeways, schools, parks, public parking, public housing, and other purposes that serve the needs of the general public.

Sometimes the government permits the use of eminent domain by private and quasi-public companies which serve a public need. A right-of-way for a power transmission line, pipeline, or railroad may be acquired through the exercise of this governmental right.

What is "fair" compensation under eminent domain depends on the rights acquired and the damages that the property owner may suffer. If, for example, the desired right-of-way creates an obstacle to future work on an operating farm, an additional compensation called *severance damages* may be paid. If land suffers a loss of value due to the construction of a nearby public facility, such as an airport or a sewage plant, the landowner may be entitled to *consequential damages*. Under some conditions, a landowner who feels damaged by a nearby facility can initiate a proceeding to demand that the government purchase his property. Such a case is called an *inverse condemnation*.

GOVERNMENT INFLUENCES ON LAND USE

Completely removed from the categories of rights, laws, and requirements are serveral government subsidy and assistance programs that effectively direct how land is used. If the landowner expects to receive the benefits offered by the programs, he must adhere to the programs' guidelines. Foremost in this category are the FHA and VA loan underwriting programs. Both agencies stipulate land use and building standards that must be met in order to qualify for loan assistance.

A more recent program directed by the federal government subsidizes the purchase of flood insurance in designated areas. The National Flood Insurance Program has established flood plain zones along waterways and in coastal areas. The decision to join this program has been optional for local governments in the affected areas. If an area elects to join and meets certain minimum requirements, the federal government provides subsidy support for private insurance carriers to write flood insurance policies for property owners in the area. Further construction cannot be undertaken on flood-prone land (that is, land that has been subject to flooding during the past 100 years of weather conditions) unless protective measures are taken. Enforcement is accomplished by forbidding any federally-regulated lending institution from financing any construction that is not in compliance. The result has been to remove large tracts of marginal land from possible development.

LAND RESTRICTIONS DUE TO
LACK OF SERVICE

In very recent years, a new form of land use restriction has developed due to (1) shortages of the basic utility services needed to sustain a modern community, and (2) rapid growth that, for some areas, has produced "unacceptable" problems. *No growth* laws have been enacted, producing an escalation in value for developed property and a sharp drop in value for surrounding land with potential development value.

Restrictions on Sewer and Water Lines

Sewage disposal facilities and drinking water are services usually supplied by a municipality, although in some communities water is furnished by a private utility company. Electricity and natural gas are usually—but not always—furnished by privately-owned utility companies. Regardless of who furnishes the services, many areas of the country are encountering difficulties in sustaining the growth rates of recent years. A number of measures have been undertaken to adjust to shortages, particularly in areas where water is in short supply.

Some California and Arizona communities, for example, have enacted building restrictions which virtually forbid new developments. The reasons for these restrictive laws include (1) lack of sufficient water, (2) lack of adequate sewage disposal facilities and the money needed to build suitable plants to meet federal and state pollution control requirements, and (3) the simple desire of many residents to enjoy their community as it is and not to be overcrowded.

Land developers have frequently challenged the right of communities to enact building limitations laws arguing that these laws are destructive of the landowner's rights to use his land. It will probably be many years before these legal questions are resolved. In the meantime, a potential investor in real estate must be aware of the utilities situation in the specific area of his investment interest.

Water Restrictions.   The most important utility-based limitation on land use is a shortage of water.

Water rights have long been an essential part of landownership in the western states. Indeed, without rights to water for such things as irrigation and use by livestock, ranch land can be worthless.

For development land in and near cities, the availability of water has only recently become a matter of concern. The location of early settlements was often dictated by the presence of suitable water, and the quantity needed to satisfy community sanitary requirements was not great. But today that situation has changed. Many areas are finding the quantity of water limited, particularly if rainfall is light. Other areas are finding that the cost of cleaning up the water is escalating more rapidly than the tax money available to do the job. As a result, many local governments cannot permit new water taps; in others, delays are increasing. The rate of growth—and the increase in jobs that growth can produce—is being forced to slow down.

Sewage Disposal.   The construction of sewer lines and sewage treatment plants has struggled to keep pace with the surge in housing construction across the country. Many local governments have fallen behind in their efforts to improve sewage treatment facilities in order to meet federal and state standards governing the quality of effluent that may be released into waterways. The techniques for proper treatment of waste material are now available and local shortages of this utility service are being remedied. But time—and, as always, more money—will be needed.

Electricity and Natural Gas

It was barely 100 years ago that electricity first became available for limited household use. Only since World War II has natural gas been distributed on a national scale. Yet today many homeowners and almost all businesses would call electricity an absolute necessity, and natural gas the cleanest and most convenient fuel.

Electric Power.   Even in the high-growth areas of the country, developers have traditionally had small cause for concern over the local power company's ability to furnish adequate electric power. This confidence in the ability of power companies to continue to meet the increases in demand is now being shaken. The plans of many power companies to supply future demands for power with nuclear power plants have been substantially curtailed because of the difficulties in obtaining construction approvals. Coal-fired plants are encouraged by various government agencies because coal is the most abundant of the fossil fuels. But coal-fired plants have to meet pollution restrictions which are both uncertain and costly. Plants using natural gas and oil for fuel are faced with limited supplies. It is possible that new energy resources will be developed in the eighties, but if not, the future production of electricity is expected to fall a little short of meeting the growth in demand.

For the investor in real estate, the impact of any future electricity shortage would show up in an inability to tie new outlets into the local power grid. If this should happen, an alternative source of power would be a privately-owned generator added to the building or the development—at an increase in the investment. Plans for future projects should be cleared with the local power company well in advance of starting construction.

Natural Gas.   The use of natural gas as a fuel has increased substantially since World War II. This is due partly because it is clean, easy to transport, and relatively low in cost compared to alternate fuels. In the late 1950s, the production of natural gas was placed under the regulatory powers of the Federal Power Commission, and price ceilings set on all gas moving in interstate commerce. For many years the ceilings remained stable while the cost of other fuels increased. As the inequities are adjusted, the cost of natural gas is sharply increasing, and the supply has fallen short of meeting the demand.

Fortunately for the real estate investor, natural gas is rarely a necessity. Most energy needs that have been satisfied by natural gas can be satisfied by other means. Some new housing developments are using all-electric heating and cooling (let the power company worry about which fuel is most suitable!). Both solar heating and heat pumps are being used to augment more conventional systems. Where gas *is* needed for fuel, the investor is not totally dependent on the uncertain supplies of natural gas.

ENVIRONMENTAL IMPACT STATEMENTS

The National Environmental Policy Act of 1969 requires the preparation of an environmental impact study for any major federal project that will affect the environment. The idea appealed to state legislatures, almost all of which have adopted similar requirements. Many local governments have construed state requirements to include them or have added environmental statements to their local zoning or planning ordinances. The courts have generally supported the requirements as a prerequisite to land development.

The thrust of the National Environmental Policy Act is to require an environmental impact statement (EIS) for *government* projects. But in the idea's adoption at lower levels of government, the burden of preparing such statements has been placed on the private developer. Generally required is a report on the expected impact of a new project or requested change in zoning classification on many hard-to-define areas such as noise, air quality, public health and safety, wildlife, and vegetation. The report also must estimate the impact on more easily measurable aspects of community life such as population density, automobile traffic, energy consumption, the need for sewer and water facilities, employment, and school enrollment. Not every project must first be studied—the laws generally specify how large a project must be to require an environmental statement. (This threshold varies with the locality.)

The information contained in an EIS is helpful to many agencies of the government. Copies of the statement are commonly submitted to the affected school district, water department, sewage control district, flood control district, and highway department. The EIS is also made available to the public, with open hearings held on the application. If federal or state money is involved in the project, additional federal or state hearings must be held.

Preparation of the statements is generally not subject to any qualification or competency standards. For a government project, the EIS is prepared by the agency involved with the project (sometimes with the help of a private consultant). If the development is privately owned, the statement may be prepared by the developer or by a private firm specializing in environmental studies.

The cost of preparing an EIS is usually the least of the new environment-based costs of a new project. The need to study the statement and process the application through prolonged public hearings have added many months to the preparatory time required before construction can commence. With inflation now endemic, delay means cost escalation. An additional problem is that an EIS sometimes provides a major weapon to opponents of a project—even a mere handful of opponents—who wish to stop growth rather than control it.

The following section examines methods and theories of environmental control that can shape the future planning and, thus, the growth of land use.

ENVIRONMENTAL CONTROL METHODS

The growing concern for the environment—and for all the living conditions encompassed by that word—has brought a large and not yet clearly defined body of laws and regulations. The trouble derives from (1) lack of a clear definition of what the problem is and (2) lack of agreement as to what should be done about it. As the environment has become a political issue, governments have looked first to their police powers as a means to improve or correct the problem. Earlier in this century, when land use in growing cities required some control, the states exercised their police powers first to regulate building construction. Then followed zoning ordinances, subdivision controls, and efforts to use police powers to protect the living environment. The first response to smog came under the authority of nuisance control laws. Next came emission control limits for automobiles and factories. Finally, requirements have been devised that make pollution abatement devices mandatory.

Cleaning up the environment is a problem involving more than just land use, but an essential thrust of the cleanup effort is directed at how the land is used. Four methods can be used to accomplish environmental goals, insofar as land use is concerned. These are (1) government police power, (2) private contract, (3) acquisition, and (4) social pressure. The first two methods were discussed earlier (in connection with land use restrictions), but are touched on again here in connection with efforts to improve the environment—a subject of interest not only to land investors, but also to present and potential landowners.

Police Power.   Government police power arises from the need for social organization. It can be termed an expression of sovereignty. When used as a control technique in restricting land use, the government's restricting an individual's freedom *without compensation* is generally accepted by the public as necessary for the good of society. When the same police power is used to restrict the freedom of *most* individuals comprising the general public—as is necessary for an effective emission control regulation—the individual generally fails to see the restriction as necessary for the good of society. Probably nowhere else in the United States has police power been used more strongly for emission control than Los Angeles. Yet the city's air remains polluted; governmental actions have failed to clean it. This cannot be because the city lacks the police authority to enforce the regulations. Rather, the general public most likely feels that other economic considerations carry a higher priority than a clean environment.

Private Contract.   A private contract is drawn between the local taxing authority and a landowner. The taxing authority agrees to limit property taxes to, say, a capitalized value on the open space usage, while the landowner agrees to forego any development. This type of agreement is effective in controlling the use of the land, but it has limited application. It requires a special set of circumstances wherein (1) the taxing agency is willing to forego the increased revenue that would result from an increase in land value and (2) the landowner is willing to forego the gain that could result from developing the land. But situations do occur where both parties are best served by withholding development.

Contract programs do remove tax pressures that can produce an undesirable change in land use. And such programs can help to direct urban growth into outlying rural areas before land speculation upsets proper mechanisms for land use control.

Acquisition.   When control of land use is essential to protection of the environment, the government can acquire land through purchase—which can be fee simple, a right to the land that is less than fee simple, or an easement. The obvious limitation to this alternative is that it can be very costly for the government. One way to reduce this expense is for the government to purchase, for example, a piece of farm land, and then resell the land with a restrictive clause in the deed that allows subsequent owners to use the land only for farming.

The use of easements is also an effective way to reduce the high cost involved in acquiring ownership rights. Many highways are constructed on easements, which allows the government to restrict highway signs. Special legislation has expanded the right to control signs along interstate highways. One state, Wisconsin, has acquired easements adjoining its major highways for the purpose of protecting the scenic beauty along the way.

More than the other methods of accomplishing environmental goals, the use of government power to acquire land from private owners for the primary purpose of preventing its use involves political and emotional questions. The heritage of this country is deeply rooted in the concept that private property is a basic right of the people. Strong arguments have been made that the security of private property is the very foundation of personal liberty. It is hard to deny the advantages that have accrued to this society under a system of private initiative and the right to own property. But as society has become less dependent on the land as a source of personal income, the concept of absolute rights to private property has given way to society's needs.

Some of those who strongly support the environmentalists' goals consider the theory of property rights to be illogical. They say that only labor and capital create value, that the land itself was not made by an owner and is basically a social possession. Therefore, this theory concludes, the private property owner has no compensable rights in land itself (but does have compensable rights in the improvements) and should not be paid if the land is needed for the benefit of society as a whole.

There is no question that some control over land use is a necessary tool in improving the environment. But is it wise to move so far in the effort to control that an essential element in the building blocks of the economy is destroyed? It is quite true that American Indians did not recognize private property in their societies and that they lived good and fruitful lives. And it is also true that great kingdoms survived with all the land held by a noble few, leaving treasures of architecture, art, and music to the world. But has any other economic system ever produced so much in goods and services for so many people to enjoy as free enterprise in the United States?

Social Pressure.   The fourth method of accomplishing environmental goals is through the attitudes of society. In our system, social priorities are determined by the laws and in the marketplace. Both the legislatures and the marketplace are strongly influenced by human conduct. And human conduct reflects a mixture of tradition, public opinion, habit, education, religious belief, and moral leadership. Changes in the law that reduce individual rights and freedoms to promote a safer and more liveable environment cannot be successful without the support of at least a sizable minority.

23

Note and Mortgage Instruments

Loans made with real estate as the collateral security can be traced back as far as the ancient Pharaohs of Egypt and the Romans of the pre-Christian era. Even then, some form of pledge or assignment of the property was used to ensure repayment of an obligation to the lender. The development over many centuries of this type of property assignment illustrates the interplay of individual rights, more specifically, the rights of a borrower as against the rights of a lender.

HISTORY AND DEVELOPMENT

The Mortgage as a Grant of Title to Property

In its earliest forms, a property pledge to secure a debt was an actual assignment of that property to the lender. During the term of the loan, the lender might even have the physical use of that land and was entitled to any rents or other revenues derived from the land pledged. Thus, the earliest form of land as security for a loan was the actual granting of title to the lender for the term of the loan.

Due to the primitive conditions of communication and transportation then in existence, the practice of granting title to property for a loan tended to foster a number of abuses by the lenders. For example, a slight delay in payments, which might even be encouraged by the lender, easily created a default and forfeited the borrower's rights for any recovery of his land. Sometimes borrowers who felt they had been unjustly deprived of their property appealed to the king, or perhaps to an appointed minister, to seek a hearing for their grievances and to petition for just redress. And if it was subsequently determined that a wrong had been committed, the borrower might be given a chance to redeem his land with a late payment of the obligation. Thus the *right of redemption* came into being.

However, lenders were not happy with this redemption privilege and initiated a countermove by inserting a clause in future loan agreements that specifically waived the right of redemption. The borrower had to accept this clause or be denied the loan. As our civilization developed away from the unchallenged rule of an absolute monarch into written codes of law, the granting or refusal of redemption became a matter of law or statute and is often referred to as *statutory redemption*. Variations in such laws among the states are substantial, going all the way from a total lack of redemption rights upon default up to two full years after default to pay off the loan and recover the property.

The Mortgage as a Lien

Another way in which land can be pledged as security for a loan is by means of granting a lien. A *lien* constitutes an encumberance on property. It is a declaration of a claim to a parcel of land for some purpose that is recorded in the public record. In states where the lien form is prevalent, a pledge of land as security for a loan grants no title except under default of the obligation. So when a default does occur, the lender must convert his lien rights into an actual title to the property through court action, as the particular state may require.

While there is some variation in the precise usage of the lien as a form of pledge, and the limited assignment of title as another form of pledge, all property laws concerning mortgages can be classified into one form or the other. The advantages and disadvantages of each can be weighed as legal arguments, but for purposes of finance, it is important mainly to be aware of the existing differences and to know under what laws a particular property can be mortgaged.

Lenders have learned to live with various requirements and can obtain adequate security for their loans by adapting their pledges to the many different laws. For example, they have adjusted even to the unique law spelled out in the original constitution of the state of Texas protecting a family homestead from all creditors with just three exceptions: (1) a loan for purchase of the property, (2) mechanic's and materialmen's liens, and (3) property taxes.

STATE LAWS CONTROL PROPERTY RIGHTS

Property rights in the United States are spelled out primarily under state laws, not by the federal government. Each state has written into its code of law specific rights that must be adhered to with regard to landownership in that state. The local variations and shadings in these laws reflect the background and origins of the particular region. In the East, for example, the great body of English parliamentary law and common law guided the New England and mid-Atlantic states in setting up their constitutions and subsequent statutes. In the South, on the other hand, the French legal codes were reflected in the Louisiana Territory and were especially evident in the growing city of New Orleans. In still another section of the country, the Southwest, Spanish heritage determined the laws, and these laws recognized Catholic religious ties in marriage, as well as patriarchal protection of wife, children, and family relationships. As a result, community property statutes were enacted, and for many years special protections, as well as special limitations regarding women's property rights, were in force in this region of the country.

An attempt to cover such a broad field of law as real property rights on a national basis would be out of place in this text since it is a subject more properly handled by qualified attorneys, skilled in interpreting these rights according to the laws of each state. It can be pointed out, however, that most states have laws specifically limiting any conveyance of property rights solely to written agreements and that all states require certain procedures to record conveyances of land in the public records. The result has been an increasingly accurate record of land titles, with a corresponding increase of protection for property owner's rights and those of any other interested parties.

THE MORTGAGE AND PROMISSORY NOTE

There are certain basic instruments used in real estate loans that have essentially the same purposes throughout the country. The collateral pledge that has given its name to the entire field of real estate finance is the *mortgage*. A mortgage is simply a pledge of property to secure a loan. It is not a promise to pay anything. As a matter of fact, without a debt to secure, the mortgage itself becomes null and void by its own terms; or, as the French derivative of the word mortgage indicates, a "dead pledge." Due to the differences in state laws, the precise definition varies somewhat, but for our purposes a mortgage can best be defined as a limited conveyance of property as security for the debt recited therein, which can only be activated by failure to comply with its terms.

The real proof of the debt is the promissory note, the actual promise to pay, which must accompany, or in some cases becomes a part of, the mortgage instrument. It calls out the payment terms including the rate of interest. It is the note that defaults for nonpayment, not the mortgage instrument. The expression *mortgage default* is a technical misnomer. When the promissory note falls into default, the mortgage instrument is activated and becomes the means of protecting the lender's collateral.

In 1970, the Federal National Mortgage Association decided to expand its lending activities from exclusively FHA- and VA-underwritten loans into the larger area of conventional loans, that is to say, those loans without government underwriting. In order to provide a more uniform standard of collateral, FNMA devised a mortgage instrument with a wider application than those previously used. No one form could be used throughout the country because of variations in state laws. So each state has its own note and mortgage instruments that comply with their requirements.

When the Federal Home Loan Mortgage Corporation was established, it joined with FNMA in the development of standardized forms that would be acceptable to both of these organizations, including loan application forms, appraisal forms, notes and mortgage instruments.

CLAUSES FOUND IN MORTGAGE INSTRUMENTS

Identification of *parties* in the initial clause spells out the precise names of all parties involved, the borrower or mortgagor, and the lender or mortgagee. In many states a wife must join her husband to create a binding pledge on real property. As in all such legal instruments, the parties must be legally qualified (of legal age, of sound mind, and so on) to undertake the contract. It is important for the lender to make sure that *all* parties holding an interest in the title to any pledged property are a party to the mortgage pledge.

Identification of the *property* used as security must be accurately described so as to distinguish it from any other property in the world. A street address is never acceptable, nor are boundary lines based on physical features, such as the "big live oak by the river bend." Accurate legal descriptions are normally used either by "metes and bounds" (a surveyor's description of boundary lines from a fixed starting point, thence proceeding in specific compass directions and distances around the property back to the starting point); or more commonly in urban areas, by lot and block taken from a subdivision plat registered and approved by a local governmental authority. An erroneous description of the property, even a typographical error, can render the mortgage instrument void but does not necessarily invalidate the promissory note.

Principal Amount Due

The mortgage instrument must define the property pledged as security for the initial amount of indebtedness. But the mortgage claim cannot exceed the value of the unpaid balance of the debt. As payments are made on the principal amount of the debt, the value of the mortgage pledge is correspondingly reduced. In this context, the word *estoppel* is sometimes used. Since the mortgage instrument may have a term of 20 or 30 years, and is recorded in the public records only in its original form, the question may arise as to the balance due at an interim point in the mortgage term. While most mortgage loans are repaid on a monthly installment basis and the reduction of principal due after each payment is accurately projected by an amortization table, breaks in the payment pattern can always occur. A greater reduction of principal may be made in any one year, or payments could be delinquent. The balance due becomes important when a mortgage loan is sold between lenders. At such time, an estoppel form may be required. This form is a statement of the balance due as of a specific date, acknowledged by the lender and the borrower, and in effect "stops" the subsequent purchaser of the loan from claiming any greater amount due from the borrower. Modern practice of trading in the secondary market places the responsibility of accurate reporting on the balance due with the seller of the loan, and the estoppel form is becoming obsolete.

Prepayment

A clause contained in many residential mortgages prior to 1972, and found today in most commercial mortgages, calls for an additional premium to be paid to the lender if a loan is paid off before maturity. This particular privilege has caused many arguments and misunderstandings. From the lender's viewpoint, he is making a loan of, say $60,000 at 14 percent for a period of 30 years. Under the terms of the promissory note, the borrower agrees to make certain monthly payments, which include both principal and interest. The 360 payments agreed to can amount to as much as $195,000 in interest for the lender over the 30-year period.* The lender can claim a contractual right to this interest, which has obvious value. Why should the lender then be required to forfeit this right to the interest? Earlier mortgages usually provided a compromise to this position by calling for a specific payment against the unearned portion of the interest at the time of early principal payment in order to obtain a release of the mortgage claim. This *prepayment premium,* or conversely, prepayment penalty from the homeowner's viewpoint, varies widely within the industry and may run from 1 to 3 percent of the balance due at the time of prepayment up to all interest due for the first 10 years of the loan. A more common provision allows up to 20 percent of the original loan to be paid off in any one year without any premium for the unearned interest, plus 1 percent of any balance in excess of the 20 percent paid in the same year.

With the rise in popularity of "consumerism," many attacks have been made on the prepayment provision insofar as residential loans are concerned. A number of lenders, following the leadership of FNMA and supported by subsequent FHA rules eliminating prepayment premiums, have dropped all such requirements for residential loans. The reasoning behind this action is that when the principal sum has been returned to the lender, he is free to put this money back to work in a new loan and thus suffers no compensable loss.

Acceleration

One of the essential clauses in a mortgage instrument provides for the payment in full of the balance due; that is, the *acceleration* of each monthly payment to the present date, in case of a default in the mortgage terms. While there can be other possible reasons for a default in the mortgage terms, such as improper usage of the property or selling of the premises without specific permission of the mortgagee, the most probable cause of default is nonpayment of the debt secured. Without an acceleration clause, it is conceivable that a lender would be forced to foreclose his claim each and every month as the installment payments came due.

The acceleration clause is sometimes referred to as the *call clause.* This is not an accurate description. There are several clauses in a mortgage instrument that state conditions which, if violated, can cause a default on the agreement and result in the calling of the loan. The ac-

---

*Monthly payment on a $60,000 loan for 30 years at 14 percent interest is $711 ($711 × 360 = $255,960). To repay a $60,000 loan, the interest cost is $195,960 over a 30-year term.

celeration clause simply makes it possible to call for the entire balance due at one time, but is not in itself a condition that can cause default.

Right to Sell

As a general rule, mortgaged property can be freely sold by the owner or mortgagor, either with an assumption of the existing debt by the new buyer, or by paying off the balance due on the existing mortgage. In a sale the common assumption is that the original borrower remains liable on the obligation along with the new buyer. Some lenders may grant a release of liability to the original borrower, but they are under no obligation to do so.

When interest remained at lower and more stable rates, lenders were more cooperative in allowing sales and assumptions of their loans. But as interest rates moved upward in the late sixties, more lenders eyed the loss of value in their older loans, which had been made at much lower rates. And many began to insert clauses in their mortgage instruments that required specific approval by the lender before the borrower could make any sale of the property that included an assumption of the loan. The price of that approval often proved to be an adjustment of the interest rate upward on the balance of the loan to a percentage rate closer to the then existing market rate. This interest adjustment is sometimes demanded without releasing the original borrower from the obligation.

The reservation of the right to approve a sale by the lender should not be confused with the term *interest escalation*, although this can be the result. More specifically, the escalation of interest is called for in a promissory note when payments become delinquent or when default occurs. The purpose of increasing the interest in such cases is to help offset the increased costs to the lender in collecting a delinquent account or in undertaking foreclosure proceedings.

Insurance

Mortgages require property insurance coverage for the lender's protection. This is also termed *hazard insurance*. Principally, it includes fire and extended coverage and is required by the lender where any buildings are involved in an amount at least equal to that of the loan. To make certain that insurance payments are made, the lender generally requires a full year's paid-up insurance policy before releasing the loan proceeds, plus two months of the annual premium paid into an escrow account. Then with each monthly payment, one-twelfth of the annual premium must be paid. The original policy is held by the lender, and it is part of the lender's responsibility to maintain the coverage with timely payments made from the borrower's escrow account.

Insurance companies in most states have another requirement controlling the minimum amount of coverage that can be carried to establish full coverage in case of a loss. Since most fire losses are partial in extent, it is not unusual for a property owner to carry only partial insurance hoping that any fire would be brought under control before the damage exceeds the amount of insurance coverage. To distribute the cost of insurance more equitably over all policyholders, many insurance companies require that the insured maintain insurance of not less than a given percentage of the actual cash value of the bulding at the time of the loss. These clauses are known variously as coinsurance clauses, average clauses, or reduced rate contribution clauses. A common minimum amount of insurance to provide full coverage is 80 percent of the actual cash value of the building at the time of the loss. By carrying less than the agreed percentage of insurance, the property owner cannot collect in full for a loss, but will have to bear a part of the loss personally. The insurance company will be liable only for such percentage of the loss as the amount of insurance carried bears to 80 percent of the actual cash value of the property at the time of the loss. The insurance company's liability may be expressed by the formula:

$$\frac{C}{R} \times L = A$$

Where: C = the amount of insurance carried
R = the amount of insurance required
L = the amount of the loss
A = the amount for which the insurance company is liable.

In periods of rapidly rising property values, any failure to maintain proper insurance coverage can expose the lender, as well as the property owner, to uninsured losses.

Another insurance problem to be considered in a mortgage involves determining just how the proceeds should be paid in case of an actual loss. Earlier mortgages required payment of the insurance money to the lender, who in turn then decided how to apply the funds; that is, whether to permit the funds to be used for restoration of the property, which is the usual procedure on smaller losses, or to apply the insurance proceeds to the payoff of the loan. As time has passed, recent mortgages have given the borrower a stronger position in the distribution of insurance proceeds, as is apparent in the FNMA/FHLMC standard conventional mortgage terms.

Taxes

Lenders long ago learned that the real first lien on any property is in the hands of the property taxing authority; that is, the agency that levies the *ad valorem* property taxes. It can be categorically stated that the full documented and properly recorded "first" mortgage instrument securing the lender's position takes only a poor second place to a tax levy. And in some states, this tax levy includes an assessment by a properly authorized neighborhood maintenance association!

It is evident then, that the timely payment of property taxes becomes another essential requirement in mortgage loans. Lenders usually require that an amount equal to two months of the annual taxes be paid into an escrow account by the borrower before the loan is funded. One-twelfth of the annual taxes is also added to each monthly payment of principal and interest. In this manner, the lender accumulates sufficient cash each year to pay the borrower's property taxes directly to the tax authorities and thus is protected against any tax priority lien on the pledged property.

In regard to federal taxes, these take priority over state laws regarding property and do carry lien rights and highest priority. However, federal taxes, including federal income taxes, become property liens only when they are filed as a delinquent assessment against an individual or corporation, not when the tax liability is incurred. A federal tax lien is a general lien and may apply to any and all property owned by the taxpayer. The *ad valorem*, or property tax, is a specific lien (applying only to the designated property liable for the tax), and becomes a lien against the property from the minute the taxing authorities levy the assessment.

Foreclosure

The right of the lender to foreclose on a property is limited by the terms of the mortgage instrument and by the applicable state laws. In general, foreclosure is the last recourse of the lender, often a costly procedure and usually an open admission that an error in judgment was made in making the loan. Lenders will normally put forth considerable effort to cooperate with a borrower who has unforeseen financial problems and needs some relief. But the lender must depend on the borrower to seek the relief, and this is more easily arranged before a serious delinquency occurs. Lenders have an obligation to their own investors, depositors, insurance policyholders, trust funds, and so on to exercise control over their borrowers' accounts and not allow a property mortgage note to slide into default so that such laxity would compromise the lender's security. When failure to comply with the terms of the note and mortgage occurs on the part of the borrower, generally due to nonpayment of the obligation, then the lender must seek foreclosure of the property.

The real purpose of a foreclosure is to sell the property under the authority of a court order, usually referred to as a *sheriff's sale,* and to distribute the proceeds to the various creditors holding claims on the property. Contrary to popular belief, in a foreclosure proceeding, the lender has no more right to take title to the property than anyone else.

Accordingly, the court orders a property to be sold in a foreclosure proceeding, and whoever offers the highest cash price at the subsequent public sale acquires a deed to the property by court order, in some places referred to as a *sheriff's deed.* In practice, the lender is allowed to submit a claim; that is, the balance due on the promissory note, as part or all of the cash offer for the property. In many states, the lender need not even offer the full amount of the claim if it is deemed too high.

In a foreclosure action, the proceeds realized from the sale of collateral are distributed to claimants in the order of an established priority. The handling of a foreclosure is unlike that of a bankruptcy. In a bankruptcy, the referee attempts to distribute the debtor's assets in an equitable manner between the secured claimants and the unsecured claimants. In a foreclosure procedure, the amount realized from the sale is used, first, to pay all administrative costs; second, to pay all property taxes in full; and then to pay each claimant what is due in order of lien priority. It is quite possible that the sale will result in insufficent funds to pay off even the first lien holder.

Because the lender has a claim against the property and can use that as payment in a foreclosure sale, the lender or an agent for the lender usually ends up taking title to the foreclosed property. If the claim against the borrower is not fully satisfied from the proceeds of the sale, then the lender can seek a deficiency judgment for the balance due.

The above considerations strongly suggest that the foreclosure is apt to be a difficult, distasteful, and discouraging procedure. The lender is faced with the costs of litigation, with the possibility of an unpleasant eviction, plus the risk of property damage through owner abuse, or vandalism. In addition, the lender may have to pay the costs of renovating and maintaining the property, plus payment of delinquent taxes and insurance. Foreclosure is seldom a satisfactory solution.

TYPES OF MORTGAGES

The most common forms of mortgage instruments have some important variations, namely, in how and when they are used. The underlying purpose of providing a pledge of property as security for a loan remains the same, however. Some of the principal variations are explained in the following discussion.

Deed of Trust

The *deed of trust* introduces a third party, a trustee, into the pledging instrument. Under these terms, the borrower actually makes an assignment (the wording is very similar to a warranty deed) of the property to the trustee, but restricts the effectiveness of the assignment to when a default occurs under the mortgage terms. The trustee is normally selected by the lender with the right of substitution in case of death or dismissal.

The deed of trust form is used in many areas and is almost universally used in Texas as a means of simplifying "homestead" law procedures. It substantially reduces the problems of foreclosure, limiting the process to an action by the trustee, with proper notice and in accordance with prevailing laws, rather than by litigation conducted in a court hearing.

Open-end Mortgages

The open-end mortgage permits a lender to advance additional money under the same security and priority as the original mortgage. This type of mortgage is often employed in farm loans where the lender maintains continuing relations with his customer-borrower. As the borrower pays the mortgage principal down, he or she may wish to add a new barn, or perhaps a new loading corral to the property. The additional loan can easily be accommodated under the terms of an open-end mortgage.

In some areas a borrower may elect to leave a minimal mortgage balance of, say, one dollar outstanding on the mortgage loan. This record of balance due, no matter how small, sustains the life of the mortgage instrument and, most significantly, its priority over any other subsequent lien except, of course, property taxes. This provision gives rural banks a means of making loans to their farm- or ranch-owning customers without the expense and delay of researching a title and recording a new mortgage instrument with each loan.

Construction Mortgages

A loan to build a house or other building is a construction loan, sometimes called *interim* financing. The security requirement is the same—a first lien on real property—but in this type of loan, proceeds are disbursed as the building is constructed. Under the construction mortgage, the borrower or builder draws a portion of the total loan at various stages, or at set time intervals, such as monthly, for work completed. It takes a construction-wise lender to make sure his disbursement of funds does not exceed the value of a building at each stage of construction.

A construction loan is considered a high-risk loan. It carries high-interest rates and is seldom intended to extend beyond three years. Commercial projects, such as a warehouse or apartment, usually require assurance of permanent financing or a *takeout commitment*; that is, an agreement by a reputable lender that the lending organization will make a permanent loan upon completion of the project.

Homebuilders frequently build for speculative sales, in which case the construction lender must look to the actual sale of the house to pay off the construction loan. This increases the risk for the lender who may require the builder to obtain a standby commitment for a permanent loan before commencing construction.

Mortgages with Release Clauses

When money is borrowed for the purpose of land development, it is necessary to have specific release procedures to enable the developer to sell lots, or a portion of the land, and deliver good title to that portion. This is the purpose of a release clause. The conditions are stated so that the developer can repay a portion of the loan and obtain a release of a portion of the land from the original mortgage. In a subdivision of building lots, the developer would be required to pay a percentage of the sales price of the lot, or a minimum dollar amount against the loan, for each lot released. The lender would calculate the payoff so that the loan would be fully repaid when somewhere around 60 to 80 percent of the lots are sold.

Under regular mortgages, there is no provision to allow a partial sale of the property. So a development loan requires considerable negotiation to work out all the details necessary for success. The lender will want some control over the direction of the development; that is, lots must be developed and sold in an orderly manner that will not undermine the value of any remaining land. A time pattern must be negotiated to allow realistic limits on how fast the lots must be sold. The clause that permits the release of a portion of the mortgaged land is also called a *par-*

tial release since the remainder of the land continues to be held as security for the loan.

Junior Mortgages

The term *junior mortgages* applies to those mortgages that carry a lower priority than the prime or first mortgage. These are *second* and even *third* mortgages.

The mortgage instrument carries no designation in its text describing its lien position. The order of priority, which determines the exact order of claims against a piece of property, is established by the time of the recording of that instrument. This becomes of extreme importance in a foreclosure proceeding. For example, if a property is considered to be worth $50,000 carries a first mortgage for $30,000 and a second mortgage for $8000, and that property is forced into a foreclosure sale that results in a recovery of $35,000 in cash after payment of legal fees—how, then, should the money be distributed? The priority of the liens exercises control. Assuming that no other liens, taxes, or otherwise have shown priority, then the first mortgage holder is in a position to recover his full $30,000 from the $35,000 proceeds, and the remaining $5000 is awarded to the second mortgage holder, leaving him $3000 short of recovering his $8000 loan. Due to the promissory note, the second mortgage holder may have a right to seek a deficiency judgment against the borrower to recover that $3000. However, it becomes evident that the security of the land has been wiped out in the foreclosure sale and resulting settlement.

Later in this text, the subjects of recording and of title protection, as related to the question of establishing the priority of mortgage liens, will be discussed in more detail.

Purchase Money Mortgages

Primarily, a purchase money mortgage is a mortgage taken by the seller of a property as a part of the consideration. The designation is also used in some states with homestead laws to distinguish it from any other form of mortgage that would not carry the same lien rights. In this mortgage form, the proceeds of a loan are used to acquire the property.

Chattel Mortgages

Although we have been discussing mortgages primarily in terms of real property as security, the term *mortgage* can also be used to describe a pledge of personal property such as furniture or a car. This personal property can be referred to as *chattel*. Chattel, then, may be defined as a movable object—any property, exclusive of land or objects permanently attached to the land. With a chattel mortgage, the pledge of personal property as security for a loan can be similar to that for real property. It is the movable quality of the collateral and the difficulty of properly identifying an object such as a table or a washing machine that make the pledge a less secure procedure than it is in regard to real property.

Nevertheless, the form is widely used in small loan companies and for installment financing. Some states, it should be noted in this connection, use a conditional sales contract procedure for installment purchases that does not legally pass title to the chattel until it is fully paid for, thus eliminating the need for a mortgage pledge.

Package Mortgages

The *package mortgage* occurs in a hybrid form and attempts to include in the mortgage indenture both real property and personal property. It is used in residential loans when considerable built-in equipment is included with the house. Such a mortgage would list various household appliances, such as an oven, a range, a dishwasher, or disposal equipment, that might be considered attached to and a part of the real property, but that can be removed rather easily. By adding these various items to the mortgage as security, the lender may better protect his complete property loan. Although the procedure is often ignored or not enforced, it is definitely a violation of the mortgage term to sell or dispose of a mortgaged range or dishwasher without the express consent of the mortgagee.

Blanket Mortgages

A mortgage is not limited to pledging a single parcel of land. Sometimes the security pledged for a loan may include several tracts of land. When more than one tract of land is pledged in the mortgage instrument, it is called a *blanket mortgage*.

24

Mortgage Procedures
and Land Titles

MORTGAGE PROCEDURES

The practices and procedures by which mortgage rights are established
and protected vary among the states, but certain elements are common
to all. In the following discussion, the common procedures and reasons
for them will be considered.

Recording

Of all the statutes written regarding ownership of land, the incentives to
record a transaction have had the greatest long-range effect on improving records of landownership. In fairly recent times and due to the lack of
controlling legislation, courts have held that a valid title to land was actually passed by such procedures as a handwritten entry in the family Bi-
ble. How can a mortgage lender determine who really owns a piece of
land? The answer lies in the recorded instruments of land transactions
filed in the county records wherein the land is located. As the laws have
made the recording of land transactions a necessary procedure and as our
methods of handling this documentation have improved, the actual
determination of proper title is becoming more and more accurate.

What is *recording?* In legal terms it is a form of notice—notice to the world—that a transaction of some kind has affected the title to a specific piece of land. Another form of legal notice is actual possession of the land, and historically, possession is the highest form of notice. The procedure for recording a transaction is to take the document to the record office of the county where the land is located and pay the fee for filing. The county officer responsible for the recording copies the instrument in its entirety for the record book and certifies on the original as to the time, date, volume, and page or pages that contain the record.

Most state laws that relate to instruments affecting land titles and the recording of them do not challenge the contractual rights of any parties to buy, sell, or encumber a piece of land. What they actually do is to declare any land transaction invalid against a third party *only in regard to the title to land if it is not recorded.* For example, A can agree to sell ten acres of land to B and actually deliver a deed for the ten acres to B. The contract may be valid and the consideration (payment for the land) accepted, but actual title to the land is not secure until the deed has been recorded. If the seller A, in this example, should suffer a heavy casualty loss and be subjected to a court judgment against him before the deed to buyer B has been recorded, the ten acres of land would be subject to the claim of A's new creditors since the title would still be in A's name on the public record.

It is important to emphasize that the failure to record an instrument affecting land title does not invalidate the instrument insofar as the parties involved in the transaction are concerned. It places the burden on whichever party is asserting a claim to the land to give notice of his or her claim in the public records, or lose the effectiveness of that claim against any other claimant. The rules apply to all instruments applicable to land titles, conveyances, claims, or debts against the land itself or against the landowner, and, of course, all mortgage instruments. Contracts for deed and leases are instruments affecting land title and can be recorded, but for various reasons of privacy or other interests often are not recorded.

State laws are usually lenient as to what instruments can be recorded, but most require that the signature to the instrument be acknowledged before a duly authorized officer of the state such as a Notary Public, or be properly witnessed. Because any instrument affecting a title to land is a legal matter that can involve many state laws, it is customary, though not always required, that such an instrument be prepared by a licensed attorney. The preparation of any instrument conveying a land title is considered the practice of law in most states and, therefore, is restricted to that state's licensed attorneys. Few, if any, lenders would permit a loan to be made based on a mortgage instrument prepared by anyone other than a qualified attorney regardless of the requirements for recording.

Mortgage Priorities

The expression *first mortgage* or *second mortgage* is so commonly used that it is not unusual for a person to expect to find such an identification spelled out in the mortgage instrument. Such is not the case. The priority by which a mortgage, or any other claim to land, is established is by the time of recording. And this is determined not only by the day of recording, but by the time of that particular day.

In handling a mortgage instrument, the lender is most concerned about the proper priority of his security claim; that is, what prior claims, if any, could jeopardize the lender's claim to the land. Most lenders do not rely on the record alone but require an insuring agent to guarantee the priority of the claim backed by an insurance policy, called a *title policy.*

The statutory priorities given workmen and material suppliers in most states may be a source of additional problems for construction loan mortgages. For example, in a mortgage to secure construction money, any work permitted on the land prior to the recording means that a workman may have a claim on the land itself in case of nonpayment. Such a claim held by a workman or contractor need not be recorded to establish its priority, but there must be some positive proof that the work was accomplished before the mortgage was recorded. One method of establishing priority for the lender is to photograph the raw land, have the date of the picture certified, and retain the print as proof that the land was untouched prior to recording the mortgage. States vary in their mortgage handling requirements; some do not recognize work commencement date as a priority time, only the date a mortgage is recorded.

Any claim to land that is of lower priority; that is, recorded or incurred at a later date, is said to be junior to the prior claim. Thus, as noted earlier, second and third mortgages are sometimes referred to as junior mortgages.

Subordination

Another method of establishing priorities for mortgage instruments is by contract. For various reasons it may be beneficial to the parties involved in a land transaction to establish a claim of lower value or lesser importance to another, a procedure called *subordination.*

An example might be a hypothetical case where a piece of land is sold to a developer who plans to erect an office building for lease to one of his customers. The seller of the land, for taxes or other reasons, prefers to take his payment in ten annual installments. But the developer needs to mortgage the land immediately with first priority for payment going to the mortgage lender for construction money to build the office building. In such a case, and assuming credit-worthiness of the developer, the land seller would agree specifically to subordinate the landownership claim to the lender's mortgage, securing the ten annual payments with a second mortgage.

Assumption

In periods of tight money and escalating interest costs, more homes are sold with assumption of existing loans plus seller-assisted secondary financing. The rights of a seller to offer his or her house with an assumption of the existing loan vary considerably and depend on the conditions agreed to in the mortgage instrument.

A legal distinction that should be noted is the difference between selling a property with an *assumption* of an existing loan and selling *subject* to an existing loan. When a buyer assumes an existing loan, he or she becomes liable for all obligations, including payment, to the lender. This is not true of a sale made subject to an existing loan. When a transaction uses the terminology "subject to" an existing loan, then the buyer acknowledges the existence of a loan but accepts no obligation for its repayment.

The right to increase interests when a loan is assumed stems from the covenant that restricts the right of a borrower to sell mortgaged property without the approval of the lender. In legal terminology, this restraint on a sale is called a *restraint on alienation*. Thus, a right to sell clause in a mortgage is sometimes referred to as the *alienation clause*. Most states prohibit any *unreasonable* restraint on alienation—a limitation that has been mostly concerned with discriminatory practices. For example, a restrictive covenant in a property deed that forbids any future sale to a female would most likely be classed as an unreasonable restraint on the owner's right to sell. The question of whether or not a lender's right to increase an interest rate with the power to otherwise deny the right to sell constitutes an unreasonable restraint is now being tested in state courts. At this writing, at least 17 states have prohibited or placed restraints on the lender's right to increase interest when a loan is assumed. In 1982, the U.S. Supreme Court ruled in favor of federal chartered savings association's right to increase interest rates as a condition for a loan assumption to be approved.

The policies applying to loan assumptions in regard to the lender's right to adjust an interest rate, or call the loan due if the property collateral is sold, are undergoing some major changes. At the time of this writing, the following situation existed.

- *FHA and VA Loans*   Assumption permitted without an increase in the interest rates allowed. Consideration is being given to allow these loans to be made callable upon sale of the property.
- *FNMA/FHLMC Uniform Instrument*   Clause 17, Transfer of Property: Assumption, grants the lender a right to adjust the interest rate as a condition for approval of a loan assumption. In the 17 states that have passed legislation, or are subject to state court decisions, that either prohibit or restrict the right of a lender to adjust an interest rate upon assumption, FNMA policy is to buy only those loans that have a 7-year call clause. That is, in those states FNMA reserves the option to limit the term of the loan to 7 years.*
- *Conventional Loans*   Conventional loans written on the lenders own mortgage form generally provide for a due-on-sale clause that gives the lender a right to either call the loan if the property is sold, or as a condition for approval of an assumption, to increase the interest rate to a market level.
- *State vs. Federal Law*   Federal chartered savings associations, commercial banks and credit unions have always insisted on the right of federal regulations and laws taking precedence over state laws to the contrary. This has been true in the past in regard to the acceptance of usury ceilings on interest rates—if state laws were more restrictive than the federal rules, federal chartered institutions were guided by the federal rules. On June 28, 1982, the United States Supreme Court handed down an important decision that clearly gives federal regulatory bodies the right to pre-empt state laws in the handling of due-on-sale clauses in mortgage loans. Thus, the Federal Home Loan Bank rule allowing federal chartered savings associations to write mortgages that contain clauses allowing the loan to be called in the event of a subsequent sale was upheld. Further, if the mortgage agreement states that the loan can be assumed providing the lender gives approval and that a condition of that approval could be an adjustment in the interest rate, then the lender can exercise this contractual right. While the U.S. Supreme Court ruling applies only to federal chartered institutions, the effect on state laws and court decisions will most likely be towards greater leniency in allowing lenders to adjust interest rates upon assumption, or call the loan if the adjusted rate is not acceptable to the buyer.

---

*FNMA dropped 7-year call clause in October, 1982.

LIMITATION STATUTES

In the codes of law established by the various states, *time limitations* have been established on the validity of most claims or debts. These limitations may vary somewhat, but usually place time limits within which a creditor can file a claim for an open account, such as one to two years. Usually there is a longer limit within which a written promissory note can be recovered, perhaps five to ten years. Time limits for secured debts may be extended for even longer periods.

There are also limiting statutes imposed for general contractors and subcontractors filing claims for unpaid work and materials on construction projects. Failure to file a claim, usually in the form of a lien recorded in the county records, within the prescribed time limits, would make that claim invalid insofar as the land itself is concerned. It does not void the debt, however.

There are also time limitations in most states affecting title to real property. These have been established in an effort to clarify claims to ownership of land. The time limitations vary with what is called the *color of title* that can be asserted to the land claimed. Two factors are essential in establishing a valid claim to land over a period of time within the statutes of limitation: (1) actual possession and use of the land, and (2) possession and use considered adverse or use without the express consent of the opposing claimant.

To exemplify a short time limitation let's assume that a purchaser bought a house from the heirs of a family who previously owned the property. All the known heirs agreed to the sale of the property and joined in signing the deed; the purchaser duly paid the full price agreed to. Then several years later someone claiming to be an heir comes forward to assert his interest in the house that was sold. Because a deed was delivered in good faith and the consideration was paid, the new claimant might be limited to three years within which his claim would be considered by the courts.

The longest time limits are usually granted in any transaction involving minor children or mentally incapacitated persons. States draw a line, most commonly at 20 years, and simply rule that possession of land for that period precludes anyone else asserting a claim against it.

The result of these limiting statutes is an effective scrubbing of the records after the prescribed number of years. Title insurance policies lapse after the maximum years within which claims can be filed, but not until the insured no longer has an insurable interest which includes the warranties under the deed.

Many property owners are careful to establish their own property lines with special markers and to assert their own usage and ownership of land by restricting access to private roadways, etc., for perhaps one day a year, so as to prevent or offset the workings of time limitation statutes.

LAND TITLES

Ownership of land is a right. It is not a deed, it is not a title insurance policy, it is not living on the land. All of these characteristics are important evidences of ownership, but the right itself must be proven in some manner in order to justify the buyer's consideration and the lender's confidence in its collateral. To accomplish this requires a research of the chain of title.

In today's complex living patterns, the free and unfettered ownership of land that once existed in earlier rural areas is difficult to find. Possession is about the only element of ownership that remains clearly distinguishable, and even that has become more difficult to determine.

The usage of land is complicated by leases on mineral rights (oil, gas, coal, and so on) and by restrictions set up by some state governments forbidding the use of water except by separate grants of water rights, as well as by federal restrictions as to what can or cannot be grown on the land. The enjoyment of the land is also subject to many restrictions in urban areas, particularly in the form of zoning laws, health and safety restrictions, and possible conflicts in neighborhood associations.

The rights to dispose of land are complicated by the practice of bequeathing life estates, say, to a widow upon the death of a husband; or by the assignment of property by will to a charitable foundation or educational institution; or by a gift of land to a community for a specific use such as a park, with the land reverting back to the estate of the former owner should his wishes be violated.

With all these complications in land ownership, it becomes necessary to find a way to establish where and in whose hands ownership and control of the land actually lie. In order for a mortgage instrument to be valid and to provide security for a loan, it is necessary that sufficient rights to the land be pledged and that the pledge be made by the person or persons holding the rights to do so. Loans are made against various portions of real property ownership, such as oil production loans on oil leases, development loans on mining claims, and crop loans on surface and water rights. It rarely happens today that much more than a portion of the ownership rights is pledged, but that portion must include the essential rights that would enable a lender to use the property as a last resort in recovering the balance of his loan.

The area under study in this book is land development and the buildings occupying the land, which would mean the ownership rights to at least the surface, the access rights thereto, and protection against infringement by any other user of rights to that land. The researching of these rights of ownership to land is the special province of land title companies, which are basically insurance companies. Title companies sell insurance policies that guarantee to the purchaser a good title to a certain piece of property. The guarantee is in the form of a promise to protect the land title against any adverse claim not otherwise excepted from the policy, or to reimburse the policyholder for loss up to the face amount (purchase price of the property) in cash, should the title fail for any reason. At the time the initial owner's policy is issued, a second policy covering the same property may be purchased that makes a similar pledge of title protection to the lender or mortgagee. The mortgagee's policy runs with the mortgage; that is, the insurance is in the amount of the balance due on the mortgage note, automatically covers any subsequent holder of the note, and is in effect until the note is paid off. The owner's policy has different terms—it insures the owner for the face amount of the policy for a specified number of years, usually the statutory limit of the owner's possible responsibility for the title. The owner's policy continues to protect the owner even after the property has been sold because he or she still carries a responsibility to defend the title that may be passed on under a general warranty deed. The fact that a title policy may exist on a piece of property provides no protection at all for a new purchaser. The new purchaser can only be protected with a new policy issued in his or her name.

A second method of obtaining title information and of determining the validity of a mortgage pledge is to employ an attorney to research the title. In this procedure, the attorney will order an abstract from an abstract or title company. The abstract is a certified collection of all instruments that have been recorded and, therefore, have affected the chain of title since the inception of that title. The inception of the title could be a land grant by a foreign monarch who once claimed the land, and more commonly by a state granting title to a purchaser, or it could be by quit claim deed from the federal government. From its original grant, the land may have been broken into many segments and passed through many hands, and the abstracts can be quite voluminous. The result of the research is an attorney's opinion on the title stating any adverse claims to the land that are exceptions to the title. The opinion will then identify those title problems that must be corrected, or "cured" before a mortgage can be made securely.

In certain areas of the country another method is employed to handle property titles, a method flowing from the Torrens Act procedure. This is a process whereby a state has adopted a program for recording title, mostly for urban property lots, by registering property title in the public record established for that purpose. The procedure is very similar to that used in registering the ownership of a car. Any sale of the property must be registered, and a new certificate of title is then issued by the state. The plan has some inherent advantages in minimizing legal expenses and title costs in the sale of property, but because of the complex nature of land ownership, this plan has not become too widespread in practice.

Accepting the fact that land titles in today's urban society are seldom completely clear, the mortgage lender has learned to live with certain kinds of exceptions. For instance, title insurance companies have standard clauses of exceptions that they customarily make in any insurance policy they issue. One of these exceptions has to do with the rights of anyone then in possession of the property. The title company does not physically inspect the property, leaving that to the buyer. Since the seller is usually in possession of the property when it is sold, his rights are clearly determined when he signs a warranty deed granting title to the buyer. If a tenant is in possession, it is necessary to establish his rights before a sale is consummated.

Another standard exception made by the title company is in the zoning requirements or sometimes in regard to deed restrictions. The title company is not insuring any specific usage of the property; it is only making certain that the ownership rights of possession and disposition are clearly assignable.

The title insuring policy will usually list any easements crossing the property, which are generally utility easements and street rights-of-way. The easements are exceptions to the insurance policy and are simply claims to the land, which are accepted as normal and necessary.

Often the title company will list certain requirements in the initial title opinion that involve a question of encroachments on the property lines, or perhaps a dispute among heirs, or a problem arising from a divorce settlement that is undecided. The requirements must be resolved to the satisfaction of the title company, or the insurance policy can be refused, or it can be issued with the unsatisfied requirement listed as an exception to the coverage.

What these questions involving title problems lead to is not always a completely clear title, but what is called a *merchantable* or *marketable* title. There can be exceptions or unsatisfied requirements, which, at the discretion of the mortgage lender, may be so unimportant or insignificant to the total property value that they can be ignored. The ultimate question is whether or not a knowledgeable buyer would be willing to accept the minor title defects in a subsequent sale should foreclosure become necessary.

In some states, such as Ohio, title companies offer a choice of assurances regarding the land title. A purchaser may require proof of title in the form of a *title guarantee* which is essentially a certification of the information on the subject property as recorded in the county office. The recorded description of the property is accepted and a survey may not be required. If the purchaser requires that the title company also insure the title for a monetary value, an additional charge is made for such coverage.

25

Contracts Used in
Real Estate Transactions

There are a number of legal instruments used in handling the buying and selling of real estate. The instruments and procedures are not uniform, differing with local customs and in compliance with various state laws. While terminology and nomenclature may vary over the country, the general purpose of the basic instruments is rather similar.

EARNEST MONEY CONTRACT

An earnest money contract is the initial sales contract—a formal agreement by the seller to sell and the buyer to buy. In other types of business transactions, this preliminary step is not necessary; that is, once an agreement is reached between a buyer and seller, the only contract needed is a conveyance instrument. In real estate, however, the buyer needs time to ascertain whether or not proper title can be delivered, and the seller needs time to prove that it can. Hence, an earnest money contract formally commits the buyer to purchase and the seller to sell provided proper title can be delivered.

To show good faith, it is customary for the buyer to make an earnest money deposit. How much? This is negotiable and may be just a token amount or up to 10 percent of the offering price. The deposit may be held by the real estate broker involved or, perhaps, by an escrow agent. A common practice is to place the deposit, which is considered a part of the purchase consideration, with the company selected to close the transaction. Technically, the earnest money deposit belongs to the buyer who posted it, pending approval of the title. If the title fails after the earnest money has been posted, it can then be returned to the buyer. However, if the buyer for some reason changes his mind and decides to withdraw from the contract, the earnest money is normally forfeited to the benefit of the seller and the real estate broker as may have been agreed to in the contract. There is an alternate remedy in the event of the buyer reneging on the contract, and that is a suit for specific performance. Such a suit is to ask that the court order the buyer to abide by the terms of the contract and deliver the consideration as agreed. Specific performance can be asked against a seller who may have a change of mind, but normally, a failure of the title (meaning adverse claims that make delivery of a marketable title impractical within the time limits involved) automatically releases the seller without being subject to a damage claim.

An earnest money agreement is a binding contract between the signatory parties but is not normally a recorded instrument. Thus, in some states an earnest money contract does not affect title to property, while in others it may convey an *equitable title.* Holding an equitable title means the right to accede to title if certain conditions are met. *Legal title* is that of actual ownership.

In parts of the country an earnest money contract can be prepared on preprinted forms by a real estate broker. In other areas, the preparation of an earnest money contract is considered the practice of law and must be prepared by an attorney.

DEEDS

A deed is a conveyance instrument. Its purpose is to transfer an ownership interest from one party to another.

While the first requirement of a deed may seem obvious, it was not always so. A deed must be in writing. This requirement goes back to 1677 when England passed a law known as the Statute of Frauds stating that real estate transfers must be in writing in order to be enforceable. Prior to that time, when people were much less mobile and the few property transactions that occurred might pass land from generation to generation, transfers could be made by a public declaration in the presence of witnesses. The procedure was subject to fraud in that witnesses were often bribed or pressured to change their statements. The requirement that property transfers be made in writing was subsequently adopted in the United States.

To properly convey title to property, a deed must contain certain words and phrases. First, the party delivering title, known as the *grantor*, must be identified and be legally qualified (of legal age, sound mind) to deliver the title. Also, the *grantee*, the party receiving title, needs to be identified. There should be a consideration specified, but not necessarily an exact amount.* A phrase such as, "For ten dollars ($10) and other good and valuable consideration," is often used. Consideration need not be money: a transfer for "love and affection" is quite proper (unless the gift is intended to defraud creditors). The deed must contain words of conveyance which *grant* such quantity and quality of the estate as is being transferred. The land being conveyed has to be identified with a clear and acceptable legal description. The grantor must sign (execute) the document and have it *acknowledged*. Most states require that a document be acknowledged before it can be recorded, while a few states permit proper witnessing as an alternative. Some states require both. And finally, the deed must be delivered and accepted by the grantee before title actually passes (although the grantee does not normally sign the deed).

A deed is very important as it conveys title to real estate. Because of this it should be prepared by a qualified attorney. Preprinted deeds are available in stores and may be used if correctly completed; but this also is a question for an attorney. The person receiving a deed should not depend entirely on the grantor's knowledge of the legal requirements. It is quite possible for a grantor to prepare a deed on a form that is ordinarily used in another state and not correct for the state wherein the land being transferred is located.

The three more commonly used forms of deeds are (1) the warranty deed which carries a guarantee of title, (2) the special warranty deed with a limited guarantee of title, and (3) the quit claim deed, which can be described as a release or a transfer of the grantor's interest if he or she has any interest.

Warranty Deed

A warranty deed, or general warranty deed, contains all the necessary covenants and warranties and is considered to be the best deed a grantee can receive. In this form of deed the grantor agrees to warrant and defend forever the title he is granting. States differ a bit in how the guarantee should be worded, but the intent is the same: the grantor agrees to de-

---

*Nebraska and New Jersey require the actual amount of the consideration to be shown on the deed.

fend the title against adverse claims "forever." Forever is limited by state laws (called limitation statutes) as to the length of time after which an adverse claim to land can be tried in the courts. It is to protect the grantor's liability under the warranty that title insurance becomes necessary.

Special Warranty Deed

The special warranty deed contains only a limited guarantee, or warranty, that the property has not been encumbered during the period of time it has been held by the grantor with the exceptions as stated in the deed. The purpose of the instrument is to convey property from an administrator, or trustee, who has held title for the benefit of another party and does not have responsibility for what might have passed before.

Quitclaim Deeds

A quitclaim deed identifies no rights to property and makes no warranties. What it does do is convey any rights the grantor may possess; if the grantor has no rights, nothing is conveyed. If a fee simple title is held by the grantor, the fee simple title is conveyed. *Quitclaim* means to renounce all rights. And this means to the date of the quitclaim. Should the grantor acquire some rights at a later date, there is no obligation to convey these to the grantee. A principal use of the quitclaim deed is to clear a title which may appear to have been encumbered in some manner due to an inheritance, the actions of dower and curtesy rights, or perhaps a community property right. Another use of the quitclaim deed is an assignment by the federal government in a sale of government land—there being no prior owner, the government simply quitclaims to the grantee. Another form of a government assignment of its interest in land is called a *patent*, which is issued to the first owner of property.

Other Types of Deeds

Sheriff's Deed and Referee's Deed in Foreclosure.   A deed issued to a new buyer when property is sold as a result of a foreclosure action. The only assurance the sheriff gives is that he has not encumbered the title; otherwise the deed conveys only the title held by the foreclosed party.

Guardian's Deed.   Used to convey the interest of a minor in real property and should state the legal authority (usually a court order) that permits the conveyance.

Gift Deed.   The consideration clause replaces the money amount with a phrase such as, "for natural love and affection." The deed may be a general warranty, special warranty, or a quitclaim depending on the extent of the warranty that the grantor desires to commit.

CONTRACT FOR DEED

A contract for deed is a promise that a deed to property will be delivered at a later date. It is a form of agreement that passes under a number of names: installment contract, land contract, conditional sales contract, contract of sale, agreement to convey, and one that is even less descriptive—real estate contract.

In essence a contract for deed is another method of selling real estate. It is exactly what its name implies, a contract for a deed and no more. It is used to sell real property on an installment payment basis without delivering title to the property until payment has been made. Properly drawn, a contract for deed is enforceable against either signatory party, as is any contract under the state's codes providing for contracts. However, it is not a deed to real property and grants to the buyer only the rights of possession and enjoyment; and these rights exist only as long as the grantor holds control of the land.

Since contracts for deed grant at best a limited interest in the property to the purchaser, a default on payment can result in the loss of all prior payments plus the right to the use and occupancy of the land. This remedy is considered too harsh in some states. Florida and Maryland, for example, require a contract for deed to be foreclosed like a regular mortgage. Some states allow the buyer in a forfeiture action to recover the amount paid to the seller less a reasonable allowance for rent. States such as Ohio, that allow the buyer to record a contract for deed, give recognition to an interest in the land other than that of the seller. Recording would give the buyer an *equitable title* to the property. Equitable title is defined as a right one holds to eventually accede to title to the property. Legal title is present ownership. Since recording a contract for deed would place on the public record a cloud to the title insofar as the seller is concerned, some contracts are written to prohibit the instrument from being recorded. This practice is not permitted in all states.

If fully understood by both parties, the contract for deed can be helpful in transferring property usage when a buyer has temporary credit problems or the seller does not yet hold a fully marketable title. However, this form of contract has gained a poor reputation through abuses, failure to fully disclose the facts, and outright frauds. The real pitfall lies in the possible inability of the seller to deliver a valid title after full payment has been made. During the installment paying period, anything that might happen to the seller, such as a damage claim resulting in a heavy adverse judgment, a divorce causing property settlements, dissolution of a corporate seller through bankruptcy, or any lien filed against the property under contract, can defeat the intent of the contract and can cause the seller to be unable to deliver a good title. If the seller cannot produce a good title to the property at completion of payment, the buyer may have a claim for damages against the seller, but has no direct claim to the property involved.

Contract for deed sales are most commonly used in the sale of resort-type lots and also in smaller rent houses where a tenant becomes a buyer if he completes the payments. In the latter case, the property owner may wish to give a tenant the right to buy the house, but because of some prior credit problems or some temporary family troubles of the tenant, the owner does not want his land encumbered by the tenant if a default occurs.

In regard to the resort-type lot sales, there have been flagrant abuses in the past. In 1969, the Department of Housing and Urban Development established the Office of Interstate Land Sales Registration as a policing agency for developers of property containing more than 50 lots in any one development and less than five acres per lot. The thrust of the legislation is not to establish sales patterns or minimum lot requirements, but to make sure the developer fully discloses the development plans and the legal status of the land title itself. And the buyer must acknowledge the receipt of all the information required, which also has the effect of protecting the developer against unwarranted claims from the buyer.

SEVEN

Analysis
Techniques

26

Preliminary Screening of Property

The market for investment properties generally offers some alternatives. There may not be as many properties available as the buyer would like, but for those properties that are being offered for sale, it is necessary to have a simple method of weeding out the less desirable. It takes time and money to evaluate investment property. Spend that time where it can produce the most likely results.

EVALUATING THE MARKET

There are several methods by which a prospective investor can sort out properties. These vary some for different kinds of properties but are directed toward evaluating the local market conditions. It is important that the investor have good information on the local market area. This is why some time should be spent talking with real estate practitioners and with other people knowledgeable of the real estate market long before that first investment is made. What are going market values? What kinds of returns are investors presently realizing? What future trends in the market can be perceived? The following suggestions are offered as guides to developing good information on the local investment market—the kind of data that will allow the investor to quickly screen available properties and thereby save his or her time for the better deals.

Multipliers

One of the least complicated methods of evaluation is to base the value on the gross income (meaning total sales receipts). In this method the "not to exceed" price to pay is a multiple of the gross annual income (the real annual income, not a projected one). For example, an apartment project can be valued at 5 to 8 times its gross annual income. Thus, a 100-unit apartment averaging $360,000 per year in gross income (gross rental receipts) might be valued at anywhere from $1,800,000 (5 × $360,000) to $2,880,000 (8 × $360,000). The figure is not precise but gives a range and provides a method of deciding if the offering price is worth pursuing. A motel property may use a multiplier of 3 to 5 times its gross annual rental income—not restaurant or bar receipts, just room rentals. This gives a preliminary value only, but one that can be helpful in avoiding costly investigation. One advantage of this method is that most property owners are willing to disclose their gross receipts to a prospective buyer early in the discussions. Details of expenses and the resulting cash flows, however, are harder to come by and can be analyzed later, if such is justified.

Per Unit Cost

A simple limit on any purchase (of multiple unit buildings) is the total price divided by the number of units to arrive at a per unit cost. An apartment project in any given market area will have an upper limit as it relates to the unit, say, not to exceed $35,000 per unit. Thus, a 100-unit apartment could not exceed a price of $3,500,000 and be a practical investment in that market area.

Per Square Foot Cost

Since many investment properties do not have "units" for measurement, an upper limit on the cost per square foot can be used as a guideline. Thus, the purchase price of a warehouse or an office building without fixed units for rent can be limited to a "not-to-exceed" cost per square foot. (So can apartments and motels, but per unit costs are more common for these.) The value placed on an office building, for example, might be limited to $30 per square foot of rental space; or the measure could be on gross square footage (rentable and utility space). Of course, there is a difference. While the easier measurement is the gross square footage, the more important economic measurement is how much of that space can be gainfully rented? So it is common to find a dollar limit of value placed on the rentable area; this figure relates more easily to the going market rents per square foot for that location. Again, these limits are only estimates that provide a logical cutoff for a preliminary screening.

COMPARATIVE DATA

In order to arrive at the type of upper cost limits just described, it is necessary to have some basis in fact. This can be learned from people in the business and by keeping a record on which this data can be accumulated for future averaging and comparison. Two kinds of information are needed: (1) selling prices and (2) operating income and expense figures. Following is a suggested form that allows both pieces of information to be accumulated on a single page. Keep one for every property you investigate. Over a period of time, you will have the basis for future decisions.

COMPARATIVE DATA SHEET

Name _____

Location _____

Type of property _____

Price _____ No. of units _____ Square footage _____

Price per unit _____ Price per sq. ft. _____

Ratio of price to gross income _____

Operating Data

			Percent
Gross operating income			100
Less: Operating expenses			
Taxes			
Insurance			
Less: Debt service			
Cash flow before taxes			

Comments:

This form can be prepared on a 5 × 8 card or on a sheet of paper for filing. As the information accumulates, it becomes much more valuable in providing a basis for comparison of various investments as they come on the market. The key figures in the operating data are the percentages.

They should remain reasonably consistent in spite of inflation. There is one exception, however: utility costs are rising at a more rapid rate than most of the others. But the average cost of operations still should not exceed a level that will allow some profitability; otherwise, Why invest?

Cash on Cash

A simplified method that can be used for a preliminary evaluation is the cash return basis—if the correct figures can be obtained without substantial verifications. This method compares the cash out with the cash in. How much cash does it take to acquire compared with how much actual cash is available in income from the property? The method reduces the facts to the amount of the equity investment and the return on that equity in actual cash at the end of the year—the cash remaining each year after payment of all expenses and debt service. As a preliminary method, the procedure avoids going into the details of what the expenses amount to, whether the debt is excessive, or the condition and location of the property. It aims at the heart of any investment: How much do I receive for each dollar that I invest? For real estate, it is not overly accurate as it does not take into account many of the problems that may underly an investment or the very real tax advantages that can accrue to real estate investments. But it does give a basis of comparison and as such can be useful.

EXAMPLE

Cash on Cash

A property is purchased for $480,000 with cash for the equity amounting to $50,000 and the balance financed. The operating statement appears as follows:

Gross operating income	$85,000
Less: Operating expenses, including taxes and insurance	32,500
Net Operating Income (NOI)	$52,500
Less: Principal & interest pymt.	47,100
Cash Flow	$ 5,400

Return on cash investment:
$$\frac{5,400}{50,000} = .1080 \text{ or } 10.80\%$$

Ultimately, the investor must study the much broader range of facts and circumstances which affect an investment before taking the step of acquisition.

THE KINDS OF INCOME

The term *income* needs definition because it means different things to different people. A dictionary defines income in broad terms as the gain from capital or labor, or both. When considering a real estate investment a more specific definition is needed. It is the purpose of this section to explain the major forms of income as they relate to real estate. These are (1) taxable income, (2) spendable income, and (3) equity income. The source for determining the different types of income starts with *Net Operating Income.*

Net Operating Income

A more detailed discussion of financial statements is undertaken in the next chapter. However, a simplified Operating Statement follows which shows the essential elements used to calculate Net Operating Income, or NOI.

Gross scheduled rental income	195,000
Less: Vacancy and credit loss	12,500
Gross Operating Income	182,500
Less: Operating expenses	82,500
Net Operating Income	100,000

There is a problem with the nomenclature used to identify the various accounts on a financial statement; so a further word of explanation is necessary. Net Operating Income is the result after deducting all operating expenses from Gross Operating Income. Operating expenses for this purpose include property taxes and insurance; it does *not* include mortgage loan interest. NOI is really the most important figure for determining the profitability of an operating property. It is not concerned with the debt service, which is a matter of financing. It is important that the cost of financing not be confused with the operating figures. In the past, an excellent property has frequently been overburdened with too much debt, and even the finest management could not operate the property with a positive cash flow. It is the NOI that shows how the property fares as a profitable operation. Separate the *operating return* from the *investment return* for this purpose; it is much easier to make an accurate comparison. The separation is important because the calculations for taxable, spendable, and equity income *begin* with the NOI and *not* with the cash flow after payment of debt service.

Taxable Income

Real property investment carries certain tax advantages. Although tax laws are subject to change, they still allow the deduction of interest paid on mortgage debt during the tax year and a deduction for cost recovery of the total building investment (not just the equity interest in it). It is the cost recovery allowance that offers a strong incentive to invest in improved property (land itself is not deductible) as it is a noncash deduction; that is, no cash outlay is needed to claim the deduction. Further, in an inflation-prone economy, real property has a good record of increasing in value rather than depreciating. Thus, the deduction for investment cost saves taxes while the value of the property may actually increase. Care should be taken to separate building cost recovery from that taken for personal property (carpeting, drapes, appliances, and so forth). The personal property is most often consumed in the rental of the property and represents a cost rather than an increase in asset value. (Cost recovery calculations are explained in Chapter 16.)

The calculation of taxable income is illustrated in the following example: it begins with the NOI.

Net operating income	$100,000
Less: Interest paid on loans	45,818
Less: Cost recovery deduction	41,344
Taxable Income	$ 12,838

The important deduction for the investor to weigh is the amount of the cost recovery. The deduction has required no additional outlay of cash, and the building that is being depreciated is most likely increasing in value. Further, in the early years of ownership, the permissible cost recovery is accelerated and often exceeds the income, permitting a tax deduction against other income. *Caution:* The offsetting of tax losses from one property against the profit of another or any other income is called an *accounting transfer.* The IRS has long tried to limit the application of tax losses to not more than the income from the property (that is, no transfer of losses from one property to another). Rules still permit taxpayers to transfer losses against other income. But even without this right to an accounting transfer of taxable losses, the value of the cost recovery deduction is such that persons in higher tax brackets may recover their initial investments from tax savings in a few years. For example, if a $100,000 investment property can be acquired for the outlay of $10,000 cash, and the accelerated cost recovery achieves a deduction of $8,000 per year, a person in a 40 percent tax bracket can recover almost the full $10,000 cash investment from tax savings over a three-year period.

Indeed, real property investment offers a solid advantage for anyone paying income taxes.

Spendable Income

What sort of cash can an investor recover from investment property? What cash can be spent for other things? The advantage in this respect, perhaps, is not so great as with other investment forms. Truly, real estate is not at its best as a short-term investment, although there are spectacular exceptions. But let's look at what can be considered *spendable income*. Following is an example of the possible disbursement of the Net Operating Income:

Net operating income	$100,000
Less: Principal & interest paid	56,420
Less: Income taxes due	5,670
Less: Capital improvements	14,820
Net Spendable Income	$ 23,090

Note carefully that a property burdened with too heavy a debt load can pay out more than the NOI (a negative cash flow). In such cases, the owner must be prepared to add additional capital to cover the obligations. This is acceptable if the ultimate goal is to achieve a profit on the sale at an appreciated price.

Equity Income

The basic concern of most investors is not the problem of taxes, nor the amount of spendable cash. The basic concern is how much gain can be realized on the equity investment. It is in this category that the leverage advantages—the ability to control a larger property with little cash down—of real estate show substantial benefits.

The equity interest realizes an income protected to some degree from income taxes by the noncash deduction for cost recovery. The debt service payment continues to reduce the mortgage debt and thus increases the equity interest. And perhaps most important of all in today's market, the appreciation in the property value accrues exclusively to the equity interest. In the following example of Net Equity Income and Net Equity Gain, only the interest, not the principal portion of the debt service, is deducted from NOI. Also, the calculation for property appreciation is based on an assumed adjusted basis of property value for tax pur-

poses of $900,000—a fairly reasonable value for a property that can pro-
duce $100,000 in NOI per year.

EXAMPLE

First, take a hypothetical example of a property to determine the equity
interest:

Property value	$900,000
Less: Mortgage loan due	575,000
Value of Equity	$325,000

Say this property produces an annual NOI and deductions as follows:

Net operating income	$100,000
Less: Interest on loans	45,818
Less: Income taxes due	5,670
Net Equity Income	$ 48,512

Now, let's calculate how much the equity interest can increase in the one
year of operation:

Gain	Dollar Amount	As a % of 325,000
Net equity income	48,512	14.9
Appreciation (at 7% per year)	63,000	19.4
Total Equity Increase	111,512	
Equity Growth Rate Per Year		34.3%

It is the rather spectacular increase that can be achieved in the value
of the equity from appreciation alone that has attracted many investors
to buy property. Even though the investor loses money each year he or
she expects to make it all back when the property is sold. The idea works
fine if only the number of dollars is considered. But think about the purchasing power of those dollars. If the only gain is derived from inflation of
property values, it is quite possible that your gain in purchasing power
will be little to nothing. As long as property values increase at a greater
rate than the average rate of inflation, the gain is real: otherwise, the gain
can be an illusion. Nevertheless, there is a big advantage: the inflation-
induced appreciation in value will keep your investment afloat as values
increase, which is certainly not true of savings accounts, money market
funds, or Treasury bills.

27

Financial Statements

The average financial statement found in the real estate business (that is, for the presentation of income properties) is so imprecise that the investor should devise an individualized procedure for recording necessary facts and figures. The investor should utilize an existing form or develop one that best suits his or her own purposes. Then take the figures that may be presented for a property under consideration and restate them on the standard form selected. By using this method the investor could indicate which figures had been verified and what information still had to be obtained.

The problem stems from the owner-operator's freedom to identify income and expense accounts under any nomenclature and to allocate income and expense as may best suit him or her. This complaint is not an invitation to add government regulations—please no!—but an effort to recognize the difficulties that a newcomer to the field may have in understanding the real income and expenses.

There is another reason for using a standard form to restate figures offered by a property owner: it is much easier to compare alternative property investments if the analysis follows the same pattern. This, of course, is also true for the experienced investor.

First, let's look at examples of the basic forms. There are only three to be considered:

BALANCE SHEET

The balance sheet details the assets and liabilities of a person or business. The difference between what is owned (the assets) and what is owed (the liabilities) is the net worth or equity that belongs to the owner. The information given can be in great detail or in simplified groupings of assets. For example, the asset "cash" can be broken down into the amounts in each of several bank accounts plus the cash on hand in the office, or it can be listed as one total amount. An asset like "property" can list individual properties owned, or the value of the properties can be calculated and lumped together as a total. A simplified balance sheet is shown on the next page which follows a general accounting format.

Items listed on a balance sheet can usually be verified through inquiries but are subject to some basic questions. A discussion of the major accounts follows:

Assets

- Cash—seldom misstated and fairly easy to verify.
- Rents or accounts receivable—can be verified through auditing procedures.
- Inventory—supplies on hand can be physically counted.
- Land—usually valued separately as it is a nondepreciable asset. Value may be acquisition cost or market value. No standards apply.
- Buildings—value may be at cost or market (or anything in between). No standards are required.

Liabilities

- Accounts payable—can be verified by audit procedures.
- Mortgage debt—easy to verify.
- Deposits and other escrows—income property operators often require tenants to make certain security deposits that are held during their tenancy. The cash involved is intended for return to the tenant upon termination of occupancy (unless needed to cover a repair obligation or other damage) and should be listed as a liability, not an asset.

Where there are no standards or solid means of verification, good accounting procedure requires that the method of valuation for an asset be disclosed by footnote or other explanatory means. However, the explanation is often ignored.

Assets		
Current assets		
Cash	$ 5,500	
Rents receivable	$ 3,100	
Fixed assets		
Land		$ 78,000
Buildings	$385,000	
Less: Depreciation	$ 91,000	
Buildings (net)		$294,000
Total Assets		$380,600

Liabilities		
Current liabilities		
Accounts payable		$ 2,800
Long-term debt		
First mortgage	$300,000	
Less: Principal paid	$ 41,000	
Balance due		$259,000
Total liabilities		$261,800
Net Worth		
Partnership equity		$118,800
Liabilities plus Net Worth		$380,600

PROFIT AND LOSS STATEMENT

A profit and loss statement is a listing of income, less expenses, resulting in either a gain or a loss for the period being reported. In its most common form, it is an end-of-the-year statement that includes the applicable cost recovery deductions and makes an allowance for the necessary income tax liability. Following is a typical example:

Income from operations	$148,878
Expenses incurred	62,569
Net Operating Income	$ 86,309
Interest expense	$ 45,324
Cost recovery	36,531
Net Income	$ 4,454
Provision for income taxes	2,048
Net Profit	$ 2,406

A profit and loss (P & L) statement should be an actual presentation of the financial transactions that have occurred. However, the figures could be presented in the form of a projection of future anticipated activity. This is called a *pro forma* statement. A P & L statement is easily confused with the third form of statement we are considering, the operating statement. They are quite similar in general appearance but differ essentially in the income tax information that is included. Income taxes are a matter of individual calculation and are varied to better suit an owner's special tax status. The P & L statement reflects cost recovery and depreciation by whatever method the owner has selected and shows the income tax due on any profit earned. These items are not found on an operating statement. Of course, there is no law or regulation that prevents a property owner from offering a profit and loss statement using cost recovery schedules that are most favorable to the operation of the property, rather than the basis used by the taxpayer for tax returns. It is up to the investor to apply his or her own analysis in such cases.

OPERATING STATEMENT

The most commonly found piece of financial information offered to a prospective buyer of income property is an operating statement. And it is probably the most abused of the three statements under consideration. The reasons stem from the wide variety of opinions as to what and how information should be disclosed. Operating statements follow no standards as to (1) nomenclature, (2) allocation of expenses, (3) the disclosure of cost recovery and replacement expenses, (4) time period covered, or (5) even what income and expense figures are necessary. There are state laws against fraud and misrepresentation, but interpretations usually differ and care is needed to make sure figures offered are basically correct.

The general format of an operating statement as it is commonly used in the real estate business follows:

Scheduled gross income		$100,000
Less: Vacancy and credit losses		7,000
Gross operating income		$ 93,000
Less: Operating expenses		
Taxes	$ 6,500	
Insurance	3,100	
Utilities	6,900	
Advertising, licenses	1,100	
Management	5,000	
Payroll, including taxes	14,000	
Supplies	1,200	
Services	1,100	
Maintenance	1,900	
Other	500	
Total expenses		$ 41,300
Net Operating Income		$ 51,700

HOW TO USE FINANCIAL STATEMENT

For the prospective investor, a base of information is needed with which to compare alternative investment opportunities. Within the area of property investment that is of most interest, cull from every possible source all the financial information that you can obtain. Ask property owners, real estate brokers, appraisers, lenders, trade associations— anyone who might have information available and might let you examine typical statements on the type property in which you are interested. One of the easiest, and perhaps least accurate, sources of information would be properties currently being offered for sale.

As information is collected, utilize a standard analysis form similar to the one illustrated on page 271. Transfer the figures to the proper accounts on the standardized forms and, most important, convert the totals to a percentage of the gross operating income (the real income from the property). Over a period of time and as the base of information grows, you will find that the expense and income items begin to form a pattern. For example, utility costs in your particular neighborhood routinely amount to 6.35 percent of the gross operating income (or whatever percentage is derived).

Most management firms develop these cost sheets for both income and expense items as a percentage figure and use them to make comparisons for new properties that they are expecting to manage. The percentage gives a good standard mark to show what accounts are running excessively high, which may be showing average figures, or which are too low.

The statement shown on page 271 is the form recommended by the Realtors National Marketing Institute and uses their nomenclature. It is a good format for the investor who is looking for a standard to use. Note that the form distinguishes between "Gross Scheduled Income" and "Gross Operating Income." The former is what the property might expect to receive if all units are occupied at full rents; the latter is what is actually received. The accounts identified cover all expected income and costs with the possible exception of a "replacement" cost which may be included with "Repairs and Maintenance." However, replacement is distinct. It is the cost of replacing items such as refrigerators, ovens, drapes, and carpeting in properties where these are consumed by tenants. Such items have useful lives in excess of one year and, therefore, must be capitalized and depreciated. But so often cost recovery of them is not included as a separate cost. Rather it is lumped with the building recovery, which in itself is not a real cost in today's inflation-accented economy. The cost of replacement of appliances and furnishings is a real one, and most often the replacement is at a higher cost.

NOMENCLATURE AND ALLOCATION

One of the confusing aspects of all financial statements is the lack of uniform identification for the various accounts—both income and expense accounts. For example, the account referred to on the operating statement as "Gross Scheduled Rental Income" may be variously identified as "Gross Potential Income," "Gross Rent Roll," "Gross Income," or even just "Income." It is important that the potential investor know precisely what is meant by each accounting item and then transfer the figures to a statement of his own choosing. Do not hesitate to ask what is included under an account heading. Originality in naming accounts can be used to conceal important information.

Another accounting problem arises from the different ways that information is allocated. For example, Exactly what expenses are included in "Property Management"? Does this include typing and filing services or the printing of forms? Maybe forms are included in "Supplies"? How is the payroll allocated if repairs and maintenance work are handled in part by employees? The same applies to other services needed, such as lawn maintenance and janitorial work. The differences in allocation of costs is not critical for determining overall profitability, but it does become im-

		%	2	3
1	GROSS SCHEDULED RENTAL INCOME			
2	Plus: Other Income			
3	TOTAL GROSS INCOME			
4	Less: Vacancy and Credit Losses			
5	GROSS OPERATING INCOME			
6	Less: Operating Expenses			
7	Accounting and Legal			
8	Advertising, Licenses and Permits			
9	Property Insurance			
10	Property Management			
11	Payroll - Resident Management			
12	Other			
13	Taxes-Workmen's Compensation			
14	Personal Property Taxes			
15	Real Estate Taxes			
16	Repairs and Maintenance			
17	Services - Elevator			
18	Janitorial			
19	Lawn			
20	Pool			
21	Rubbish			
22	Other			
23	Supplies			
24	Utilities - Electricity			
25	Gas and Oil			
26	Sewer and Water			
27	Telephone			
28	Other			
29	Miscellaneous			
30				
31	TOTAL OPERATING EXPENSES			
32	NET OPERATING INCOME			

A Standard Form for an Operating Statement

portant in determining which costs might be excessive and where savings can best be accomplished. The questions are more related to property management than to the investor's initial analysis. However, the astute investor may detect a good opportunity in a losing operation if he or she is able to locate the weak spots. One or two areas of excessive costs can destroy profitability in a competitive market. If the owner fails to notice an area of weakness while the investor does, it is most likely that a better bargain can be made.

PREPARATION OF STATEMENTS

Because there are no required standard ways to prepare a financial statement, the integrity and capability of the person preparing the information is of great importance. Few persons preparing statements are willing to misrepresent or engage in fraudulent activity to induce a sale. That is not the main problem; sales can always be arranged subject to a confirmation of the reported figures. The big problem is the free-wheeling nature of some accounting methods and the lack of knowledge on the part of many persons who attempt to prepare financial statements. If the statements *appear* neat, complete, and the figures total correctly, it is easy to accept them. But it is best that you seek out the source of the information and assess his or her qualifications before proceeding further. Following are comments on those persons most likely to offer financial statements on real property investments.

Certified Public Accountants (CPA)

A CPA is the top professional in the field of accounting and is able to present the most acceptable form of financial statement. As indicated in a previous chapter, a CPA must meet minimum educational requirements and pass an exhaustive examination in order to attain state-granted certification as a Certified Public Accountant. A CPA is least likely to be subjected to any unusual pressures in determining how the facts are to be presented as he or she can be deprived of his certification (depending on the state laws) if improprieties can be proven. Only a CPA is authorized to prepare an *audited* statement.

Audited Statement. This is the most demanding form of presentation of financial information. The CPA must verify assets and liabilities as well as review and offer an opinion of the cash controls and accounting methods used by the client. The figures must be presented in a form acceptable to the CPA, and he or she must sign a statement certifying the audit.

Prepared Without Audit.   A CPA or lesser designated accountant may prepare a financial statement without going through a complete audit procedure. It need be no less accurate than an audited statement but because it does not carry a certification of audit it is less acceptable to many people, particularly lenders.

Owner-Prepared Statements

Whether or not suspicion is justified, a financial statement prepared by a property owner is *always* suspect. Owners seldom possess sufficient accounting expertise to prepare an adequate statement. Besides, it is simply human nature for a prospective buyer to be skeptical of the financial information offered by the seller. However, an owner's statement is often used as a starting point for discussion with the expectation that verification can be undertaken *after* a preliminary evaluation establishes genuine interest.

Sales Broker–Prepared Statements

A financial statement prepared by a broker trying to sell income property lacks credibility, unless the broker has a solid record of analysis expertise. Commercial brokers often use operating statements that they have prepared from the seller's records as a means of developing buyer interest. This form of statement usually has a broad disclaimer statement attached which is a signal to the investor that more accurate information will be needed if there is a real interest in buying.

METHODS OF ACCOUNTING

Two methods of accounting are commonly used in both business and personal affairs. These are the cash method and the accrual method.

Cash method

This is the simplest method and the one most commonly used by individuals keeping their own records. The cash method simply reports all cash at the time it is received and expenses or other disbursements at the time of payment. During the business year, the cash method may not provide all the information needed to properly evaluate operations; that is, income may be accruing that is yet to be collected, and bills may be piling up that have not been paid.

Accrual method

This is the most widely used method for business accounting. It records income when a billing has been made or a rental becomes due. The anticipated receipts are accumulated as an *account receivable* item and deducted from the receivables when paid. Obligations are recorded when incurred and posted to an *accounts payable* ledger to be deducted as the bills are paid off. This method gives a more accurate indication of the business progress at any given time.

CAVEATS FOR THE INVESTOR

There are some obvious "red flags," or warning signals, that an investor can pick up from a cursory glance through financial statements submitted on a potential acquisition. Many of these are listed next.

Rounded figures

Under the excuse of simplification, some operating statements are offered with figures rounded to the nearest $100 or, in some cases, to the nearest $1,000. This is also an easy way to cover up figures that are only estimates and not factual. If figures are "for real," they hardly ever come out in even numbers.

Lack of explanatory footnotes

It is seldom that the full story can be told with figures alone. Usually, statements prepared by professional accountants anticipate possible questions that may arise about how figures are determined or how they are allocated. A simple footnote can greatly clarify such questions and can be very helpful to the investor. A lack of any explanations is cause for asking in-depth questions if there is an interest in the property.

Time span covered

One of the first bits of information that should be noted is the period of time represented by the proffered statement. If it is other than a normal period, usually the previous 12 months, the reasons for the time period used should be determined. Is the operation a seasonal one with only the peak period represented? Or is there some unusual expense that may recur but has been bypassed in the period reported?

Management costs

It is not unusual for a seller to eliminate all management costs from the operating statement in order to increase the profit figures. The rationale is that a new purchaser will probably manage the property himself and set a new salary or withdrawal base, or not take any income as a management fee. Whatever is withdrawn for time spent on management is really profit anyway. This reasoning is not wrong, but it overlooks the fact that management costs money and takes time—and some allowance should be made for that by the new investor.

Utility costs

An ever more important cost component of operating properties and one that must be checked carefully is utility costs. Are all of the meters feeding the property being recorded? Or, as is the case in some government-subsidized projects, Are any other meters serving adjacent or unrelated property included in the figures?

Use of national averages

Occasionally a statement will be presented on the operations of a property, say a motel, using cost figures developed from the national averages for that particular type and size of property. These are an interesting study in "what might be," but of little value in the evaluation of a specific property.

Projections on an existing property

This is similar to the "national averages" idea for a statement. If an existing property with an operating record is presented on a basis of projected figures (rather than the actual figures), it is clearly an indication that the owner does not want the truth to be known. However, do not be overly critical of the reluctant owner. Small income properties become closely entangled with the owner's personal tax situation. It is quite possible that the owner does not want to disclose his personal tax methods to the general public who may be looking at the property. An initial financial statement is sometimes considered to be more of a sales tool—a "come-on"—and is not to be taken too seriously. If the prospective buyer shows serious interest, then more detailed and complete figures can be furnished.

A hard stumbling block in some instances is an owner who insists that no real figures will be furnished until a prospective buyer shows genuine interest by signing an earnest money contract or posting some form of good faith money. The intent, of course, is to discourage curious but unqualified buyers, but this tactic can disenchant a serious buyer as well.

CONCLUSIONS

The basic financial statements used in business are the balance sheet and the profit and loss statement. Real property investments are often offered for sale with the use of a variation of the P & L statement—an operating statement. The operating statement shows income and expenses but does not detail the tax treatment for the property. There are many problems associated with financial statements and their use for analysis purposes. For example, there is no standard to facilitate comparisons between properties and there are differences in the names used for various operating accounts and in the way income and costs are allocated. The prudent investor must know who is preparing the financial statement and be able to depend on his or her character. There is some flexibility offered by the IRS in accounting methods and reporting periods for the individual taxpayer which may be advantageous. Financial statements should be questioned when they are presented in rounded figures or when they lack explanatory information. The true figures can be manipulated a bit by shifting the time span covered to an optimum period, eliminating management costs, and inaccurately reporting utility costs. The use of national averages as a means of obtaining cost figures and the use of a projection to present figures on an existing property are both clear signs of a reluctance to submit the actual figures. Do not hesitate to ask questions when accurate information is needed.

28

Investment Analysis

In the analysis of any form of investment, there are some procedures that do not have the force of the more basic "cash on cash" or "dollars out for dollars in" ideas, but are just as meaningful. It behooves the astute investor to understand the meaning of such concepts as capitalization, leverage, and the time value of money, and most certainly to be acquainted with the terminology. In this chapter we will examine capitalization and leverage and in the next the more complex subject of the time value of money along with the present worth of a dollar.

CAPITALIZATION

Somehow the word *capitalization* conjures a whole range of thoughts, and to some, a mysterious way of determining the true value of an investment. The snappy expression "cap rate" is often thrown around as something anyone should know how to calculate. The real mystery is how it all became so confused.

For property evaluation, the word *capitalization* describes the conversion of a given amount of income into a purchase price for that income property. How much would you be willing to pay for a property that is leased and can produce a steady income of $5,000 per year? Would you pay $10,000 for it? Most likely, as you would be asking a return of 50 percent on your investment. Would you pay $50,000 for it? Maybe, as then your return would amount to 10 percent.

The conversion of the $5,000 income stream into a value for the property is done by dividing the income by the rate of return. Thus, the value of $5,000 at a 50 percent rate of return is calculated as follows:

$$\frac{5,000}{.50} = 10,000 \text{ capitalized value}$$

(*Note:* For those a little rusty on math, *percent* means *hundredths* and rate percent means any given number of hundredths. Thus, 5 percent, or 5%, means .05 or 5/100, in which 5 is the rate. So to convert 50%, as used in the example, to a denominator, it is necessary to change the percentage to its decimal equivalent of .50.) In the same way, if the $5,000 income stream is to be capitalized at a 10 percent rate of return we have the following:

$$\frac{5,000}{.10} = 50,000 \text{ capitalized value}$$

The theory of capitalization is that the investor must select a desired rate of return (one that is considered competitive with alternative investments adjusted for the risk involved) and apply that rate to the expected income. In this way a value can be determined which helps the investor screen properties and provides a comparison for the asking price.

How does one select the rate of return (the "cap rate")? There is no question that the optimum rate of return can be simplified to "as much as possible!" But we are dealing with a method of measurement rather than a goal in this procedure. So let's examine two practical ways of selecting the acceptable cap rate.

Comparison With Other Rates

The normal, and most practical method, is to use a rate of return for this computation that compares favorably with whatever other investments are available to you. Larger investors have an advantage in this respect as larger investments in money markets can command much higher returns than smaller sums. If the comparison is with savings rates offered by depository institutions, then consider that a passbook account may achieve 6 percent, savings certificates (with no stated minimum denomination) up to 8 percent, and money market certificates in minimum amounts of $10,000 have fluctuated as much as 10 percentage points (16 percent to 6 percent) in a three-month period (March to June, 1980). But the investors with over $100,000 can negotiate with the lending institution and normally command considerably higher rates than the smaller savers.

Further, is it fair to compare a long-term real estate investment with the return from a short-term money market investment? And what about the investor's time? Probably more time will be needed to administer the real property, and the investor should be compensated for it.

As you can see, comparison is not a simple matter. It becomes a decision that the investor must weigh as it relates to his or her personal situation. A suggested position is to expect a real estate investment to produce a return of at least 5 percent over a savings certificate. If a required rate of return is used as a measurement of value, it is important that the rate selected be realistic—in other words, an attainable goal.

Risk Components

A capitalization rate may be determined by measuring each of the components and adding them together (a summation method). There are four parts to the risk evaluation which are described as follows:

1. *Safe rate* is the rate of return that can be expected from a risk-free investment. The measurement of risk, from an investment standpoint, is based on a government bond. It is not that the federal government rates so well with its budget and money management, it is simply that only the federal government can print all the money it may need to pay its debts! Keep in mind that this measurement is based on dollars, not on purchasing power. Savings accounts insured by an agency of the government also rate as near risk-free and are easy alternatives for any investor. For use in this example, we will take the long U.S. bond average rate, presently near 10 percent, and consider that as the base "safe risk" rate of return.

2. *Hazard rate* is the increase in return (over the safe rate) needed to justify the increased risk of the investment. For real estate, the hazard ranges from 1 percent to 4 percent.

3. *Nonliquidity rate* is the percentage of increase in return needed to offset the lag time during which no return may be realized from the investment. The usual range is from 1/2 percent to 2 percent.

4. *Management rate* is compensation for the owner's time spent in managing the property investment. This rate averages about 1 percent.

Now, to accumulate these four components using some typical rates of return:

Component	Return Required
Safe rate	10.00%
Hazard rate	2.50%
Nonliquidity rate	1.50%
Management rate	1.00%
Capitalization rate	15.00%

LEVERAGE

In its definition as one of the six basic machines (the others being the wheel, pulley, inclined plane, screw, and wedge) the lever, as a rod pivoted on a fulcrum, allows the movement of a much larger weight with a less than equal force. So, in investment, any procedure that allows control of a larger amount of capital with a less than equal amount of capital can be considered leverage. For real estate, leverage is concerned with the ratio of equity cash to borrowed money. Leverage is also expressed as a ratio between the borrowed funds and the total purchase price; the greater the amount of borrowed money compared with the equity cash, the greater the leverage.

To illustrate the effects of leverage on an investment, consider a simplified example. An investor is offered a property for $100,000 that is capable of producing an annual income of $12,000. If the investor purchases the property for cash, the return on the investment amounts to 12 percent:

$$\frac{\$12,000}{\$100,000} = .12 \text{ or } 12\%$$

Now, the investor decides to borrow $75,000 at 10 percent interest and use only $25,000 of his own cash to acquire the property. How does this affect the return? First deduct the cost of the borrowed money:

Return on total investment	$12,000
Less: Interest cost ($75,000 × .10)	7,500
Return on Equity Investment	$ 4,500

To determine the rate of return for the equity:

$$\frac{\$4,500}{\$25,000} = .18 \text{ or } 18\%$$

Obviously, an advantage accrues to the investor when the interest rate for borrowed money is less than the anticipated return from the property. In the above example, the investor increased his return on equity from 12 percent to 18 percent—a 50 percent gain—by borrowing money. Leverage that produces an increase in the return on equity is called *positive leverage*. When the rate of interest and the return from the property are at the same rate, the result is *neutral leverage*. While neutral leverage would have no effect on the rate of return for the equity investment, it would reduce the amount of equity cash needed to purchase the property. When the interest rate for mortgage money exceeds the overall rate of return from the property, the result is *negative leverage*. For example, if the interest rate for the borrowed funds increases to 18 percent, a loss is incurred as shown in this example:

Return on total investment	$12,000
Less: Interest cost ($75,000 × .18)	13,500
Loss	($1,500)

Clearly there is a risk to the investor in properties that are overleveraged. Few properties, with the possible exception of high-grade net leased properties, present the certainty of future income that can guarantee a margin of profit between the fixed-cost borrowed funds and the overall return from the property. A slight drop in the property income can sharply decrease the return on equity investment.

Another more recent development that must be considered is whether you can obtain borrowed money at a fixed rate of interest. Since 1978 when the federal regulators began to lift the limits on interest that could be paid on savings accounts, the cost of funds to lenders has increased. Further, the growing amount of lendable funds that is generated through the financial markets relying on money market interest rates has created considerable volatility in the lending field. After several years of paying high interest rates for short-term funds that are then loaned long term at lower interest rates, lenders have had to "change gears." More mortgage loans will be made with adjustable interest rates in the future. Thus, investors seeking to utilize borrowed funds will be faced with the uncertainties of fluctuating interest costs along with possible fluctuations in the property income. Certainly, one of the major advantages of leverage, the use of a fixed interest loan to acquire property, is diminished somewhat by the adjustable rate mortgage.

29

Time Value of Money

All investors expect a return *on* their investment and a return *of* their investment. But when? Money used to acquire property is probably not earning as an immediate a return as it would if placed in a savings certificate. What is the worth of that delayed return? Income anticipated from property investment may not be available until some future time. How much more would that future income be worth if you had it in hand today? Or turning the question around, How much is a dollar delivered one year from today worth right now? The answer reflects the *time value* of money and is calculated at a selected rate of return, usually the current market rate generally available to the investor.

To further explain the time value of money, let's first examine the simple math used to compound interest. For this example, use a $5,000 savings certificate paying 8 percent interest per year. At the end of the first year the interest earned would be:

$$\$5,000 \times .08 = \$400$$

By adding $5,000 and $400 we know that the total value of the savings certificate at the end of the first year is $5,400. A simpler method of arriving at the same figure is to add "1" to the rate of interest and multiply thus:

$$\$5,000 \times 1.08 = \$5,400$$

If the compounding is carried on to a second year we have:

$$\$5,400 \times 1.08 = \$5,832$$

The addition of the numeral "1" gives us an important mathematical factor, which is $(1 + i)^n$. That moved a little fast, so go back a bit. Described in words, the factor is "one plus interest rate." The "n" denotes a power, which in this formula is the number of *periods* that the interest earned is compounded. That is, How many periods are there in which earned interest is added to, or compounded with, the principal amount? Now to convert the simple formula to reflect the $5,000 savings certificate at the end of two years:

$$\$5,000 \times (1 + .08)^{2*} = P$$

For those a bit rusty in math, the parentheses means to combine the figures within. Therefore:

$$\$5,000 \times 1.08^2 = P$$

Now square the 1.08 figure (multiply 1.08 times 1.08), and the result is 1.1664. To restate the formula for final computation:

$$\$5,000 \times 1.1664 = \$5,832$$

What we have learned is that $5,000 left in a savings certificate earning 8 percent interest is worth $5,832 after two years. That is compounding.

Now consider discounted value or present worth. If a person is offered $5,000 to be delivered just two years from today, what is the worth of that future income today? One approach is to figure how much money would have to be placed in that 8 percent savings certificate today to equal $5,000 two years from now. This calculation is called *discounting*, or *discount value*. It measures the time value of money. Most real estate investment offers income over future years. It is the value of that future income in dollars today that is used to measure the present value.

Going back to the question: How much money would have to be placed in that 8 percent savings certificate today to equal $5,000 two

---

*In the language of mathematics, the "2" is called an *exponent* and in this example it means to the second power or to multiply the factor by itself. If the exponent is 2, it is most commonly called *squared*. If the exponent is 3, the proper expression is *cubed*. Any number over 3 is expressed as a power, such as $(1 + i)$ to the fifth power is $(1 + i)^5$.

years from now? The math is not difficult. The *same factor* that was used to compound the return of interest is used to discount $(1 + i)$, but it is used as a *divisor* for the discounting calculation. If a two-year period is considered, the factor is carried to the 2nd power, or squared, just as before. The formula:

$$\frac{\$5,000}{(1 + .08)^2} = \text{Discounted Value}$$

Resolving the factor:

$$\frac{\$5,000}{1.08^2} = \text{DV}$$

And, one more step:

$$\frac{\$5,000}{1.1664} = \$4,286.69$$

So, we know that $4,286.69 placed in a savings certificate that pays 8 percent interest will amount to $5,000 in just two years. Compound the interest yourself to prove it! We also know that if someone offers a $5,000 return on an investment that will become available in two years, that all it is worth today is $4,286.69, providing we figure that 8 percent is a fair and reasonable return.

It is this simple mathematical formula that is used to calculate the present worth of any future income. The interest rate that is used depends on the investor's decision as to what returns are available in other forms of investment, or What is the market rate of return? The calculation must be made for each future period, for each future year that the property will be held as an investment. Each future year represents a power in the factor used to divide the income.

For example, if the property being considered offers a $5,000 return each year, payable at the end of each year, the present worth of that future income stream is calculated as follows. Note that the example uses and 8 percent return.

First Year		Second Year		Third Year		Fourth Year		Fifth Year		
$\frac{5,000}{1.08}$	+	$\frac{5,000}{1.08^2}$	+	$\frac{5,000}{1.08^3}$	+	$\frac{5,000}{1.08^4}$	+	$\frac{5,000}{1.08^5}$	=	Present Value of Income Stream
$\frac{5,000}{1.08}$	+	$\frac{5,000}{1.1664}$	+	$\frac{5,000}{1.2597}$	+	$\frac{5,000}{1.3605}$	+	$\frac{5,000}{1.4693}$	=	PV
4,629.62	+	4,286.69	+	3,969.20	+	3,675.12	+	3,402.98	=	19,963.61

Thus, $25,000 offered at the rate of $5,000 each year has a present worth of $19,963.61, if an 8 percent return is used. There is one more step: the property that is under consideration has a resale value. In this example, we are assuming a period of ownership of five years for the property. What is the probable resale value of the property at the end of five years? Let's assume the value would be $75,000, and it will be received after five years of holding. It is called the *residual value*.

$$\frac{75,000}{1.08^5} = \text{Present Value}$$

$$\frac{75,000}{1.4693} = \$51,044.72$$

To determine the present worth of this property it is necessary to add the present value of the future income stream to the present value of the residual:

PV of income stream	$19,963.61
PV of residual	51,044.72
Present Value of property	$71,008.33

Of what value is the present worth calculation? Is the $71,008.33 value a realistic purchase price for the property? Not necessarily. It is a realistic *measurement* with which to assess an asking (or a selling) price. What it means based on the cash flows is that if you cannot buy this property for *less than* $71,008.33, you would be just as well off financially if you put your money in that 8 percent savings certificate.

All this may be true, but savings certificates do not increase in value with inflation and real property usually does. Doesn't this make a big difference? Yes, it certainly does. But how do you place a mathematical value on inflation? Only by estimate—and this estimate can easily be used to adjust both the future income stream and the residual value of the property. For example, assume a continuing 10 percent inflation. Each year the $5,000 income flow will increase by 10 percent, first to $5,500, then to $6,050, and so forth. And the residual value would be estimated at the inflated value expected to exist in five years. Then apply a rate of return (an interest rate) commensurate with the market return for similar investment risk to discount the inflated values down to a present worth.

Obviously, the inclusion of an inflation rate in the calculations is necessary if the investor recognizes one of the major advantages of real estate in today's markets. It also introduces an uncertainty as to what the future might bring; it introduces a speculative or uncertain element into the mathematical projection. There is, of course, another basic uncertainty in real estate investment analysis that must be recognized. This is the quality of the cash flows. How certain is the amount to be earned?

Present worth computations are used with greater certainty in calculating the value of a bond investment. A bond presents a fixed interest rate and an assured return of the principal investment after a period of years. Inflation is not a factor with bonds as repayment is made of the face amount in dollars when payments are due. Relative purchasing power of the dollar between investment and repayment is certainly important but normally is not a component in the calculation.

As long as the investor understands the inherent difficulties with applying a sound mathematical procedure to the uncertainties of future income and future inflation rates that relate to real estate, the present worth analysis can be useful. If the measurement base is uniform (meaning the same rate of return and inflation rate) and applied to different properties, a meaningful comparison can be derived.

EIGHT

Real Property Investments

30

The Business Organization

The form of business organization that is used to undertake an investment in real property is important. The concerns of an investor have to do with management control, liability for losses, and the taxation of income derived from the investment. Five forms of business organization are considered here:

1. Sole proprietorship.
2. General partnership.
3. Limited partnership.
4. Corporation.
5. Tax-option corporation (Subchapter S).

While it does not classify as a business organization in itself, the *real estate syndicate* is examined in the last section of this chapter. The syndicate is a popular method of promoting group investments.

SOLE PROPRIETORSHIP

The simplest form of business organization is the sole proprietorship. An individual can own land and/or operate a business in his or her own name, under a trade name, or under an assumed name. Most states require that a trade name be publicly registered or recorded if it differs from the individual's name, thereby reducing the possibility of misrepresenta-tion to creditors or others. An advantage of the sole proprietorship is that the owner has absolute control over management decisions and an absolute right to dispose of profits or assets as he or she sees fit. However, the sole proprietorship offers an owner no protection against financial losses or claims that may arise from the operation of the business. In some states, any nonbusiness assets that belong to the owner may be attached in satisfaction of a judgment or lien. (The laws which govern are those of the state of residence or of the state in which the business operates.)

Income Tax Reports.   All taxable income of a sole proprietorship must be reported as part of the individual owner's income or loss. It must be reported for the same calendar year (or fiscal year) used for the per-sonal income tax return. The business report is submitted on Schedule C, Form 1040, "Profit (or Loss) from Business or Profession."

Accounting Period Used.   Individual tax returns normally cover a calendar year; that is, the 12-month period from January 1 through December 31. However, individuals may choose to use a fiscal year ac-counting period which encompasses a 12-month period ending on the last day of any month except December. The election of an accounting period must be made when the first tax return is filed. Changing the period requires IRS consent.

Accounting Method Used.   The individual may select any account-ing system he wants, but is required by law to keep whatever records he will need to prepare a complete and accurate income tax return. These records include receipts, cancelled checks, and other evidence to support the records. The most common accounting methods are the cash method and the accrual method. (See Chapter 27.) The taxpayer must select one method for each business when it begins to operate. (The *same* account-ing method need not be used for all of a taxpayer's businesses.) Once a method has been selected, any change requires IRS consent.*

Disposition of a Sole Proprietorship.   If the assets of a sole pro-prietorship are disposed of, they must be classified into four separate categories. The gain or loss for each category must be computed separ-ately. Guidelines* are as follows:

- *Capital assets.* Sale results in a capital gain or loss.
- *Depreciable property used in the business.* Sale results in a gain or loss

---

*Further information may be obtained from IRS Publication 538, "Tax Information on Accounting Periods and Methods."
*Further information may be obtained from IRS Publication 544, "Sales and Other Dispositions of Assets."

from adjusted basis as a Section 1231 transaction (must be held for over one year to qualify for capital gains treatment).

- *Real property used in the business.* Sale must be reported separately, but the tax treatment is the same as for depreciable property.
- *Property held as inventory or stock in trade.* Sale results in ordinary income.

GENERAL PARTNERSHIP

The laws of partnerships stem from civil law, common law, equity, and law merchant. In 1914, the Commissioners on Uniform State Laws drafted the Uniform Partnership Act, which codified the general rules prevailing at the time. This Partnership Act is the basis for all state laws regarding partnerships.

The Partnership Act defines a partnership as "an association of two or more persons, who carry on a business as co-owners for profit." Partnerships can be classified as *trading* and *nontrading*. Nontrading partnerships are those formed by professionals, such as lawyers, accountants, and physicians. But it is the trading partnership that this text discusses. These trading partnerships can be further classified as *general* or *limited*. (Limited partnerships are discussed in a separate section of this chapter.)

Formation of a Partnership

A general partnership can be formed by either oral agreement or a written contract between (or among) the partners.

By Oral Agreement. A valid partnership can be formed with an oral agreement, although some states limit the life of such a partnership to one year. Courts have held that a partnership formed by oral agreement may hold title to land even though state laws require land transfer agreements to be in written form. The reason is that courts have interpreted the law to govern the form of the land *transaction*, not the form of the *partnership*.

By Written Agreement. Even though oral partnerships are valid in some states, a written understanding is preferable. A written agreement should obviously contain the name of the partnership, the names of the partners, the duration of the agreement, and the partnership's place of business. Not so obviously, it should also clearly indicate the capital contributions of each partner, their duties, a method for settling disputes, a procedure for cash withdrawals required by the partners, the way in which profits or losses will be divided, and a method by which the partnership may be dissolved. Some states have statutory requirements regarding the names that can be used for a partnership, and most require that any fictitious or assumed name be published or filed with a designated authority. The Partnership Act does not prevent a corporation from becoming a partner. On the contrary, the Act defines the word *persons* as "individuals, partnerships, corporations, and other associations."

Partnership Operations

In a general partnership, the partners determine the responsibility for management. Each partner might have a specific area of management responsibility, with major policy decisions made by a majority vote of the partners. The partnership agreement should define the duties of each partner, as well as any shared responsibilities.

Liabilities.   In a general partnership, each partner is liable for all obligations incurred on behalf of the partnership by any of the partners. The partnership agreement can limit liabilities *among* the partners themselves, making each partner responsible for his own commitments. But, the responsibility of each partner to the general public and to the partnership's creditors cannot be limited by internal agreement among the general partners.

Disadvantages of a Partnership

The most obvious disadvantage of the general partnership is each partner's unlimited liability for the partnership's losses. Insurance coverage is rarely available to protect the partners against bad management or poor judgment. Another disadvantage of a partnership is the limited life of the partnership agreement. Unlike a corporation, a partnership may be terminated by the death of any one partner or by the withdrawal of a partner. Termination can also result from mutual agreement among the partners, an act in default of the partnership agreement by one or more of the partners, or through bankruptcy.

The partnership form does not provide an investment interest that is easily liquidated or readily sold. Each partner has, in effect, both undivided interest in the partnership's property and an equal right of possession. The close relationship among the partners, which is all-important for successful operation, is not readily replaced. Generally, partnership agreements contain restrictions on each partner's right to sell his interest to outsiders.

Advantages of a Partnership

A partnership is formed primarily to combine the capital and expertise of two or more people. And it does so in an effective manner. All partners have a voice in the management; all participate directly in the success of the partnership's operation. Partnerships are not required to file reports or pay franchise taxes to the state, while corporations must. And the partnership is not a taxable entity for income tax purposes.

Partnership Income Tax Reports

Although a partnership pays no income tax, it must file an information return (Form 1065) each year. This return shows the results of the partnership's operations for the tax year, separating the items of income, gain, loss, deduction, or credit which affect each partner's individual income tax return. (These items are the partner's *distributive share.*) A partnership may use a different tax year from that used by individual partners. In that case, partnership income is treated by the partners as having been distributed on the last day of the partnership year. Each partner must include his distributive share of partnership items on his individual return for the tax year in which the last day of the partnership year falls. A partner reports his share of the partnership's ordinary income or loss on Schedule E, Form 1040.

The manner in which profits and losses are distributed is usually set out in the partnership agreement. If there is no agreement on sharing a specific item of gain or loss, each partner's share is determined in accordance with that partner's proportional interest in the partnership. Partnership income and gains are taxable to each partner—to the extent of his share—*whether or not they are distributed.* This is an important point to consider when selecting a form of business operation, particularly if cash flows must be retained in the business for a number of years while operations are getting off the ground. The distributive share of partnership losses is *limited* to the adjusted basis of each partner's interest at the end of the partnership year in which the losses occurred. Partnership income or losses may be allocated to each partner only for that portion of the year that the taxpayer is a member of the partnership. The IRS claims the right to reallocate the distributive shares of partnership income, losses, or other items to the proper parties if the allocation lacks substantial economic justification.

When a taxpayer-partner has the right to exercise an election, the partnership—not the taxpayer-partner—makes the decision. These decisions include the method of accounting, the method of computing depreciation, the use of installment sales provisions, and others. The elections apply to all partners collectively. (There are exceptions to this procedure, notably when foreign taxes are involved or certain exploration expenditures are incurred.)

Guaranteed Payments.   If a partner is paid a salary for services rendered, or interest for the use of capital, these guaranteed payments are generally deductible as business expenses to the partnership. But guaranteed payments for a partner's services in forming the partnership, selling interests in the partnership, or acquiring property for the partnerships are *not deductible* as a business expense to the partnership. Any guaranteed payments to a partner must be reported on that individual's return as salary or interest income.

Special "At Risk" Rules.   Certain types of business activity have been singled out by IRS rules which limit the amount of losses that may be deducted for the tax year. These activities include motion pictures, various agricultural activities, exploration for oil or gas, and the leasing of personal property or depreciable real property other than buildings. Deductible losses on any of these investments are limited to the amount the taxpayer has at risk (with respect to the activity) at the close of the partnership's taxable year. *At risk* is defined as the sum of three contributions by the taxpayer to the activity: (1) cash, (2) the adjusted basis of other property contributed, and (3) any amounts borrowed for use in the activity for which the taxpayer is personally liable. So far, land and buildings have been excluded from the at-risk rules.

Distributive Items.   When the IRS uses the term *distributive item*, it means the various forms of income and loss that may be taxed in different procedures for the individual partners. Schedule K of Form 1065 contains a list of partnerhip's distributive share items. A copy of this list (Schedule K-1) shows each partner's share of the distributive items. Items commonly reported on Schedule K include:

1. Ordinary income or loss.
2. Partner's salary and interest.
3. Net short-term capital gain and loss.
4. Net long-term capital gain and loss.
5. Gains and losses from property used in trade or business and from involuntary conversions.
6. Qualifying dividends.
7. Contributions.
8. Net self-employment income.

9. First-year expense deduction.

10. Expense account allowance.

11. Tax preference items.

Each partner's distribution share of the partnership's income, gain, loss, deduction, or credit must be shown *separately* on his own Form 1040. These items are treated generally as if each partner had realized or incurred them personally. If a partner itemizes deductions on Form 1040, he may include the distributive share of items such as partnership's contributions, which are not deductible in computing partnership income.*

LIMITED PARTNERSHIP

The *limited partnership* puts a ceiling on the financial liability of each person designated as a limited partner. It has become a popular method of organizing real estate investments and raising equity capital. The limited partnership can be formed only by written agreement, which must be filed with the state authority charged with its regulation.

The origin of the limited partnership is the Uniform Limited Partnership Act, which has been adopted by every state except Louisiana (which has its own Act covering limited partnerships). The essence of a limited partnership is that it consists of one or more persons, known as *limited partners*, who do not participate in the management of the business and are personally liable to creditors only for the amount of their capital investment in the partnership. The limited partnership also has one or more persons, known as *general partners*, who are responsible for the management of the business and are personally liable for financial obligations of the partnership without regard to their investment.

The Limited Partnership Act states that a general partner possesses all the rights—and is subject to all the restrictions and liabilities—of a partner, in a general partnership. However, the Act provides additional restrictions on the general partner; for example, he cannot act contrary to the partnership certificate, and he cannot admit someone as a general or limited partner. The death or retirement of a general partner generally terminates the limited partnership, but this can be overcome through a specific provision in the partnership agreement.

According to the provisions of the Act, a limited partner does not become financially liable as a general partner *unless* the limited partner participates in the management and control of the business. The limited partner is authorized to inspect the books of the partnership and to

---

*Further information may be obtained from IRS Publication 541, "Tax Information on Partnership Income and Losses."

receive, on demand, full information on all matters affecting the partnership. The limited partner may lend money to the partnership and can
transact other business with the partnership. The limited partner may
make a capital contribution of cash or property to the partnership but
cannot contribute his services.

Courts have held that a limited partnership may be dissolved if it is
operating at a loss. The Limited Partnership Act establishes priorities for
distributing assets upon dissolution of a partnership, giving general
creditors first rights over limited partners, and limited partners priority
over general partners.

Disadvantages of a Limited Partnership

Problems that can arise in a limited partnership are like those found in a
general partnership, including the difficulty of selling a partnership interest and the possibility of early termination of the business through
death or withdrawal of a general partner. The general partner takes the
same risks as in a general partnership, plus the possibility of challenge by
the limited partners if management decisions are less than prudent.

Limited partners, who generally contribute most of the capital,
have very little voice in the management of the partnership. This may be
an advantage or a disadvantage, depending on the quality of the general
partners. The capability of the general partners is so important in this
form of business organization that the limited partner-investor should
very carefully investigate the experience and management track record of
each potential general partner.

Advantages of a Limited Partnership

For both general and limited partners, the limited partnership offers the
same direct pass-through of profits and losses for taxation purposes that
is found in a general partnership. The limited partnership is not a taxable
entity and files only an information return.

For the limited partner, there is the added advantage of limited
liability. And the limited partner has minimal management responsibility, which may release his time for other endeavors. The general partners
can also provide expertise in a specialized form of business activity that
might otherwise be beyond the reach of the limited partner.

Limited Partnership Income Tax Reports

The limited partnership—like the general partnership—files the Form
1065 information return. Each partner, general or limited, must report
his distributive share of the partnership's ordinary income or net loss on

his personal return (Schedule E, Form 1040), regardless of whether or not income is disbursed.

Although the tax rules do not specifically single out the limited partnership as a target, it is this form of business organization that is most subject to the special at-risk rules that limit deductible losses.

Since the limited liability of a limited partner is the same as the shareholder's liability in a corporation (a shareholder's liability for financial losses being limited to the amount of his investment), the distinction between a limited partnership and a corporation can become extremely hazy to the tax collector. If the IRS believes that a limited partnership has been formed for the purpose of avoiding corporate taxes, an additional assessment may be made. To make this determination, the IRS looks for four telltale traits of the corporation—continuity of life, centralized management, limited liability, and freely transferable ownership interests. The IRS may attempt to assess corporate taxes on a partnership, when the latter shows predominantly corporate attributes.

CORPORATIONS

The corporation, a form of business created by state chartering laws, is an artificial "person" with rights and powers to transact business of a limited and designated nature.

The Corporate Entity

In their earliest U.S. forms, corporations were chartered by special acts of the state legislatures. As this procedure became increasingly cumbersome, the states enacted corporation statutes to provide a more expeditious method of forming a corporation. Although several model procedures have been developed, including a Model Business Corporations Act by the American Bar Association, there is still no uniform statute to guide state lawmakers.

The courts have played a considerable role in developing the law of corporations. While there are diverse opinions on the true nature of a corporation, the dominant theory conceives of the corporation as a legal entity separate and distinct from its shareholders. A corporation may enter into contracts with its shareholders, and sue and be sued by them as a separate legal entity.

A corporation is held to be a "person" under some provisions of the United States Constitution, but a corporation does not have the status of a "citizen" for all legal purposes. For example, a corporation cannot move freely into any state to conduct business, while a citizen may. On the other hand, a corporation cannot be deprived of its property without due process, which is the same protection accorded citizens.

In a landmark decision in 1819, the United States Supreme Court ruled that a charter granted by a state to a corporation is deemed to be a contract between the state and the corporation.* Thus the relationship between the state and the corporations runs through the entire field of corporation law.

The Corporate Structure

The ownership of a corporation lies with its shareholders and is evidenced by shares of stock. Stock is issued and sold by the corporation, as regulated by state laws and by the SEC if stock is sold publicly. One corporation may issue several classes of stock, including *common stock* and *preferred stock*, with each giving the holder different rights.

The shareholders elect directors who, as a group, are responsible for the corporation's finances and operating policies. Corporate directors can be held personally liable for negligence in corporate matters and for any illegal actions by the corporation.

The board of directors selects the officers of the corporation, who are charged with managing the corporation's day-to-day operations. Officers may or may not be directors or shareholders of the company.

Corporations may borrow money from banks, insurance companies, or other lenders. The loans may be unsecured or secured by a pledge of certain corporate assets. Corporations also have borrowing methods that are not generally available to others. For example, corporations can sell promissory notes (more commonly known as *commercial paper*) in the open market. And they can issue and sell bonds as a method of borrowing money. These bonds vary, depending on their purpose, collateral, and repayment commitment. One common type is a mortgage bond, which is secured by a pledge of specified real property owned by the corporation.

Types of Corporations

Corporations are chartered for a variety of purposes. They are considered here under three categories: (1) for profit, (2) for nonprofit, and (3) government and quasi-government.

Corporations for Profit.   The corporation most commonly used for real estate investment is operated for the purpose of making a profit. It may be a *close corporation* or a *public issue corporation*. Close corporations

---

*Dartmouth College vs. Woodward, 4 Wheat. 518, 636, 657, 4L.Ed., 629.

have only a few closely knit shareholders (such as family) or even just one shareholder. Public issue corporations are authorized to sell stock and bonds to the general public and are subject to a number of state and federal regulations on such sales. Most states also have special rules for incorporating particular classes of business such as banks, insurance companies, and savings associations.

Nonprofit Corporations. Certain state statutes provide for the formation of corporations that are *not* established for profit. These include charitable, educational, recreational, religious, and social organizations, all of which are convenient methods of holding and operating property. Nonprofit corporations do not distribute dividends to members on their invested capital.

Government Corporations. A government corporation is created for public purposes. It is considered an agency of whichever government forms it—federal, state, or municipal. It can be used in administering the government or providing a service such as a utility. The government corporation can be used to conduct a business operation; the Tennessee Valley Authority, the Federal Home Loan Mortgage Corporation, and the U.S. Postal Service are prime examples. Quasi-government corporations—those partly owned by the federal government and partly by the general public—operate businesses that are considered too large or too much in the public interest to be entrusted to private hands. Examples of the quasi-government corporation are Comsat, which handles the communications satellites, and Amtrak, which operates passenger railroad trains.

Disadvantages of the Corporation

For the real estate investor, the major disadvantage of the corporate form lies in the method of its taxation. There are two problems:

1. *Double taxation.* All corporate income is subject to corporate income taxes, after which the remaining income may be distributed to shareholders as dividends. Ordinary dividends received by shareholders are subject to a second taxation—they are taxed as ordinary income to the recipient. There is a $100 exclusion from taxes on dividends received from qualifying corporations.
2. *No pass-through of tax deductions.* The corporation—not the shareholder—is entitled to the normal deductions for depreciation and other losses. Corporate losses—unlike partnership losses—cannot be included in the shareholder's taxable income.

Another disadvantage of the corporate form is the investor's lack of a voice in management. From a practical standpoint, the investor will have little control over management unless he is a major shareholder.

Advantages of the Corporation

The advantages of the corporate form are that (1) the shareholder has limited liability and (2) shares of stock are generally more liquid than an interest in any other form of business organization. Stockbrokers and stock exchanges promote the buying and selling of corporate stock. There is an "Over-the-Counter" market for stock that is not listed on the major stock exchanges. Many shares in smaller companies are traded daily in these localized markets.

Corporate Income Tax Reports

Corporations must file with the IRS an annual income tax return—Form 1120—and pay the taxes due. It is beyond the scope of this text to consider the substantial body of corporate tax law, but some requirements for the individual shareholder in the reporting of dividends and other corporate distributions must be discussed.

Corporate Distributions

The four classifications of corporate distributions are (1) ordinary dividends, (2) return of capital, (3) capital gain dividends, and (4) tax-free distributions. Each class is treated differently for tax purposes.

Ordinary Dividends.   These are paid out of the earnings and profits of the corporation and are reported as ordinary income to the shareholder. Any dividend received by the shareholder, whether on common or preferred stock, is treated as an ordinary dividend unless the paying corporation indicates otherwise. The first $100 of ordinary dividends received from qualifying corporations is excluded from taxable income. Examples of nonqualifying corporations on which the dividend exclusion is *not allowed* are foreign corporations, exempt farmers' cooperatives, real estate investment trusts, and any Subchapter S corporation that elects to be treated as a partnership.

Return of Capital.   A distribution that is not made from earnings of the corporation is treated as a return of the shareholder's investment. A return of capital is not taxed until the basis in the stock is fully recovered. Any return of capital that exceeds the amount of the basis is taxable as a capital gain—whether long term or short term depends on the holding period of the stock. Corporations usually advise their shareholders when the distribution represents a return of capital.

Capital Gain Dividends.   These are paid or allocated to shareholders' accounts by regulated investment companies, mutual funds, and real estate investment trusts. The company or fund normally indicates how much of the distribution is a capital gain dividend. These distributions are reported as long-term capital gains *regardless* of how long the stock has been owned. These dividends must be reported if they've been *allocated* to the shareholder—even if they haven't been *received*.

Tax-Free Distributions.   A tax-free distribution is usually in the form of additional shares or rights in the corporation which do not alter the stockholder's previous proportional share in the corporation. Examples include the stock split—where the corporation distributes additional shares of its own stock to its shareholders—and a reorganization of the shares. A tax-free distribution is not reported on the shareholder's tax return.

TAX-OPTION CORPORATIONS (SUBCHAPTER S)

A limited partnership is a hybrid between a corporation and a partnership in terms of *liability*; a Subchapter S corporation is a similar hybrid, this time in terms of income taxes. Essentially, a Subchapter S (Internal Revenue code) corporation is any normally chartered corporation with no more than 25 shareholders (husband and wife treated as one shareholder) that has elected to be taxed as a partnership. The Subchapter S corporation files an annual information return allocating its total income among the shareholders, who must then report the income (or loss) on their personal tax return whether or not the distribution has been received. Under this procedure, the corporation does not pay corporate income taxes.

The IRS regulations covering the Subchapter S procedure recognize that corporate taxes can unfairly penalize the corporate form of business ownership. This is particularly true for small, closely held corporations whose shareholders are expected to distribute profits in a manner that is "reasonable" under IRS interpretations. Three items create difficulty with interpretation—salaries, interest paid to shareholders, and dividends.

Salaries.   The small corporation usually begins with all or most of its shareholders working full- or part-time for the company. As employees of the corporation, they are entitled to reasonable salaries, which are a normal business expense and, therefore, deductible from corporate income. If the IRS considers these salaries to be excessive, however, it can disallow the excess, then assess corporate taxes on the amount of the excess. The excess salary is then treated as a dividend to the recipient.

Interest.   The capital structure of a corporation may include interest-bearing loans made by the shareholders. For example, if a corporation requires $300,000 to commence business operations, the shareholders may purchase $150,000 of stock, and lend the corporation an additional $150,000 at 9 percent interest. The annual interest payment on the loan would amount to $13,500 and should be deductible as a normal business expense. However, the Internal Revenue Code has a rule stating that if a corporation is *undercapitalized*, interest payments made to shareholders may be disallowed as an expense, and then treated as a dividend.

Dividends.   To defer the effects of the "double tax" on corporate income, a corporation might delay the payment of a dividend. Accumulated earnings increase the value of the company and could lead to a higher selling price for the stock. A shareholder might thus benefit from the corporate income, since he would pay a tax at the capital gains rate on the sale of stock rather than at the ordinary income rates applicable to dividends. Here again, the tax laws have a counteracting provision that permits taxation of *excessive accumulated earnings*. Furthermore, there are special rules for taxing a "collapsible" corporation; that is, a corporation created for a limited time, with most of its earnings distributed through sale of its stock.

Qualifications for Subchapter S Treatment

To overcome some of the problems that arise in corporate taxation, the shareholders of a small corporation may elect to have corporate income taxed directly to them rather than to the corporation. To qualify for this election, the corporation must:

1. Have no more than 25 shareholders, none of whom is a nonresident alien.
2. Have only one class of stock.
3. Have each shareholder sign the form electing taxation as a partnership.

4. Derive no more than 20 percent of its income from rents, royalties, interest, and dividends (passive income).
5. Obtain IRS approval.

Advantages and Disadvantages

The Subchapter S corporation has the tax advantages of the partnership form and the limited liability advantage of the corporate form. If the business operates at a tax loss, Subchapter S allows a pass-through of the loss as an offset to the taxpayer's other income. But if the business is operating at a profit and is not able to distribute that profit because of internal cash demands, a disadvantage arises in that the shareholder must pay income taxes on undistributed earnings.

There is one obvious limitation to the Subchapter S corporation in the real estate field: no more than 20 percent of the income may be derived from rents. However, the IRS considers as *income*—not rent—those payments received for the use and occupancy of rooms in a boarding house, apartment, motel, or trailer court, where services are provided for the convenience of the occupants. And there are a number of real estate activities that produce *profit* other than rents, including the sale and leasing of properties for commissions, the development and sale of lots, property management, and consulting services. Gain from real estate sales is not subject to the 20 percent limit.

Subchapter S Tax Reports

The corporation must file a tax return on Form 1120S for each year that the election under Subchapter S is effective. Shareholders must include their prorated shares of the corporation's taxable income and gains in their returns, whether or not the amount is actually distributed. However, a shareholder must report income differently from a partner. If the shareholder's tax year is different from that of the corporation, any distribution of current taxable income must be reported in the tax year it is actually received. (For a partnership, any distributive share of partnership items is reported in the tax year in which the *last day* of the partnership year falls, regardless of the date actually received.) The Subchapter S shareholder reports any *undistributed* taxable income in the personal tax year in which the tax year of the corporation ends. While the cash distributions from a Subchapter S corporation are considered dividends, they do not qualify for the $100 dividend exclusion.*

---

*Additional information may be obtained from IRS Publication 589, "Tax Information on Subchapter S Corporations."

REAL ESTATE SYNDICATE

The syndicate is introduced here, under "Business Organizations," because it has become a popular method of investing in real estate. It is not in itself a form of business or ownership. A syndicate can be a general partnership, a limited partnership, a corporation, or even a landholder (as a joint tenancy or a tenancy in common). In practice, the syndicate provides a way for individuals or firms to combine their investment capital to undertake a larger project that might be possible for any one of them alone. It is used as a means to raise equity cash or to sell investment property. When used for real estate investment, the term *syndicate* most often means ownership in the form of a limited partnership. But this section considers the syndicate as a method of investment, rather than as a form of ownership.

Regulations

Depending on the number of persons involved, the wording of the agreement, and the manner in which it is sold, the sale of participating interest in real property can be considered a sale of securities. Both federal and state laws control the sale of securities to the general public. These laws are designed to protect the public from fraud and misrepresentation, and to require full disclosure of the facts by sellers of securities.

Insofar as real estate is concerned, regulatory authorities are concerned whenever a certificate that is sold to the public represents some *future* interest in land. It can be called an earnest money agreement, a security deposit, an advance payment, or a preconstruction sale of a right to some unit of property. The name does not matter. What matters is that if the sales document is a piece of paper granting some right or interest in land without a specific assignment of title, the document of sale may be held to be a security and, therefore, subject to registration requirements. Violations of the securities laws can bring fines and felony prosecution. Charges can be brought against any or all of the parties involved in the sale of an unauthorized issue, including the original promoter, the sales personnel (who may not even be aware of the noncompliance), and the mortgage lender.

The state statutes in this area vary considerably. But registration of syndicated offerings is required by most states. And if the offering is made to potential buyers across state lines or to more than 35 persons within a state, then registration is also required with the federal regulator, the Securities and Exchange Commission.

A regulatory agency's acceptance or approval of the registration to sell participating interests is no assurance of a safe or successful investment. All this approval means is that the registration laws have been complied with, and all pertinent facts have been fully and accurately disclosed. The true worth of an interest in a syndicated venture is an estimate that the investor must make.

Types of Syndicates

Two basic methods are used to form a real estate investment syndicate.

1. *Sale of existing property.* Under this method, the property is identified for the investor. For example, a builder or developer (usually called the *syndicator*) owns or controls (by option or contract of sale) a suitable investment property. The syndicator then sells participating interests in the property to a group of investors.

2. *Sale of interests in property to be acquired.* The syndicator sells interests in a syndicate organized for the purpose of *acquiring* good investment properties. This procedure is also referred to, quite accurately, as a *blind pool.* Because it allows so much freedom to the syndicator in the use of other people's money, many states, including Texas, forbid sales of this type of syndicated interest.

Disadvantages and Advantages

The following discussion considers a syndication from the investor's point of view. The investor is most likely to be a limited partner in the syndicate, rather than the syndicator. As a general partner, the syndicator would have financial control and responsibility for performance.

Disadvantages.   The property's description and operating figures are usually compiled by the syndicator, who has a strong interest in selling the property. The result can be a biased presentation. The syndicator usually controls the management of the property, but he may be a far better salesman than property manager. The division of profits can be loaded in favor of the syndicator by the use of unduly high salaries, expense accounts, unnecessary payroll additions, and other ill-advised business expenses. The limited partner has no voice in the management.

Advantages.   The same points that represent possible weaknesses in a syndicate investment can also become advantages. Everything depends on the integrity and capability of the syndicator-operator. If the syndicator is well-qualified and has a good record of accomplishment in real estate operations, the syndicate investor can enjoy the advantages of a

TABLE 30-1

Comparison of Business Organizations

Characteristics	Partnerships		Corporations	
	General	Limited	General	Subchapter S
1. Liability of owners	Partners—unlimited	General Partners—unlimited Limited Partners—limited	Shareholders—limited	Same as General
2. Transferability of interests	Not transferable	General Partner—not transferable Limited Partner—transferable	Transferable, subject to limitations with other shareholders	Same as General
3. Management	All partners have equal voice, unless otherwise agreed	General Partners have equal voice Limited Partners have no voice	Shareholders elect directors to manage	Same as General
4. Taxation	Not a taxable entity—net income prorated and taxed to each partner personally	Same as General	Income taxed to corporation Dividends taxed to shareholders	Net Income taxed to shareholders whether distributed or not
5. Method of creation	Established by agreement of the parties	Same as General, plus filing form in public office	Charter issued by state	Same as General, plus filing agreement with IRS
6. Duration	Termination by agreement, withdrawal, death, or bankruptcy	Term provided in the authorizing certificate	May be perpetual	Same as General

professional management team while shouldering no direct responsibility.

There are other advantages. If the syndicate is a partnership, each member can share in the tax deductions permissible for depreciation and the benefit of capital gains upon the sale of the property. If the syndicate is a limited partnership, the liability of the limited partners is fixed at the amount of their investment. By participating in several syndicates, the investor may spread out the risk factor through a more diversified investment portfolio. Finally, the investor in real property should receive a higher return than is normally available from stocks, bonds, or savings accounts, as well as some protection against inflation through the appreciation potential of real estate.

COMPARISON OF BUSINESS ORGANIZATIONS

Table 30–1 on the opposite page provides a quick reference for comparing the general characteristics of the major forms of business organization. An investor's selection of the best business form depends on many additional facts—goals, personal income and tax obligations, and the other people involved.

31

Raw Land and Its Development

An investment in raw, or undeveloped, land offers risks and speculative gains that differ from other forms of investment. First, raw land provides no income against which to offset the expenses of holding it. Thus, carrying charges incurred while holding the land may be added to the capital investment or possibly deducted from other income. Land can increase in value at a fairly slow rate which means the investor must be able to pay the carrying costs when due and hold on until a fair return can be achieved. On the gain side of the investment, few types of property investment have the potential to soar in value as does well-located raw land.

LAND SELECTION

Care must be taken in the selection of a tract of undeveloped land to be held for appreciation to ensure that it lies in the general path of population growth, that potential zoning problems will not grossly inhibit future use, and that utility systems and transportation patterns will support future use. The key word is "use"—basic land value is increased in direct relation to its growth in usefulness. It is the change in the land's usage capability that causes value to increase (or decrease).

FINANCING LAND ACQUISITION

Loans to finance the acquisition of undeveloped land are not generally favored by lenders. Repayment of the loan is tied in some measure to the ability of the borrower to sell the land. And *when* this objective might be accomplished is an uncertainty that bankers do not like to contend with. However, the landowner can realize a much better profit margin from the leverage offered by borrowed money. For these reasons, the *seller* of undeveloped land is often the lender, providing financing in the form of a relatively small required down payment and low amortization payments for a limited span of time. To understand the value of leverage in land acquisition intended for resale, take an example of a tract costing $5,000 per acre. Assume that after three years the land can be sold for $8,500 per acre, giving a $3,500 per acre gross profit.*

(Figures are "per acre")

Selling price	$8,500
Less: Acquisition cost	5,000
Gross Profit	3,500
Less: Selling expenses	600
Less: Three years' taxes and insurance	650
Net Profit	$2,250

To compute return on investment:

$$\frac{\$2,250}{3 \text{ years}} = \$750 \text{ per year}$$

$$\frac{\$750.00}{\$5,000} = 15\% \text{ return per year}$$

If the acquisition is made with $1,000 equity cash and $4,000 in borrowed funds, the return is calculated as follows:

Selling price	$8,500
Less: Loan principal repaid	4,000
Less: Equity cash used	1,000
Gross Profit	$3,500
Less: Selling expenses	600
Less: Three years' taxes and insurance	650
Less: Three years' interest ($4,000 @ 13%)	1,560
	$ 690

---

*For simplfication, the time value of money is not considered in this example.

To compute return on investment:

$$\frac{\$690}{3 \text{ years}} = \$230 \text{ per year}$$

$$\frac{\$230}{\$1,000} = 23\% \text{ return per year}$$

The result of the borrowed money is a 50 percent increase in the return on the equity capital invested. However, borrowed money sharply curtails the time frame within which a profit may be realized in the example. Assume that the selling price of $8,500 is not realized within the projected three-year span. The buyer for cash must continue to pay taxes and insurance at the rate of $216.67 per year, which would take another ten years to reduce the return on the investment to zero. But the buyer using $4,000 in borrowed money is converted into a loss position in the fourth year of the holding period if the $8,500 selling price has not been realized. Thus borrowed money increases the return for the equity owner if a sale can be made within a reasonably short time span, but it also limits the length of the holding period within which a profitable sale can be made.

In example, the increase in land value from $5,000 per acre to $8,500 over three years represents slightly more than a 23 percent per year appreciation rate. The returns shown in the example are hardly adequate to justify the substantial risk involved. There is little assurance that a favorable sale can be consummated within the time span to achieve optimum profits. Some investors feel that land values must *double* every three years to justify the risk. While the risk *is* quite high for an investment in undeveloped land, the right combination of growth factors can provide higher profit margins than from any other kind of real estate venture.

TIMING

Timing is the key to success in holding land for profitable resale. The longer land is held, the greater the holding costs. Appreciation does not increase land values at a steady rate. Rather, increases come in spurts as potential use changes. Over a period of years, a tract of land may proceed through a whole litany of potential uses. It may first be suitable for single-family residences, then for higher density housing, then for light commercial use, then for a high-traffic shopping center or office building, and finally for high-rise structures. With each change in potential use, the land value jumps upward. So the basic question is: At what point can a specific piece of land be sold with a maximum differential between its cost (plus holding charges) and its selling price? The answer depends on the local situation. Astute landowners try to project the length of time until the next change in usage may occur, then decide if the costs of holding will be justified by the resulting increase in value.

The appreciation described here should be distinguished from the appreciation in value that is more and more being created by inflation. There is little real gain to an investor from inflation. The rise in land value attributable to inflation is offset by the loss in purchasing power of the dollars realized at the time of sale. To create profit, land values must increase at a greater rate than that induced by inflation.

HOLDING LAND

There is no requirement that a land investor—or "speculator," if you prefer—must stand idly by and wait for the land to increase in value. On the contrary, many dealers in land find it advantageous to make some use of the land during the holding period. There are a number of ways for the landowner to recover at least some income from the property to help pay the taxes. The problem is to find a use for the land that neither encumbers it with a long-term lease commitment, nor alters the land itself in a way that could discourage a higher use later on.

Following are some suggestions for interim land use, which have general application in all regions. Note, however, that what is practical for a particular tract of land depends on its location and nearby population density.

1. Recreational facilities—pitch-and-putt golf courses, playing fields for rent, kiddie land parks, or small race tracks.
2. Parking lots—a standard holding procedure for high-value downtown land.
3. Carnivals, rodeos, and other special shows may rent land for short-term periods.
4. Mobile home parks in some areas have been used as a good way to "warehouse" land. Utilities can be designed for higher land use at a later time.
5. Golf courses—used by some large developers to hold land for later development.
6. Farming partnerships for crop production, with season-to-season leases.
7. Timber can be harvested and logs sold for firewood from forested tracts.

8. Sod or turf production for replanting can be developed on land that is not intended for further use as farm land.

It is the local demand for usable land that best determines what interim use is most practical. In some cases the temporary use develops sufficient profit to justify continuing its operation. There is always the possibility that the higher use for the property may not materialize, and the interim use may be the only viable alternative. So even if the landowner must make a sacrifice to accommodate an interim use, it is a good hedge against the future if the cost is not too great.

LAND DEVELOPMENT

Land may be acquired for holding; it also may be acquired for development. For the purpose of this discussion, *development* includes building streets and installing utility systems to service houses or commercial buildings that may be constructed at a separate time. Land development is an integral part of the design and construction work involved in most large apartment complexes and many commercial projects. Small builders, however, depend on developers to do the land planning, construct the service facilities, and then sell the finished lots to others.

Financing land development is an easier procedure than financing the acquisition of raw land. Savings associations, which must classify a loan for undeveloped land as "commercial" (that is, nonresidential) in their loan portfolios, can consider a development loan as "residential" if that is the obvious plan for the land's development. As indicated in Chapter 7, the savings association's charter requirements and tax advantages strongly favor residential-type loans. Savings associations have an additional incentive to finance development projects for houses: their initial financing puts them in a "first refusal" position to supply the financing for construction loans to the builders and permanent loans to the home buyers. The advantages that accrue to a savings association from maintaining a close relationship to a development project apply equally to all lenders. But, commercial banks and some insurance companies—which *will* make land development loans and building construction loans because they are short-term (less than three years)—are not so interested in making longer term loans to the home buyers.

Another relationship that has developed between large institutional lenders and land developers is the joint venture. The lender makes a sound loan for the development and acquires a continuing market for its financial services. The developer has access to capital resources that might not otherwise be available to handle a large development project.

An interesting angle on land development can be seen by looking at the permissible loan limits. Depending on the lender, the maximum loan may range from 60 percent to 80 percent of the land's value. When acquiring undeveloped land, these loan limits mean that the buyer must put up 20 percent to 40 percent of the *acquisition* cost. In a development loan, the lender will generally accept an appraised value of the *finished* lots as the land value. The cost of the land, plus the cost of development of that land, should not exceed 75 percent of the finished lot price. Therefore, an 80 percent loan based on a finished lot price could provide a loan in excess of the acquisition cash expended by the developer. In practice, however, most lenders prefer to limit the loan amount to the actual cash needed to pay for the land and to build the streets and utilities. For experienced and reputable developers, the loan limits can amount to a 100 percent loan!

Mortgage Clauses

A land development loan is usually made with a mortgage lien in favor of the lender covering the entire tract of land. Two covenants that have special application to a development loan are involved. These are the plan used for development and the requirements for partial release of the completed lots.

The Development Plan.   In some cases, the lender specifies the order in which the mortgaged property can be developed. The purpose is to assure the continuing value of the entire tract during the development period. The plan must be agreeable to the borrower-developer and is generally a logical procedure to encourage a complete development.

The Release Clause.   The initial mortgage on the entire development tract must provide a mechanism to permit the sale of lots to others as the lots are developed. This is most commonly accomplished by requiring a minimum payment of cash to the lender for each lot released. The minimum required payment, for example, may be 85 percent of the initial price of the finished lots, plus 50 percent of any amount realized in excess of the original price. The lender's purpose is to obtain full repayment of the loan before the last—perhaps marginal—lots can be sold. Thus, much of the developer's profit can be tied up until the entire project is sold out.

Lots

The discussion of finished lots applied to land that is developed for the purpose of constructing buildings. Not all lots offered for sale are developed; that is, suitable for building. In some states—primarily

Florida, Arizona, and California—developers have acquired large tracts of land in relatively remote areas and divided them into lots of from one to ten acres each. These lots are then offered for sale through mass advertising programs, with small down payments and the balance in monthly payments over five to ten years. Many of these tracts are years away from practical development and have disappointed many buyers.

To prevent misrepresentation and outright fraud in this type of land sale, Congress created the Office of Interstate Land Sales Registration (OILSR) in 1968 to operate under the Department of Housing and Urban Development (HUD). The OILSR has since established specific rules and requirements under which land developers may offer their lots for sale. Severe penalties can be assessed against developers for failure to comply with the requirements. Essentially, the requirements call for full disclosure of information regarding the landownership, tax rates, proximity of schools, available utilities, and plans for future development. The development plans become a part of the sales package; if promised, completion is mandatory. However, the OILSR requires only that the facts be presented to the buyer; it is then up to the buyer to appraise the value offered. If the entire development tract is tied up in a master mortgage lien that cannot be released for, say, another ten years, the sale of an individual lot is permissible as long as that fact (and all others) is disclosed.

Government regulations of this type are not directed towards the prudent investor who examines in detail all aspects of a property and always inspects the property before signing a contract to buy. The purpose of these regulations is to protect the general public from unscrupulous promoters.

TAX TREATMENT FOR THE SUBDIVISION OF LAND

A tract of land that is subdivided into individual lots or parcels for sale or exchange is entitled to capital gains treatment of the proceeds if certain conditions are met. The qualifications for capital gains treatment are as follows:

1. The landowner cannot be a dealer in real estate.
2. Improvements cannot be made to the lots to enhance their value, nor can such improvements be made a part of the contract for sale.
3. The property must have been held for five years prior to the sale, unless it was acquired by inheritance (heir) or by will (devisee).
4. The owner cannot offer the subject lots—or any other real estate—for sale in the ordinary course of his trade or business.

5. If the sale is for less than six lots, the entire amount of the gain is treated as a capital gain. If the sale is for six lots or more, 5 percent of the selling price of the sixth lot and all additional lots are taxed as ordinary income.

Capital gains treatment for the sale of lots is confined to the small land-owner who disposes of an occasional tract of land no more often than every five years.

32

Leasing and Operating Income Properties

The leasing of space for use by others is the major source of revenue from an income property investment. There are three principal forms of leases used:

1. *Term lease*—generally of limited duration with fixed monthly rentals that allow periodic escalation. Suitable for apartments, office buildings, shopping centers, and warehouses.
2. *Net lease*—the burden of building management is passed to the tenant with the rental payment calculated for a return on the landlord's investment covering only very limited services, if any. Most appropriate for use in any type of building with a single tenant.
3. *Percentage lease*—rental payments are based on a percentage of the tenant's gross *sales*, usually with a base rental required and escalation permitted. Can be used with tenants selling merchandise but more difficult to administer where services are sold.

Further discussion of the three lease procedures follows.

TYPES OF LEASES

Term Lease

The *term lease* is also called a "gross lease" or a "flat sum" lease. Lease payments are made periodically—usually monthly—at a constant rate. The lease term is short, from one month to perhaps three years in length. The basis for the rental payment is the size of the space and its location. Rent may be based on the number of square feet of space or on the frontage available. Or it may be simply a flat sum that is acceptable to both landlord and tenant. Rent under a lease "by the month" can be readily increased to offset the property owner's cost increases. A one-year or longer lease can provide for an automatic increase each year or two, or it can contain an escalation clause.

The services provided for tenants by the landlord vary with the lease conditions, but commonly include the exterior maintenance of the building and parking lots, furnishing of all or a part of the utilities, trash disposal, and payment of all taxes and insurance for the building (but not its contents). It is these services that have shown erratic cost increases and have popularized the use of general escalation clauses in all kinds of leases, particularly for term leases at otherwise fixed rentals.

Escalation Clauses.   In more stable, less inflationary periods (generally prior to 1970), the use of escalation clauses in lease agreements was confined to covering an increase in taxes and insurance. Now there are almost no limits to the types of cost that may be included under escalation clauses. The reason, of course, has been the uncertainty of future costs generated by continuous high levels of inflation. Landlords are wary of long-term commitments to furnish space and services to tenants, because future costs are not determinable. As a result, the term lease often allows for annual adjustment in rent to compensate for increases in taxes, insurance, utilities, maintenance, and management. To provide a measure of protection for the tenant, the escalation provision usually requires the landlord to produce (1) some form of documentation of increases in operating costs and (2) details on how these costs are being allocated to each tenant. This allocation can be done on a basis of the square footage under lease or as a percentage of the space actually occupied in the building. Escalation clauses have gained acceptance to some degree because they permit the landlord to fix rental payments close to actual operating costs, rather than to guess at future cost increases and inflate present rentals to protect against those increases.

Net Lease

A *net lease* pays a net return to the landlord (generally computed solely on the amount invested), while the tenant pays all costs, including taxes and insurance. The existence of a net lease is usually seen by the IRS as evidence of property that is held for investment, rather than for trade or business. The net lease is favored by investors who construct or buy buildings for lease to a major tenant such as a discount store, a super-market, a service station, or a major department store. The landlord—as the owner—retains the right to all tax benefits available to property owners, unless the lease is for a term longer than 30 years. The IRS, for tax purposes, may attribute ownership to the tenant if the lease term exceeds 30 years.

There is some variation among real estate professionals in the way they use the word "net" when talking of a lease. One interpretation is that the single word "net" means that the tenant pays all expenses *except* taxes and insurance. The term "net, net" means the tenant pays all expenses *and* the insurance. "Net, net, net"—or "triple net"—means what has already been described as a net lease; that is, the tenant pays all costs, including taxes and insurance.

Escalation clauses are generally included in those net leases which require the landlord to pay for either taxes or insurance. Otherwise, the lease is generally written to provide a fixed return for the investor over the term of the lease.

Percentage Lease

The most common lease form for stores and shopping centers is the *percentage* lease. Rental payments are based on gross sales figures, not on any computation of profit. The use of sales figures to determine rental charges is most common for stores where products are sold, rather than where services are rendered (which occurs most often in office buildings). Sales figures can be easily verified through (1) a lease clause that permits the landlord to audit the tenant's records or (2) a certified copy of the tenant's sales tax reports.

There are three ways that rental can be computed in a percentage lease:

1. Straight percentage of gross sales.
2. Minimum base rental *plus* a percentage of gross sales.

3. Minimum base rental *or* a percentage of gross sales, whichever is larger.

A minimum rental is desirable, as it provides the landlord with the protection of an assured income to cover mortgage payments and operating costs. Without a minimum, it is possible for a tenant to achieve a volume of sales that gives an adequate profit but does not provide the landlord with sufficient rental to cover the costs of leasing the space.

An escalation clause appears in most percentage leases, but is usually more flexible than a term lease's escalation clause. After all, under a percentage lease any increase in sales prices due to inflation (or any other cause) should result in an increased rental payment. Most commonly, the escalation provision adds to the minimum rent requirement all or part of any increases in taxes, insurance, or other agreed upon expenses. The escalation clause may permit the tenant to *recapture* an increase in the minimum rent (if due to escalation of costs) when the percentage rent exceeds certain specified levels.

Percentage leases give the shopping center owner a good incentive to cooperate with the tenants in advertising and promoting the center. Careful tenant selection and judicious placement of the stores within the center can achieve maximum benefit of the shopping traffic; greater sales can thus be realized.

Typical Rental Percentages

The following list of major types of stores shows a typical percentage range for leasing each type. Rents vary considerably in different areas of the country and even within a local community. However, the percentages *do* give some indication of how landlords determine the rental structures and what rates have been generally acceptable to various classes of store owners. The right to recapture payments for taxes, insurance, or other expenses is found most often in larger leases and is noted in the table as "Recapture."

Type of Business	Normal Percentage
Convenience markets (small)	4% to 6% Recapture
Supermarkets	1 1/2% to 2% to minimum Recapture. Then 1% after minimum
Department stores	2% to 3 1/2% Negotiable
Discount houses	1% to 1 1/2% Recapture
Drug stores	2% to 4% with exclusions for low-margin items

Restaurants and fast foods	5% to 6%. Can drop to 3% to 4% after minimum
Liquor stores	4% to 6% Recapture
Barber shops, beauty shops, services	7% to 10%
Hardware stores	4% to 6% Recapture
Auto supplies	3% to 5%
Sporting goods	5% to 7%
Men's stores and women's stores	4% to 6%
Shoe stores	5% to 6%
Gift stores	7% to 10%
Toy stores	4% to 5%
Service stations	3¢ to 8¢ per gallon

Leases Adjusted by Cost-of-Living Index

In some areas of the country, rentals are subject to periodic adjustment based on an index referred to in the lease agreement. Since this kind of arrangement is not subject to regulation except in those places and properties subject to rent control laws, there are a variety of methods in use. A tenant is better protected with an agreement that ties an adjustment in rent to a published cost-of-living index; that is, one not subject to the landlord's discretion. In a few cases, notably some New York office leases, the rent is adjusted by the owner's "cost-of-living" figures. Such discretionary adjustments can foster unfair abuses.

POINTS TO CONSIDER IN A LEASE

The relationship between a tenant and landlord is initially established by the lease agreement. The more problems that can be anticipated when a lease is drawn up, the better likelihood that they can be minimized with point-by-point agreement in the lease covenants. Always of concern in a lease arrangement is the allocation of responsibilities and of the expenses incurred in the operation—Who pays for what and when? The following discussion considers the major areas of concern.

Lease Covenants

Lease conditions determine *who* pays for *what*. Following is a point-by-point consideration of the relevant expense allocations:

Taxes.   Except under a net lease with special terms, property taxes are paid by the owner. Some leases call for an escalation in the rental structure if taxes increase. The exact responsibility for payment should be spelled out in each lease, including (1) whether the tenant pays all, some, or none of the base year's taxes, (2) when taxes are paid, and (3) how taxes are paid. If the tenant's operations create an increase in the tax assessment, this should also be anticipated by the lease. (Any taxes due on the tenant's property may become a claim against the landlord if protection is not provided.)

Insurance.   The landlord usually pays for hazard insurance for his own property. A tenant *does* have a right to know how his leasehold interest is being protected against loss, and he may require the landlord to provide to him a copy of the insurance policy. If the cost of insurance increases, the increase may be prorated to the tenant in accordance with an escalation clause. If the activities of the tenant create an increased risk for the property, the resulting increase in insurance cost may be passed on to the tenant.

Other types of coverage must be considered in lease agreements. The landlord may require that the tenant maintain liability insurance with a protective clause in favor of the landlord. If plate glass is a part of the premises, a separate insurance policy may be required (it can be the responsibility of either the landlord or the tenant). Any other special risk or exposure that must be covered should be spelled out in the lease agreement.

Maintenance.   Under the normal division of costs between a landlord and tenant in rental property, the landlord pays for exterior maintenance and the tenant pays for interior maintenance. But the line between "exterior" and "interior" is not always easy to define; it needs to be defined in the lease. Such things as electric-eye operated doors, exterior lighting for the special use of the tenant, trash and garbage areas, and exterior protective screens or walls used only by the tenant are all subject to dispute if maintenance requirements are not clearly detailed in the lease.

Parking.   The lease agreement should detail the tenant's rights to parking facilities, both for employees and for customers. Furthermore, the lease should allocate the costs of lighting and upkeep for the parking area (in whatever shares may be agreed upon by the parties). Additional charges on a "per car" basis are sometimes written into lease agreements, especially for office buildings. Or employees may be offered parking privileges in exchange for a pay reduction, the amount depending on the accessibility of the space. At large shopping centers, the common practice is to set aside a specific area—away from major customer traffic patterns—which is reserved for employee parking.

Improvements and Trade Fixtures.   A least should specify who pays for improvements and who pays for trade fixtures. Normally, improvements are made by the landlord and added to the rental price. Improvements remain the property of the landlord. Trade fixtures usually belong to the tenant, are paid for by the tenant, and may be removed by the tenant at the termination of the lease. Trade fixtures installed by the landlord may become a part of the leased premises as a sales inducement for the tenant. If so, the landlord's ownership should be clearly determined in advance. Structural changes in the building may be agreed upon, but are generally not a part of the tenant's leasehold rights.

Terms, Payments, and Conditions.   The term of the lease should be clearly stated, as should the date or time that rental payments become due. Different payment times may apply to a base rent and to a percentage (or gallonage, in the case of a service station), so as to allow time for computation or verification. If the lease permits any adjustments in rental payments (such as the recapture of tax and insurance payments against a percentage over base rent), *when* these adjustments are allowed should be clarified in the lease. And it should specify the time that any escalation payments become due.

Many other conditions that limit leasehold rights may be included in the lease. The lease may or may not be *assignable*. If it is assignable, what are the continuing obligations of the original tenant? The lease should say. Limitations are usually placed on how the property may be used, as a protection to other tenants and to the landlord's continuing property value. Further, the right to *sublet* all or part of the leasehold interest may or may not be granted under the original lease.

Utilities and Other Services

Utilities and various other services are still very much an accepted part of the covenants found in an income property lease. But increasingly they are excluded from the obligations of the landlord. Landlords once paid for almost all utilities, arguing that utilities could be furnished to tenants most cheaply through the use of a single master meter. Today that practice has given way to separate meters for each tenant or to a strict allocation to each tenant of the month-to-month costs. Rapidly rising utility costs are, of course, the reason.

Landlords are also attempting to shed their obligations for as many nonutility services as possible.

Utilities.   Included in the category of utilities are electricity, natural gas, water, and sewer facilities. The trend among landlords is to pass on these expenses to their tenants.

Electricity is most easily separated from the landlord's responsibility through the use of a separate meter, very much as telephone service is separated. Industrial properties, warehouses, and other free-standing, single-tenant rental properties have long used separate meters to allow the tenant to pay electric charges. Apartment owners tried for awhile to use a single meter, furnishing electricity to tenants as a part of the services provided under their basic rental payment—but abuse and escalating costs have changed all of that. New apartment houses are including separate meters for each apartment, and older units are converting to separate meters where possible. When conversion is not practical, landlords usually allocate the single-meter costs so that each tenant pays a proportionate part of the total cost. Office buildings generally have not moved to the use of separate meters, but most do include escalation clauses in leases so that cost increases are allocated among the tenants.

Natural gas is not always a necessity for apartments and office buildings. But when gas is used, it is generally handled in much the same way as electricity; that is, separate meters for new buildings and allocation of cost increases for older buildings with single meters. Industrial and commercial use of natural gas is almost always measured through separate meters since it is more often a processing component than a landlord-provided service.

Usable *water* is far more precious today than it was only a few years ago. Yet even now few lease agreements for apartments, office buildings, or small commercial buildings call for separate metering of water. Rental increases in term leases and escalation clauses in commercial leases, generally have been sufficient protection for the landlord to justify continuing this service as part of the leasehold rights. Large commercial properties and industrial buildings are more easily adapted to separate water metering, and they usually do provide this separation.

Sewer facilities are usually provided (and charged for) by the same entity that furnishes water, often a municipally owned utility plant. Not too many years ago, sanitary sewer lines and storm sewers were an accepted part of a community's service to the taxpayer. Now sewer costs are skyrocketing and more and more often are included in utility bills as an additional charge.

Janitorial Services.

Sweeping, cleaning, and polishing public areas are services found in shopping centers, apartments, and office buildings. In addition, office buildings often provide the same service for tenants' office space. Older lease forms usually included this kind of maintenance as a part of the building services covered by the basic rental fee. Now some landlords are assessing these costs as a separate monthly maintenance charge that is determined by the costs incurred. Office buildings that provide cleaning services for the tenants' offices include this cost in escalation clauses.

Maintenance Service.   Plumbing and electrical repairs, painting, and other building repairs are normally the responsibility of the landlord. Lease provisions define the tenant's area of responsibility (usually interior maintenance) *and* the landlord's. As maintenance costs increase, the landlord may want to include repairs in the escalation clause, thereby permitting an increase in rent to cover the added costs. The need for repairs is unpredictable—unlike cleaning services—so they are not as easily translated into a monthly service charge. However, some leases allow for an all-inclusive service charge that includes repairs as they become necessary.

Heating and Air Conditioning.   With some forms of income property—such as warehouses, shopping centers, and other commercial buildings—it has long been possible for the landlord to require that the tenant furnish, install, and maintain the heating and air conditioning equipment. Naturally the rental structure in these cases reflects the landlord's low investment, but the tenant is responsible for the maintenance expense and the potential of lost sales (as would occur if a store's air conditioning failed for an extended period of high summertime temperatures). In an office building with multiple occupancy, heating and air conditioning are considered part of the services offered to the tenant. The general practice is to include maintenance of this equipment in escalation clauses, allowing for annual increases.

Trash Disposal.   This is an optional service that may be assigned to either the landlord or the tenant, depending on the terms of the lease. The disposition of trash has become a more and more difficult problem—suitable dumping grounds are becoming scarcer and farther removed from the source of the trash. However, there has been some recognition of the salvage value in trash, and a few companies have devised their own procedures for separating usable materials from waste. Office buildings that contain large accounting operations—and, thus, large quantities of waste paper—may recover marketable materials through a simple sorting of the trash. Printing shops produce high-quality waste paper. Restaurants and bars may have a sales potential for old cans and even glass bottles. While trash disposal is still commonly seen as an expensive nuisance, there is a growing trend for both landlord and tenant to take a closer look at what trash is being produced and to investigate the potential for selling the material.

Security Systems.   Alarmed by the increasing incidence of vandalism, assaults, and robbery, all forms of business activity have sought better methods to protect their investments. This is another service that may be the responsibility of either the tenant or the landlord. In practice, only large office buildings consider security to be the landlord's responsibility; even then, the landlord accepts no liability. Shopping centers often provide for security through a merchants' association, where each contributes a portion of the cost of maintaining a security system. Buildings with a single tenant or a small number of tenants have considered security wholly the responsibility of the tenant(s) and usually do not refer to the subject in leases. However, security is a matter of growing concern, and one that should be defined in all lease covenants.

While landlords have preferred a "hands off" approach to security, a property owner is well-advised to cooperate with the tenant in furnishing property protection. Fire warning systems can reduce both insurance premiums and the potential for loss. Sonic monitors detect sound and movement in or on the premises under the scanning instrument and then sound an alarm. Electric eyes and laser beam–type instruments can detect break-ins and possibly prevent or reduce property damage from vandalism or robbery. Centrally located control monitors manned by computers have reduced the cost of surveillance to the point where even very small companies (and homeowners) may find the service attractive.

LEASING NEW PROPERTIES

Most problems that must be resolved in a lease agreement occur whether the property has been previously occupied or is a new building awaiting its first tenant. For new properties, however, some additional questions—involving the final steps of construction and finishing out the premises to be leased—must be considered. Initial lease-up requires that both the investor-owner (landlord-to-be) and the leasing agent have a good knowledge of construction procedures and current costs. For instance, the leasing agent's promise to add an interior wall or alter a plumbing installation may appear inconsequential and, thus, inexpensive. But the addition or alteration may require changes in other areas of the building that substantially increase the cost. The following discussion focuses on the principal areas of concern in completing a new building to suit a tenant's special requirements. The general guidelines offered here apply to all newly constructed income properties, with one exception. Apartments are almost always finished (carpeted, painted, wallpapered, fixtures installed) *before* leasing unless the tenant is permitted to select the color of walls and carpeting.

Planning

If a building is preleased, the future tenant normally is deeply involved in the planning details. Any plan changes can be made before construction is completed, and any resulting addition or reduction in costs can be built into the rental structure. A common alternative procedure is for the landlord to agree with the tenant on a basic plan for the building and then charge the costs of any alterations directly to the tenant. A cost overrun on a preleased building is almost impossible for the landlord to recover and must be prevented if at all possible. The best preventive medicine is planning carefully and requiring that tenant-created alterations be paid for by the tenant.

For buildings that are constructed on a speculative basis (that is, without preleasing), planning should proceed only to the extent of providing basic minimum requirements. This is termed a *shell*, since the building at this point has exterior walls and roof, but no ceiling, perhaps no floor, no interior finishing, no utility outlets, and no interior walls. Leasing a shell to a new tenant requires detailed planning of exactly what the tenant requires and how the costs of installation will be allocated. Two basic procedures are used to assess completion costs to the new tenant. One is to pass the full cost directly to the tenant (who may even handle his own subcontracting for the work); the other, to allocate costs on a per unit basis (that is, so much for each additional running foot of wall, so much for each new electrical outlet, and so on). The following sections discuss the components that are most commonly furnished by the tenant on newly constructed buildings.

Interior Walls.   The design of office, shop, or warehouse space is best handled by the tenant who will be using the space. The building design, of course, limits the location of interior walls that will conform with the load-bearing columns or walls which support the roof. Within these limits, nonbearing walls and dividers may be located in the way that best serves the tenant's requirements. In office buildings, the most common method of passing on this cost to the tenant is to charge for each running foot of wall. The lease agreement may, for example, permit the tenant to install 200 feet of nonbearing wall under the basic rental price. Any additional wall might be charged to the tenant at $20 per foot. (Actual prices vary substantially.) Shopping centers and warehouse buildings are more apt to make a flat charge for additional walls, based on the contractors' construction bids.

Ceilings.   Ceilings are not enclosed in new construction until the property is leased because of the need to locate lighting and air conditioning outlets at required positions (which in turn depend upon the interior wall arrangement). The cost of the ceiling is generally not a separate charge in office buildings because the owner knows that the amount of the ceiling will be the same as the square footage to be leased. In shopping centers it is not unusual to ask tenants to furnish their own ceilings (with appropriate adjustments in rent), so that they may tailor the design of ceiling, lighting, and air ducts to best suit their marketing needs. Warehouses and industrial buildings normally do not require ceilings.

Concrete Floors.   With the exception of large shopping centers and some warehouse space, floors are completed prior to leasing. The reason these exceptions wait until a tenant is obtained is to permit the installation of underground plumbing, electrical outlets, and any special piping or wiring needed by the tenant. If the floor is for warehouse use, the tenant may require a stronger than normal floor to support unusually heavy loads. When flooring is constructed to meet a tenant's special requirements, the cost is usually assumed by the tenant.

Utility Outlets.   Most tenants have special requirements for the location of each utility service outlet, including electricity, water and water drainage, natural gas (if needed and available), and telephone outlets. In an office building, the normal procedure is to charge a flat fee for each outlet, based on the cost of installation. The flexibility that a new tenant has to lay out his space in the most effective manner is a major advantage of the newly constructed building.

Doors.   The location of interior doors for a newly constructed building can usually be determined by the tenant. If a tenant requires special doors or more doors than are anticipated by the initial plans, he is charged with the additional cost.

Interior Finishing.   Painting or wallpapering interior walls, the installation of lighting, and any other required finishing are normally the responsibility of the tenant in commercial leases. The landlord may insist that he approve any plans for finishing to be undertaken by the tenant. Most new office buildings and a few new apartments have some finishing requirements that will provide a uniform exterior appearance. The office building owner may supply drapes or require a certain pattern for window shades or blinds. For carpeting, wall coverings, and paint, the building may offer a selection of several basic color combinations that can be installed at the landlord's expense; variations may be charged to the tenant.

MANAGEMENT OF INCOME PROPERTIES

All income properties require management—some more, some less. An operating property is a form of business that requires the collection of rents, the keeping of records, and the protection and maintenance of the property itself. The investor must either hire outside management or be willing to spend his own time handling the management responsibilities. These responsibilities are (1) maintenance of the premises, which includes both repairs and capital improvements; (2) securing, screening, and locating tenants in the most effective way; (3) supervising all operating personnel; and (4) controlling the use of the premises by tenants and their customers.

Maintenance of the Premises

Income properties are usually maintained, at least in part, by the landlord or owner. Even though tenants may be responsible for maintaining interior walls and some of the heating or air conditioning equipment, the landlord should specify minimum maintenance standards. Various levels of maintenance are required, depending on the type of property and the conditions of the lease. Because of this flexibility, maintenance duties should be detailed in the lease agreement; for example, how often the tenant can require exterior painting.

As for capital improvements, such as the replacement of an air conditioning unit or the addition of a new sales area, the management must have written guidelines in the lease (or drawn from the leases) in order to make a fair allocation of costs to the tenants. An addition to the premises of one tenant may conflict with the premises of another, so the rights of the tenants need to be settled in advance.

Securing and Screening Tenants

Securing occupancy of a building may be done through leasing agents or through the owner's advertising and sales representation. The quality of tenants is always a major problem for the landlord and can easily determine an operation's success or failure. The quality of tenants must fit the use intended for the building; that is, the type of work and services they perform must be compatible, and the customer groups they serve must be similar. An office building catering to the medical profession is not a suitable location for a nightclub. A shopping center with predominantly low prices and discount stores is not attractive to an exclusive dress shop.

Tenants of all types must be screened for financial responsibility. Major companies are often the preferred risk, of course. But in fact most tenants are small—as well as new to the area when the initial lease is consummated—and they should be investigated for their previous records of operations and credit-worthiness. Evicting an undesirable tenant can be expensive and can be avoided by careful advance screening.

Both tenant and landlord have an interest in where an office, shop, or storage facility is located within a building complex. The choice of location can be based on (1) the flow of customer traffic (most important for a shopping center), (2) the availability of required utilities, or (3) the ease of access to transportation or to the handling of materials. Naturally the choice of locations is more flexible in a new building than in an existing building, and immediate optimum use of the space is easier to accomplish. With an existing property that has tenants, it may be desirable to reject even a highly qualified prospective tenant if locating that tenant in the only space available could jeopardize future operations and leasing.

Supervision of Operating Personnel

Property owners often try to avoid becoming burdened with personnel problems—payroll records, personal problems, the complex set of equal employment and labor relations laws, and the need for constant supervision. Large income properties can afford to employ highly competent, professional managers to handle personnel responsibilities. Medium-sized and smaller operations may prefer to use contract management companies, which are growing rapidly all over the country and provide much needed expertise. And small property owners may simply serve as their own managers, aided by one or two maintenance and service employees.

Using service contractors is another growing method of avoiding the problems of directly employing people. Many services can be furnished by contractors, including janitorial service, maintenance of heating and air conditioning equipment, periodic and minor plumbing repairs, painting, and window washing. Many large cities have contracting companies that provide all-inclusive services for operating properties.

Control Over the Use of Premises

One of the most difficult management responsibilities is that of controlling how the premises are used after leases have been signed. A loosely drawn lease may leave a tenant free to operate his shop or office any way he sees fit. A leasehold does grant the rights of possession and use, but the landlord retains the right to protect his property against the loss of value that may result from misuse. Limits on use may be (1) spelled out in the lease, (2) based on customary use, or (3) negotiated between the building management and the tenant. Careful advance planning is the best procedure to prevent conflicts in this area. Unfortunately, even careful planning is not fail-safe—businesses change, and sometimes their products or services are changed by market requirements. When things do change, the interpretation and settlement of conflicting situations becomes a management responsibility. For example, a tenant restaurant which replaces its piano bar with pornographic entertainment can diminish the value of the property for other tenants—and for the management. But pornography has proven difficult to define, even by the courts. So management must walk a thin line in dealing with the change. Consider one more example. The introduction of a new chemical process or electronic testing procedure—which may later prove hazardous to occupants, customers, or the building itself—is always of concern to an alert management.

The tenant's customers are even more difficult to control, and sometimes necessitate security agreements in the lease. This is especially true for large shopping centers, which can become hangouts for undesirable characters. This problem must also be considered as the landlord examines prospective tenants and the types of automobile and pedestrian traffic they are likely to attract to the premises.

33

Apartment Projects

INTRODUCTION TO INCOME PROPERTY

Each class of income property has peculiarities in marketing its particular services and in its operations. The previous chapter was devoted to information that applies generally to all classes of income properties. The balance of the chapters in this section will focus on the more specialized nature of each major class of property investment. How does one decide which is best? There are many considerations. Personal preference, previous experience, available financing, and local market conditions are all important. From an analytical standpoint, the market requirements are a first concern.

To begin with, the investor needs some assurance that the income property under consideration has a solid and continuing market. This requires a market research effort. For each category of property, the market analysis uses a different approach. For an apartment, local area occupancy rates and competing rental rates are the key factors. For an office building, emphasis is on the business growth potential and the ability of the area to absorb additional office space. For shopping centers, the analysis is based on population in the area, traffic patterns, and income levels. For warehouses, the trade volume of the area is the crucial consideration.

The Value of Convertibility

Many income properties, and particularly apartments, may reflect an increased value due to the potential for conversion to another use. A single-purpose building such as a bowling alley, a fast-food franchise or free-standing restaurant, a racquet ball athletic club, and others, must be analyzed for future profitability strictly based on the continued usage as indicated. Other properties, such as an older hotel with conversion possibilities as a well-located office building, or an apartment that can find increased income through leasing of space for office or sales facilities, or possible conversion to condominiums, should be valued with an eye to the future usage.

Apartment Conversion to Condominium.   Certainly one of the more popular conversions (for landlords, not tenants) is the outright sale of individual apartment units as condominiums. Not all apartment projects lend themselves to conversion because of utility problems, legal restrictions, fire code restrictions, or other construction inadequacies. For those that can be converted, the outright sale of an older apartment project at the escalated values of housing per square foot represent a substantial capital gain for the owner plus a relief from the management problems associated with operations.

There is no question that conversion of existing apartment units offers hardships for some tenants and benefits for others. The hardships may mean moving for those tenants unable to meet a down payment requirement or the financing costs of purchase at high interest rates. The benefit for some derives in an escape from escalating rental charges plus the tax benefits that accrue to homeowners in the deduction of property taxes and interest costs from income. A number of communities have taken steps to restrict apartment conversion either through prohibitive restrictions or with requirements that offer a measure of protection for a tenant unwilling or unable to move.

INCOME ANALYSIS FOR FINANCING APARTMENTS

Apartment projects range in size from small four or five family units up to 2,500 units and more. Ownership is similarly varied with most small projects owned by individuals and the larger by groups of individuals and business organizations. With no standardized accounting procedures, the diversity of ownership results in probably the greatest variety of financial information offered with any one class of property investments. Some suggested standards for financial statement comparison are offered in Chapter 27. However, the investor is cautioned to examine operating statements with competent management persons who can offer income and expense comparisons based on their own operating experience in the local area.

As a brief review, a financial statement should offer a first line showing the gross potential income, a deduction line for vacancy and credit losses (which can be an estimate if the statement is for a proposed project), and a result line (after vacancy and credit loss) which is best identified as "Gross Operating Income" (GOI). From the GOI the fixed expenses (those items such as taxes and insurance not affected by occupancy rates) are deducted along with all operating expenses. This results in the important profit line called "Net Operating Income" (NOI). It is the NOI that best determines successful operation. The distinction here is that an overload of debt service should not be confused with operating problems.

It is the NOI that concerns the lender in tailoring a suitable loan. The NOI must be sufficient to cover the periodic payment of debt service with an acceptable margin to spare. The ratio of NOI to debt service is called the *coverage ratio*, which for apartments will run from 1.25 to 1 up to 1.4 to 1. (A 1.25/1 ratio means that a $12,500 NOI would cover a debt service payment of $10,000.)

While operating experience with apartments lacks comprehensive published statistical data, there are a few guidelines. First, occupancy requirements of about 90 percent for the local area must be met before new financing is generally available. The break-even point for modern apartment projects is at a fairly high 85 percent to 90 percent considering the high cost of financing. Second, expense ratios vary with the size, age, and management efficiency. Generally, the sum of both fixed and operating expenses compared with the Gross Operating Income (GOI) ranges from a very good 36 percent up to a mediocre 45 percent. A third percentage comparison that is popular among apartment investors is that the debt service should not exceed 50 percent of the Gross Operating Income. While many investors lean toward highly leveraged real estate investments, too high a debt ratio can be particularly hazardous with an apartment project. The nature of the tenancy allows greater fluctuations in the occupancy and income than may be found in other investments. There needs to be a reasonable margin of income between the Gross Operating Income and the expenditures for expenses and debt service. Lenders usually make such a requirement in the form of a *coverage ratio*, that is, the ratio between the debt service and the net operating income. For the investor, a reasonable margin would be about 10% of GOI. To sum up this break-down, take the gross operating income as 100%: total operating expenses including taxes and insurance should run about 42%, debt service about 48%, leaving a margin of safety amounting to 10%. Investors willing to speculate on the profit achieved from a later sale need not be concerned with this particular margin!

SPECIAL CONCERNS FOR AN APARTMENT INVESTOR

Of the major forms of income property investment, an apartment offers the most transient—and therefore most unstable—form of occupancy. Leases are often on a month-to-month basis, and termination by the tenant is seldom difficult. The *continued* high occupancy rate of an apartment is more dependent on its competitive location, management, and operating policies than are income properties held for longer term business leases. The unique problems associated with apartment properties can be summarized under the following headings:

1. Location.
2. The building and amenities.
3. Optimum mix of apartment units.
4. Rules and regulations.
5. Furnished vs. unfurnished apartments.
6. "Adults only" or "children accepted."
7. Tenants and lease agreements.
8. Government-subsidized apartment projects.

Discussion of these problems follows.

Location

An apartment is, of course, a residence. Tenants expect a reasonable proximity to schools, shopping facilities, churches, and recreational areas. In addition, the apartment dweller wants easy access to transportation (freeways, buses) and to places of employment. Some successful apartment operaters consider location the most important factor in maintaining a good occupancy rate. Others consider a good location of equal importance to sound management and an attractive building.

The Building and Amenities

An attractive, well-maintained building is obviously more desirable than a rundown property. Probably more than any other factor, the physical condition of the building and the amenities (pool, tennis courts, clubhouse) govern an apartment's rental value as it competes with other apartments in the same area. High rentals generally can be sustained by the apartment that offers better physical facilities, as long as the overall charges are reasonably competitive for the neighborhood.

Optimum Mix of Apartment Units

An essential element of continued good occupancy is the ability to offer the types of apartment which meet local market requirements. In large cities, where apartment dwellers are a growing segment of total housing, the older "shotgun" approach to variations in the units offered has given way to careful research designed to determine precisely what the market requires. In small cities, it is common to mix the number of one-, two-, and three-bedroom apartments in an arbitrary manner that should offer "something for everyone." In areas of increasing competition among apartment owners, the effort is directed along the guidelines furnished by market analysis. In an area catering to young couples and singles, the demand may be for one-bedroom or studio-type apartments, with the larger units holding low occupancy. Where the market is dominated by older couples and retirees, the best occupancy can be achieved in one- and two-bedroom units that emphasize ground floor units and few stairs. There is a growing apartment market for large families that can no longer afford to purchase or rent suitable single-family housing. Families with growing children need easy access to schools as well as three- and four-bedroom units.

When an investor uses apartment occupancy rates as a guide for additional construction, it should be noted that a distortion can occur during periods of high occupancy (generally in excess of 95 percent). Under these conditions, tenants will live in a larger, or smaller, unit than is desired, until suitable accommodations become available.

Rules and Regulations

One of the most difficult problems facing apartment management is to establish and enforce equitable rules. People object to being told that their particular life-style is disturbing to a neighbor. Yet rules are very important and are primarily for the benefit of all tenants.

All rules should be clearly explained to the prospective tenants *before* a rental agreement is concluded. The tenant has the right to know what is expected of him or her. Besides that, an understanding of the rules and the reasons for them is the first step toward good enforcement. The rules should cover how and when the public areas (such as a pool) may be used, the hours within which noise levels are restricted, the proper disposition of trash and garbage, the parking requirements, any limitations on improvements and decorating within the rented unit, restrictions applicable to pets, and any limits on the activities of children. The apartment owner should keep in mind that a major cause of moveouts is incompatibility with a neighbor. Rules can help avoid potential conflicts.

Furnished vs. Unfurnished Apartments

A choice facing all apartment owners is whether to offer furnished or unfurnished units. There are three factors involved in making this decision:

A Requirement of the Particular Market.   In some neighborhoods, essentially the only way an apartment may be rented is to offer it furnished. If a survey of the market shows generally that furnished apartments are well rented while unfurnished units are standing vacant, the apartment owner has little choice but to furnish.

To Stabilize Occupancy.   Again, the market in the area controls whether or not a furnished apartment prolongs average tenancy. Generally, tenants with their own furniture will remain longer than those without. However, many tenants see the question of "furnished or unfurnished units" as a minor consideration in the length of occupancy. More important concerns for them are (1) compatibility with their neighbors and (2) their personal situations, such as their progressing income level. With a furnished apartment, tenants tend to judge the unit by the quality of the furniture, rather than by the quality of the unit itself; an exchange of furniture can thus provide a reason for continued occupancy. Another consideration in the furniture question is that unfurnished apartments can require more decorating because of damage to walls and doors as furniture is moved in and out. Also, the unfurnished apartment presents a "bare look" to the prospective tenant, which may make it more difficult to rent.

For Additional Income.   The rental of furniture to apartment dwellers is a big business in most major cities. Many apartment owners rent furniture as a sideline business. Large operators can buy furniture at wholesale, then offer it for rent at the capitalized value of the retail price. Furniture is "personal property" for tax purposes, and it may be depreciated over three to five years. The useful life of furniture varies—living room pieces are limited to about two to three years, while bedroom furniture may be useful as long as ten years. Furniture is generally rented at a price that will pay for the furniture in about one-half of its useful life. And there is often a residual value in the repair and resale of the used furniture. The return on the investment in furniture often proves to be greater than the return on the real property.

"Adults Only" or "Children Accepted"

Most apartment owners consider that children of tenants necessitate an increase in general maintenance costs for the property. Therefore, there has been a tendency to offer apartments for "adults only" when the market will permit. Tenants have successfully fought discrimination suits in some areas of the country to overcome this form of restriction. But the results of these suits have not yet dictated a uniform pattern, and the choice remains mostly in the hands of the landlord. As with most other criteria for successful apartment operations, the choice between "adults only" and "children accepted" is determined by the market.

Tenants and Lease Agreements

One of the many important advantages that come from experience in apartment management is the ability to screen prospective tenants in a fair and reasonable manner. The problem of screening has become more difficult because of the need to be nondiscriminatory. The landlord's desire to obtain immediate full occupancy must be tempered by the longer range goal of maintaining that occupancy. Noise, objectionable use of the premises, and a tendency to vandalism are all qualities that can be detrimental to an apartment owner who has an implied obligation to maintain a reasonable living standard for all his tenants. One first-time apartment owner recently bemoaned the fact that he never realized a tenant would consider the living room carpet a suitable place to change the oil in his motorcycle!

The question of whether or not to provide a written lease has turned 180° for apartment owners. The written lease was once used to provide the landlord some assurance of continued occupancy. In recent years, the lease has become a protection for the tenant to assure a fairly stable rental rate. There are many variations in lease procedures, with a month-to-month agreement being the most common. This form provides that the rental rate and other lease conditions will continue in effect for each month of continued occupancy until termination upon, say, a 30-day notice. Renewal may then be agreed upon at a higher rental rate.

Government-Subsidized Apartment Projects

The boom in government-subsidized apartment construction between 1968 and 1971 resulted in many projects going into foreclosure and subsequently being offered for sale at government-controlled auctions. Failures resulted mostly in the FHA Section 236 program, under which sponsors had little operating experience partly because the government preferred nonprofit organizations as sponsors. For the most part the non-profit organizations had a lofty sociopolitical interest in the apartment project, but usually had little management capability and little economic incentive to control operating costs. Some of these properties are now operated by management companies with a syndicate of investors as sponsor.

The refinancing of a subsidized project is often handled by the government's providing 90 percent of the minimum acquisition price at a less-than-market interest rate. However, in exchange for its financial assistance, the government requires adherence to considerable controls over the rental structure and the manner of operation. Government supervision applies to any project that carries a government subsidy in its rental structure. Investment in such a project may provide a reasonably assured return, but one that is limited by government regulations.

RULE–OF–THUMB ANALYSIS

In order to properly analyze an apartment income property, a detailed study of all information regarding operating costs, fixed expenses, and gross income, with allowances for credit loss and vacancies, must be considered in relation to the total investment required. However, investors have developed certain guidelines that are useful in providing a quick evaluation on an apartment to determine if it is worthy of further analysis. The use of these methods varies among investors and according to practices of the area of the country in which they do business, but some of the more commonly employed ratios and evaluations can be listed as follows:

Mortgage Multiplier.   The factor that converts effective gross rent to an estimated mortgage amount ranges from four to six. For example, if a project grosses $4,500 per unit annually, it could attract a mortgage loan of $22,500 per unit if a multiplier of five is used.

Loan per Room.   The required size of a room in an apartment is not standardized. One company might consider a minimum living room size for a two-bedroom apartment to be 160 square feet with the smallest dimension being 11 feet. Or a living-dining alcove combination for a two-bedroom apartment with 200 square feet would be counted as one and one-half rooms. The average loan per room will vary from $3500 to $9500.

Gross Rent Multiplier.   This is a rule-of-thumb method for converting gross project rental income into an estimate of value or sales price.

The measure varies from 5 1/2 (or 66 months' income) to 8 times gross annual income.

Site Value Ratio.   The site value ratio is the ratio of the value of the site to the total value of land and improvements. The percentage varies from 6 to 30 percent.

TAX POINTERS ON RENTAL INCOME AND EXPENSES

There are several special considerations that apply to rental income and expenses insofar as IRS rules are concerned. Rental income is, of course, the normal monthly receipts from the leasing of apartment units. There are additional items involved as follows:

Advance rent

Any rent paid in advance must be reported as income in the tax year received regardless of the period covered or the method of accounting that is used. Advance rent may not be reduced by anticipated expenses. It is fairly normal to charge the first and last month's rent at the time of letting the space to the tenant. The rent for *both months* is income to the recipient in the tax year it is received.

Security deposits

A deposit that is held as security with the expectation of returning it to the tenant at the end of the lease is *not* considered income. However, if during any year, all or part of the deposit is claimed because the tenant has failed to live up to the lease terms, the amount claimed must be reported as income. The landlord may deduct such expenses for restoration or other costs that may have been necessitated by the tenant's failure to comply with lease terms. If a security deposit is to be used as a final payment of rent, it is advance rent and classed as income when received.

Payment for lease cancellation

Any payment by the tenant for cancellation of a lease is classed as rent and becomes taxable in the year received regardless of the accounting method used.

Payment of expenses by tenant

If a tenant pays any expenses attributable to the operation of the property, the payment is income to the landlord and must be reported.

COOPERATIVE APARTMENTS

Before enabling legislation made the condominium concept available in the various states, owner-occupied multifamily housing used the form of a cooperative. A number of large cities still have this form of housing in use, but the newer pattern is the condominium. One of the advantages that some found in the cooperative method was the discipline and control that could be exercised by the cooperative owners' associations; that is, since the unit dweller does not own the property, its use and sale can be made subject to the other owners' rules. Others found this control undesirable and much preferred the rights to use and sell their dwelling unit that a property owner has in the modern condominium concept.

There are several ways that cooperative apartments are formed. Most are organized as corporations with the owner-occupants owning shares of stock in the corporation rather than title to the property. Title is vested in the corporation. The corporation handles the management of the cooperative and insulates the individual members from direct liabilty for corporate obligations. Cooperatives may also be formed as general or limited partnerships, as trusts with the tenants as trust beneficiaries, or as a tenancy in common. None of these other forms has been very widely used because of the lack of the legal insulation which is provided by the corporate form. The tenancy in common method has been replaced by the condominium.

The Federal Housing Administration and some cities sponsor low-cost housing cooperatives that are subsidized by tax revenues. Leases in these buildings are generally for short terms (one to three years) and are not automatically renewable in case of a change in the level of public funding. Further, when a tenant sells his or her share in the cooperative, no profits may be taken. The tenant can only recover any money actually invested as a down payment, mortgage amortization, or in improvements.

The Cooperator

In the corporate form of operation, the shareholder, or cooperator, receives a lease from the corporation for the unit to be occupied. More expensive units would normally require the purchase of a greater number of shares. The cooperator does not pay rent on the lease but does agree to pay a proper share of the cost of maintenance, mortgage payments, insurance, and taxes.

If one or more cooperators fail to pay their share of the costs, the remaining cooperators must make up the difference. Partial payment on a mortgage note will not prevent a delinquency! The deductibility of mortgage interest and taxes passes to the cooperators who make up the otherwise unpaid amounts.

In today's corporate form of operation, generally the worst that can happen to a cooperator-shareholder for nonpayment of his share of costs is the termination of his lease. If the corporation fails to meet its obligations, the foreclosure cannot reach beyond repossession of the apartment building and land since the shareholder is not liable for debts of the corporation.

Financing a Cooperative Apartment

The nature of a cooperative apartment project makes it much less attractive for a developer to work with than a condominium project or an apartment offering rental units. Lenders prefer to make loans to recognized builders or developers rather than to loosely organized groups seeking to build a cooperative apartment. However, some corporations are organized for this purpose and line up their cooperator-shareholders in advance. Also, the Federal Housing Administration offers an insured loan program under Section 213 that protects lenders against losses on loans made to nonprofit housing cooperatives.

Financing is arranged initially on the entire building project and remains that way. There is no later financing of individual units as ownership of the property remains with the corporation. This is a particularly difficult problem for the cooperator desirous of selling his or her unit. As the mortgage loan is reduced through regular payments by the corporation and the value of the units increases through appreciation, the equivalent of the equity interest increases much the same as with a house or a condominium. The problem arises when the potential buyer must put up the entire amount of the equity without being able to use the cooperative unit as collateral. It cannot be pledged to obtain a loan. One possible solution is for the seller to help the buyer with financing through acceptance of an installment contract for the sale. Financing is one of the major reasons why cooperatives have given way to the condominium concept.

Operation of a Cooperative Apartment

Most cooperative apartments operate with both a board of directors and an owners' association.

Board of Directors.   Since the property ownership is vested in a corporation, it must have a duly elected board of directors. The board is elected by the cooperators-shareholders based on shares held or on a one-vote-per-apartment basis. The board is the governing body and decides how the facilities will be used, arranges for the services to be provided, and handles the assessments on the cooperators. Normally, the annual budget is submitted to all shareholders for a vote each year.

Owners' Association.   The owners' association works with the board and normally handles the direct relations with cooperators. The association and its board differ from the way a condominium association works. Most important, the cooperator's individual unit is *not* his separate property, and the association *can control* how he uses it. The basis for this control is the principle that the building is owned jointly by all cooperators for their mutual benefit. A cooperator who causes undue damage or becomes a constant nuisance can have his lease terminated by the other cooperators, usually with a two-thirds vote. In such a case it is normal to return the terminated cooperator's investment.

Another power held by an owners' association in a cooperative operation is the right to accept or reject new shareholders, or *sublessees,* if the shareholder rents his unit to another. This means that whenever a shareholder wants to sell or rent his apartment unit, he must have the approval of the board for the transaction. While this right may seem to be discriminatory on the surface, it has been upheld by the courts. The reason is that cooperators share both mutual ownership of the building and joint financial responsibility. The actions of the board cannot be taken inconsistently or capriciously.

For some dwellers, the right to uphold economic and social standards is a very attractive feature of cooperative apartments. It further has an advantage for a person who prefers living in a special environment, say, without children or pets on the premises.

Tax Treatment for Cooperators

In the past, cooperators were not permitted deductions for mortgage interest and property taxes as is allowed for houses and condominiums. The thought then was that the corporation, not the shareholders, was responsible for interest and taxes. Now the tax code has been revised to allow deductions for the cooperators if at least 80 percent of a cooperative's income is derived from cooperator-shareholder rentals. The individual cooperators may deduct their proportionate share of mortgage loan interest and property taxes. However, if the land or building is leased by another to the corporation and the fee owner pays the property taxes, it is the fee owner who can take the deduction, not the cooperators.

34

Condominiums

The ownership of a condominium as a dwelling or as a business property is of fairly recent origin. It has taken enabling legislation in each of the 50 states to properly define a condominium as a piece of real estate. Through this type of legislation, an owner holds title to a particular apartment or unit in a larger building or building complex (an improved "cube of airspace"). He or she also holds title to an undivided interest—usually as a tenant in common with other unit owners—in the land on which the building stands and in the other elements of the property which are used by the owners as a group. Condominiums may be residential or commercial (shopping centers or office buildings, for example).

Condominiums did not appear in large numbers on the housing market until the early 1960s. It was not until 1967 that all 50 states had enacted the necessary legislation to permit condominium ownership as it is known today. Condominiums account for nearly three million housing units, and some projections indicate that by the end of this century, 50 percent of the country's population will live in condominiums.

THE UNIT OWNER

In general, the owner of a condominium unit holds the same tax status of any other real property owner. That is, if the property is occupied as a personal residence, the same rules as to deductibility of interest and taxes and the nondeductibility of maintenance costs and depreciation apply to the owner of a condominium as to the owner of a single-family residence. If the condominium is used for business purposes—either all or a part of it—the same rules apply as with other forms of property. Several aspects of condominium ownership are unique and should be considered.

Mortgage Interest

The owner of a condominium may mortgage the unit, and the interest paid on such a mortgage is deductible. Since the unit owner's undivided interest in common elements is inseparable from the unit, this too would be included in the mortgage.

In most instances, the lender furnishing financing for the construction of a condominium project provides for the release of a portion of the construction mortgage as the individual units are sold, and the construction mortgage is repaid from the proceeds of the sale. Thus, there is no overall mortgage to concern the unit owner. However, there are situations—especially when an existing building is converted to a condominium—when the unit purchaser assumes a specified dollar amount of an existing overall mortgage on the premises. Under these circumstances, the *share* of interest paid on such a mortgage is deductible.

If the condominium is used as a business property, the interest is fully deductible. There is a slight possibility that a portion of interest costs could be reallocated to the unit owner's association which is discussed later in this chapter.

Real Estate Taxes

A condominium owner may deduct real estate taxes paid, or accrued, for the property the same as for any other real estate.

However, assessment procedures do vary from state to state. In some states each unit owner is assessed separately along with his corresponding percentage of ownership in the common elements. That is, a single assessment is made against each owner. In other states, the assessment is made only against the unit with no mention of the common elements. In such a case, a single assessment could be made against the common elements as a whole to be paid for by the unit owner's association. The association then assesses each unit owner his or her proportionate share of the taxes which would be deductible when paid by the owner. If some of the unit owners should default in paying their share, the other owners, as tenants in common, could deduct the share of the deficit that they paid.

In states that permit condominiums to be created on long-term leaseholds, there is often a provision for the tax assessment to be made against individual units, which creates no problem for deductibility. In states that have no such provision and the tax assessment is made against the landowner (the owner of the leased land) it is doubtful that unit owners can deduct any share of the taxes. The theory is that a lessee may not deduct taxes imposed on the lessor because this should be treated as a part of the rental payments. Such rental payments are deductible only if the property is used in business and not as a personal residence.

Maintenance, Repairs, Insurance

If a condominium is occupied as a personal residence, expenses for repairs, maintenance, or insurance are not deductible whether or not the payment is made individually or as an assessment levied by the unit owner's association. These are considered personal expenditures of a homeowner. If the unit is used, all or part, for business purposes, the same rules of prorated deductibility for expenses apply as to other real estate.

An overassessment for common expenses by a unit owner's association is generally not deductible, particularly if the association has agreed to refund such overpayment or apply it to the following year's assessment. There are administrative complications in properly informing the unit members of the time when each expenditure was paid. Thus, an overassessment can be a normal result of prudent management.

Depreciation or Cost Recovery

The unit owner may *not* deduct depreciation if the unit is occupied as a personal residence. It is deductible if the unit is used as rental property.

While the IRS distinguishes between residential and commercial rental property in determining qualification under the 1981 cost recovery procedures, the rule was not clearly designed with condominiums in mind. To qualify as *residential* rental property, the building must have at least 80 percent of its gross rental income from dwelling units. The most logical interpretation is that the unit itself comprises the building and, therefore, should qualify under its own usage category.

There is one more small problem in condominium depreciation. If the unit owner's association is considered to be a taxable entity, like a corporation, and is considered to be the owner of the common areas, there could be a question if any part of the common area is used to produce income. The IRS might attempt to allocate a portion of any depreciation claimed by a unit owner to the corporation.

Capital Improvements

An assessment for capital improvements would normally be capitalized and depreciated over its useful life if the unit is rental property. This is not permitted if the unit is used as a personal residence. Care should be taken that such an assessment is not handled as a contribution to the capital of the owners' association corporation. As such, it would be neither deductible nor depreciable for the unit owners because the corporation would hold the depreciable interest in the improvements.

Sale or Exchange of a Unit

The owner of a condominium unit used as a personal residence qualifies for all of the normal tax benefits available in the sale of this type of property. The unit is a capital asset and, if sold at a gain, the gain is taxable, but a loss is not deductible. Any gain is subject to the deferral rules of Code Section 1034 if a replacement residence is acquired (see Chapter 19) and the $125,000 exclusion available to persons age 55 or older. A personal residence is not eligible for a deferment of the capital gain tax under the rules of a property exchange.

If the unit is used for the production of rental income (or used in the owner's business), it is eligible for the same tax provisions that apply to other commercial real estate—taxes can be deferred through a property exchange, and losses in a sale may be deducted as a Section 1231 asset.

THE SPONSOR OR DEVELOPER

A sponsor or developer may engage in the new construction of a condominium project or convert an existing building to this use. The owner of an existing building may desire to convert his own building, or he may prefer to sell it to a developer who can handle the conversion. There are tax questions involved; principally, How is a gain (or loss) calculated and is it classed as ordinary income or as capital gain?

First, consider the decision of an owner to sell or convert his building. From a practical standpoint, the building would have to be worth more as condominiums than as rental property. The decision to sell or convert finds most owners opting to sell for some of the following reasons:

1. An owner undertaking conversion is more likely to find the gain treated as ordinary income rather than capital gain.
2. Conversion can be expensive and may require a considerable amount of the owner's time.

3. The owner will have to pay for conversion costs, legal fees, advertising, and promotion expenses which can be considerable.

4. Income to be realized from a conversion will take longer than it would if the property is sold to a developer.

5. The converter must help obtain financing for tenants and others who want to purchase the units.

6. There is a risk in that the total projected profit may not be realized.

Tax Questions in Conversion by an Owner

Determining capital gain

Remember that a capital gain is the difference between the adjusted basis of the property sold and the realized selling price (as reduced by selling expenses). To figure the basis of each unit sold, the basis of the entire property must be equitably apportioned to each unit. While the tax rule is that the basis should be allocated in accordance with the relative fair market values of the different portions at the time of *purchase,* as a practical matter, the allocation is more likely to be made with relative values at the time of sale. Conversion was probably not a consideration at the time of purchase of the property, and anyway, the relative values would not change that much.

EXAMPLE

An apartment building is converted to a condominium, and the owner sells one unit plus a 5% interest in the common area for $50,000. The adjusted basis of the property is $600,000, and the present value (as determined by the total asking price for all units) is $1,000,000. To determine the allocation to one unit:

$$\frac{50,000}{1,000,000} \times 600,000 = 30,000 \text{ (basis of unit)}$$

The gain is:

$$\$50,000 - \$30,000 = \$20,000$$

Ordinary income or capital gain?

The IRS has a rule to distinguish ordinary income from a capital gain which makes the determination based on whether or not the "property is held by the taxpayer primarily for sale in the ordinary course of business." Owners converting their own buildings to condominiums run a considerable risk of being perceived as engaging in the business of selling condominiums, which means any gain is taxed as ordinary income. Two telltale signs indicate if an owner converting his own building to condominium units is in the business of selling condominiums or simply realizing a gain from the sale of a capital asset. One is the probable need to make substantial improvements to the building to meet local condominium building codes before the units can be marketed. The other is the considerable amount of time the owner must spend in preparing and selling the units. So even if the building has been owned for a long period of time, the owner's act of converting and selling the units can cause a gain to be treated as ordinary income.

While the subdivision of property for sale is in itself an indicator of being in the business of selling real estate, this is not a required rule for all cases. An owner is not prohibited from maximizing profits in the liquidation of an asset through conversion to unit sales. Thus, if an owner has held the property for a long period of time, is not a dealer or broker, and expends minimal money, time, and effort in arranging for a conversion, any gain from the sale of individual units could be treated as a capital gain.

One more point: an owner subject to ordinary income tax treatment in the sale of converted units loses capital gain treatment on both the *appreciation* of the building itself as well as any profit earned from the conversion.

EXAMPLE

Jones buys a 30-unit rental building for $100,000 in 1960. In 1980 he is offered $325,000 for the building which amounts to a capital gain of $225,000 (for simplification, any change in the basis is ignored). Jones decides to convert the building to a residential condominium in 1981 and realizes a net of $600,000 after all units have been sold. The profit from the conversion amounts to $275,000 (the difference between the market value of the building at $325,000 and the net realized from the sale of the units at $600,000). Both the building appreciation of $225,000 and the profit from converting of $275,000 would be taxed as ordinary income.

THE DEVELOPER

A developer who buys an existing building and rebuilds it for the sale of condominium units is normally in the business of selling condominiums, and thus any gain is considered ordinary income. About the only possible exception to this rule would be the case of a developer converting a building and selling all of the units to one individual.

A gain on the sale of an individual unit (even though taxed as ordinary income) is the difference between the realized selling price and the *unrecovered cost of each unit*. In determining the cost of each unit, the developer is expected to use the *cost apportionment* method of accounting. That is, the cost of the entire condominium conversion must be equitably apportioned to each unit and a gain reported for each sale. The IRS has refused to permit the *cost recovery* method of accounting in reporting gain from the sale of units in the conversion of an existing rental building. The cost recovery method allows the taxpayer to defer reporting a gain on the sale of individual units until the cost basis for the whole building is recovered.

EXAMPLE

Cost-Apportionment Method

A condominium project of 60 units is constructed for a cost of $2,460,000. Total square footage of saleable space amounts to 48,400 sq. ft.

Cost per square foot:

$$\frac{2,460,000}{48,400} = 50.83$$

An 840 sq. ft. condominium is sold:

Net	$55,000
Cost apportion = 840 × 50.83 =	42,697
Gain on Sale	$12,303

NEW CONSTRUCTION

There is almost no chance of capital gain treatment for the sale of newly constructed condominium units. Even if it is a one-time venture for the taxpayer, the activity involved in building and selling a condominium is sufficient to classify the taxpayer as a dealer.

Even if the taxpayer has owned the land on which the project is constructed for a long time, the construction and selling activity would most likely throw the landowner into the classification of a dealer in respect to the project. In such a case, the taxpayer could find that this method of disposing of his undeveloped land converts a potential capital gain into ordinary income.

A landowner could avoid such tax treatment on the gain from undeveloped land by selling it to a controlled corporation or partnership which would undertake the building and selling activities. Care needs to be taken in such a land sale to ensure that no development activity takes place prior to the sale. Also, the price for the land should be close to market value, rather than a price so high as to transfer the entire gain from the sale of the units to the land value.

There is one other concern in the sale of land to a corporation for the purpose of development: the IRS may treat the sale as a contribution to capital rather than a sale. If this position is sustained, the corporation does not acquire a stepped-up basis in the land, and payments for the land on an installment contract would be classed as dividends to the taxpayer. Such a contention by the IRS is much less likely if the transfer is made to a partnership. Or, if the corporation is a Subchapter S, any recharacterization of the sale (to the corporation) would not result in double taxation. Subchapter S procedures would treat the installment payment as a nontaxable distribution to the shareholder as previously taxed income.

THE INVESTOR

Investors are often sought by condominium developers to provide equity funding for their projects. Most often the arrangement is handled as a limited partnership (the developer, usually as a corporation, is the general partner and the investors, limited partners). Or it could be arranged as a development corporation with the investor receiving shares of stock in the corporation in exchange for funding. The corporate form offers two drawbacks: (1) profits are taxed twice, as corporate income and as dividends to stockholders and (2) losses are available to the corporation but cannot be passed through to shareholders for deduction against other income.

The reason an individual invests in a condominium project is the same as a developer—the expectation of a share of the profits. There are at least two considerations: (1) profits will be received in a relatively short period of time and (2) profits most likely will be taxed as ordinary income rather than capital gain. Thus, in spite of some promotions to the contrary, investment in condominium projects cannot be classed as a tax shelter. The cost of producing the units must be capitalized rather than deducted currently, and the gain upon sale is normally taxed as ordinary income.

There are a few suggestions for a taxpayer who desires to participate in a condominium project and gain some tax advantage. One is to borrow the money to purchase the equity share—investment interest is deductible up to $10,000 ($5,000 for a married person filing a separate return) each year. Consideration could be given to the various methods of placing ownership in a trust with its limited tax liability. Also, if a substantial gain from such an investment is realized in a relatively short period of time, the taxpayer should consider using income averaging to reduce tax liability.

THE UNIT OWNERS' ASSOCIATION

Tax rules permit a condominium management association a tax exemption on income from membership dues, fees, and assessments providing it meets certain requirements. IRS Code Section 528 defines a condominium as a plan of ownership under which persons own directly a portion of the building in which they reside and the land underneath it. The units are separately owned by the members of the association, and the underlying land and commonly used improvements are collectively owned by the members. Membership in a condominium management association is usually restricted to unit owners and the developer.

Following are IRS requirements for a unit owners' association to qualify as a tax-exempt condominium management association:

1. It must elect to be treated as a condominium management association *each* tax year. This is accomplished by filing Form 1120-H, Income Tax Return for Homeowners Associations."

2. It must be organized and operated for "exempt function purposes," which means the acquisition, construction, management, care, and maintenance of association property. Association property is that owned and used beneficially by the members. Facilities, such as a meeting hall, set aside for the use of nonmembers is not association property.

3. At least 60 percent of the association's income must be "exempt function income," defined as that income derived from membership fees, dues, or assessments paid by the owners. The 60 percent rule is for qualification of the association. It does not mean that all income becomes tax exempt; only the "exempt function income" is tax exempt. Income derived from other activities, such as rental of a meeting hall to nonmembers, is considered taxable income.

   In the determination of "exempt function income," excess assessments later rebated may not be counted as gross income, nor can contributions or assessments made for capital improvements be included. What counts is that the income from the members be used for a common, noncommercial activity by the collective group.

4. Ninety percent or more of its expenditures must be for exempt purposes, which include the acquisition, construction, management, and maintenance of association property. Some of the qualifying expenditures are salaries of association managers and security personnel, street paving, property taxes assessed on association property, and the upkeep of common areas and recreational facilities. Transfer of funds to investments for future expenditure (such as the purchase of a certificate of deposit) are not "expenditures," nor are excess assessments which are later rebated.

5. No part of the net earnings of the association may inure to the benefit of a private individual. The benefit members receive from the general maintenance of the facilities is not an inurement.

6. Substantially all of the dwelling units must be used by individuals for residences. The guideline is that at least 85 percent of the total square footage be so used.

A unit owners' association that receives substantial income from the rental of facilities to nonmembers is subject to income taxation on its earnings. Surplus earnings of the association may be distributed to members in cash or in the form of reduced assessments for members. Either way, the general rule is that the distribution is a dividend and taxable to the recipient. Such a corporation with outside income may be allocated a portion of the real estate taxes and mortgage interest normally paid by the unit owners, with a corresponding reduction in the amount deductible by the unit owner. The reasoning is that taxes and insurance paid by the unit owner include the common areas, a portion of which are being used for profit-generating activities. The same position can be taken with regard to depreciation that may be claimed for units used for business purposes.

35

Office Buildings

Over the past decade the largest growth in employment has been in service-related areas—legal, accounting, banking, computer information, selling and managing real estate, and many others. The need for office space to house this market has grown accordingly. As found in other types of real estate properties, office buildings come in all sizes. Some are converted houses providing offices for doctors, attorneys, or architects. Others are small single-story, single-tenant buildings housing an engineering firm, or perhaps, a real estate office. Multitenant buildings range from a few office units to the high-rise giants that give cities their unique skylines.

FINANCING OFFICE BUILDINGS

Financing an office building depends on how and to whom the property is to be leased. If a company, such as an oil company or a major manufacturer, wishes to build for its own occupancy, financing can be arranged on the credit strength of the company, almost without benefit of the building itself as collateral for the loan.

Unlike a shopping center or store, the office building occupied by an owner produces no additional income. But rent and other operating costs can be substantially reduced through more efficient office layouts.

In financing owner-occupied buildings of large size, an alternative choice to straight mortgage financing would be the sale of first mortgage bonds through an investment banker or a mortgage banker. Acquisition of large office buildings by investing institutions, such as banks or insurance companies, is a common practice. In this way, the owners simply finance large buildings from their own investment funds.

Various local, state, and federal governments and their agencies build office buildings for their own use with legislative appropriations. But some government buildings, such as post offices, are built by private investors under long-term lease contracts and are financed through private sources.

It is the other types of office buildings that are considered here—the buildings constructed or acquired by an investor which may be either preleased or speculative. That is, tenants may be signed before construction is commenced, or the building may be constructed with the expectation of finding tenants before it is completed.

Preleased Buildings

Preleasing is generally restricted to single-tenant office buildings (built to tenant's requirements), the ground floor space in high-rise office buildings, and large users of upstairs space. A prelease arrangement offers substantial advantages for both the landlord and the tenant. The landlord can use the leases to support his applications for financing, and the assurance of one or more major tenants helps him to lease the balance of the space. An important reason for the success of several major office building developers is their ability to prelease a large portion of a new building to a major company and then name the building after that company. The business operations of the major tenant attract supporting supply and service businesses to the same location.

A big advantage for the tenant in preleasing office space is the planning and finishing of his own offices. A tenant can thus create an optimum layout of the space that best suits his individual needs.

For preleased office buildings, the leases represent solid collateral for the lender. Based on the quantity (amount of money anticipated from the leases) and the quality (the tenants' credit-worthiness) of the leases, the lender may well base the loan on the lease income rather than the cost of the completed building. However, multioccupant office buildings are generally more difficult to prelease to full occupancy in advance of construction than are shopping centers. One reason for this is that an office building must be completed in one stage whereas a shopping center is more flexible and can be developed in staged increments as space is leased. This means that large office buildings can be undertaken only by major development firms who have the cash resources and credit standing to complete the building without benefit of a high-occupancy ratio of lease income to offer as additional collateral. Smaller buildings and single-tenant office buildings lend themselves much more to the individual investor. Or perhaps an office park that can be developed in stages would be a practical alternative for a small investor.

Speculative Office Space

It follows from the previous comments regarding preleased office space that a developer with no leases in hand would have an even more difficult time obtaining proper financing. Thus, speculative office space must be financed through the builder-developer's own resources. If such independent financing can be arranged, it is quite possible to "mortgage out" the building. That is, once the building is completed and leased to a good occupancy ratio (generally 85 percent or better), a mortgage loan might be obtained in excess of the building costs as the amount of the loan would be based on the rental income. Those who build office space for speculative leasing must have some assurance that a market will exist for that space. The best first step is a market analysis, prepared by a person or firm with adequate experience in the office building field. The necessary information can be listed as follows:

1. Amount of competing space in the area.
2. Quality of competing buildings (an opinion).
3. Current rental and escalation requirements.
4. Vacancies, and reasons for vacancies.
5. Record of absorption rate in the area.
6. That portion of the market which the builder may expect to capture.

From this information, a realistic projection of rental income may be made for the speculative space. It is important to remember that rental rates depend more on the market for office space in the geographic area than on the construction costs incurred. Therefore, the market analysis must precede the final construction budget. The maximum investment in the office building should be based on the projected income, not simply on the cost of construction. And the decision to build should weigh more heavily the *rate of absorption* of new office space rather than existing occupancy rates.

ACQUIRING EXISTING OFFICE BUILDINGS

Because of the stability represented by most business tenants in an office building, this type of property has found a strong market. An investor estimating the price that can be paid for an existing building analyzes the leases through the next 15 to 20 years. As lease dates expire, the rental calculation is projected on a future increase in the rental rate. For prime properties, called *investment grade*, investors have been willing to accept returns of from 4 percent to 6 percent at times when money market returns top 15 percent. The reasoning is based on two factors: (1) rentals may be increased periodically as conditions justify and (2) the value of the property will increase at a rate greater than that of inflation.

A spur to the high value and resulting lower returns for investment-grade properties (which also includes shopping centers and some warehouse properties) has been the recent growth of interest by foreign investors and domestic pension funds. Both are seeking security of principal and are willing to accept a less than maximum rate of return. Of the two investment sources, the direct involvement of pension funds in the acquisition of real estate is of special interest. Large pension funds often utilize the expertise of money managers such as can be found in banks and life insurance companies. Banks such as First City National of New York (Citibank) and life insurance companies such as Prudential, Equitable Life Assurance Society and Aetna Life & Casualty Company have moved a step further by setting up separate real estate accounts that pool pension money to buy investment properties. These pools offer their pension fund clients a share of an entire national property portfolio. Most of the pools buy existing buildings. But the supply of investment-grade properties is somewhat limited and pension money is moving into new construction.

What this means to an investor is that the requirement for financing in the future may best be met by joining hands with one or more of the institutional investors handling pension fund money. The increased activity from this source of funds comes at a time when mortgage lenders are pulling back from fixed-interest, long-term loans and demanding a "piece of the action," a share of the income, as an additional price for making a loan.

EXAMPLE OF AN OFFICE BUILDING LOAN

The impact of high interest costs and the concern of long-term lenders for continuing inflation is strongly reflected in the loan example illustrated in Table 35-1. The loan itself is a high-ratio (90 percent) commitment for a commercial loan. Because of the interest rate offered and the long term of the loan, the lender felt justified in requiring additional participation in the property income. The terms outlined in the three features of the loan agreement are called *income participation* and are usually limited to the duration of the loan. Another form of participation by lenders is called *equity participation* and is an ownership interest that endures beyond the term of the loan.

Following are the three income participation requirements:

1. The land amounting to 100,000 square feet was purchased by the lender for $5 per square foot and then leased back to the owner of the building for a ground rental of $70,000 per year.
2. As additional ground rental, the lender took 2 percent of the gross annual income, which amounted to approximately $26,600 more.
3. With the repayment of the loan calculated on a $14 per square foot rental, the lender demanded 15 percent of any rentals earned in excess of $14 per foot as a hedge against inflation.

With the substantial participation protection available to the lender in this loan agreement, there was no requirement for personal endorsement on the part of the borrower.

TABLE 35-1

Projected Statement for Office Building

(Based on 100,000 sq. ft. net rentable space costing $60 per ft. to build—total investment: $6,000,000)

Capital Investment		
Equity investment (10%)	$ 600,000	
90% mortgage loan	5,400,000	
Total Investment		$6,000,000
Annual Operating Calculations		
Gross Scheduled Income		
100,000 sq. ft. × 14 per ft.	$1,400,000	
Less 5% vacancy and credit loss	70,000	
Gross Operating Income		$1,330,000

Annual Operating Calculations (cont.)	
Expenses:	
Operating costs including land rent @	
39% of GOI	518,700
Net Operating Income	$ 811,300
Debt service:	
13% interest for 25-year term	
Constant: .1353 × 5,400,000	730,620
Profit before participation	$ 80,680
2% of Gross Operating Income (Lender)	26,600
Cash Flow Before Taxes	$ 54,080
Return to Owner:	

$$\frac{54,080}{600,000} = 9.0133\%$$

SPECIAL CONSIDERATIONS FOR OFFICE BUILDINGS

Each type of investment property has some differences in market requirements and in certain distinguishing features that should be reviewed.

Location

One service provided by a modern office building to its tenants is access to supporting service industries. Attorneys favor locations near courthouses or major clients. Doctors locate near hospitals or other medical facilities. Main offices for banks locate near legal and accounting services. Hotels locate near good transportation systems. All of these advantages—and many more—occur in the downtown areas of major cities. "Downtown" is still the number one location for major office buildings. But since World War II, a trend away from the downtown areas has developed due to new freeway patterns and the growth of suburban areas and regional shopping centers. There are now four prime areas for office buildings:

1. *Downtown areas of major cities* (which still command the highest rentals).
2. *Airport locations.* Passenger and freight traffic generated by major air terminals has brought about a need for supporting office space to service airlines and their customers.

3. Regional shopping centers. These are not always ideal locations, but can be good if a full complement of supplemental services (bank, restaurants, apartments, and so forth) are available to tenants. An office building is best located on the periphery of a shopping center, with easy access for nonshoppers.

4. *Along freeways or heavily traveled main roads.* Urban freeways have sprouted rows of new office buildings that cater to those who appreciate their ease of access (although congestion in some "growth areas" is negating this ease of access). The majority of office workers depend on cars for transportation, and many favor locations away from the more inaccessible downtown sites. In most major cities, freeway patterns have brought large developments that integrate office buildings with shopping centers and apartment complexes, thereby catering to suburban neighborhoods.

Parking

The automobile created the need for freeways. With freeways came the growth of outlying areas, to the detriment of downtown growth. The problem has not been accessibility so much as it has been parking. Most downtown areas, locked into high-cost land use patterns, have not managed to keep pace with the growth in demand for parking space—and loss of occupancy for office buildings has been the result. Most building codes for new buildings now require certain minimum parking space for each square foot of rentable office space, which has further encouraged development in outlying areas where land costs are lower.

Most outlying office buildings and those in shopping centers offer free parking for tenants and customers. Buildings along freeways close to the downtown area, and those in the downtown area itself, usually make an additional charge for parking space to both tenants and their customers or clients.

Use of Available Space

Office buildings are most commonly leased on a "per square foot" basis. However, there are two methods of calculating the square footage that is being leased. One is the *net* leasable area, which comprises the amount of square footage within the actual perimeter of the office space being leased. The other is a calculation of the *gross* leasable area, which allocates to each space actually rented a proportionate share of the corridors, wash rooms, elevator space, and maintenance areas. This latter method is also called the *New York Plan.* The normal ratio between net and gross leasable area holds that 80 percent of the total area is usable for tenants' offices, with 20% allotted to corridors and service areas.

Service features in office buildings—a rooftop restaurant, health club, lounges, meeting rooms, and the like—are "plus" factors in leasing space. But they are often costly to maintain and may necessitate additional rent. Some major office buildings offer a subsidy payment for a good restaurant operator to provide quality service for the tenants.

Leasing Conditions

Office space is leased to major tenants for as long as 25 years. Smaller tenants often use a five- to ten-year term. Seldom does a term last less than three years. An excessively short lease term does not allow time to amortize the cost of standard tenant improvement allowances. Time extension options should be avoided, if at all possible. They make future leasing plans uncertain and should therefore be granted only if an option is required by a major tenant and the building owner has some protection on future rent.

Expansion options should also be discouraged, as they may also conflict with future leasing plans. Some tenants who anticipate expansion are willing to pay a premium to hold adjoining space for future growth. However, it is proper to advise any tenant who is occupying space under option to another individual or group that there is a commitment outstanding for that space.

Escalation clauses for the landlord are especially important here. More than other forms of income property, office buildings have a special vulnerability to rising costs, since they customarily provide all utilities, heating and air conditioning, and janitorial services for the tenant as part of the lease agreement.

Lease agreements should provide a covenant covering rules and regulations for the tenants' proper use of the building. These rules are for the benefit of all tenants, and building management must be able to enforce them. When the office building is a part of a larger shopping center or other multibuilding complex, rules may be drawn up and enforced by a tenants' association or a merchants' association.

Tenants

Experienced management is needed to screen prospective tenants and assign to each the most suitable space in an office building. The local market is controlling, but there are a few general guidelines.

It is difficult to mix medical and general office tenants. General office tenants usually object both to the overloading of elevators and passageways by incapacitated persons and to the odors common in medical facilities.

Professional people, such as lawyers and accountants, prefer that a certain prestige be associated with their location. They do not favor noisy and unorthodox neighbors, such as discos and nightclubs.

Businesses that attract large numbers of the general public can create parking problems and congestion within a building if these businesses are not located for easy access.

Companies that take multifloor occupany and require frequent elevator travel between upper floors should be located so as to cause minimum delays for the other tenants.

36

Shopping Centers and Stores

More than any other type of income property, shopping centers are financed through preleasing arrangements. After leases are obtained for the space and subsequently assigned, developers are able to command loans that might otherwise be unavailable to them. Often merchants themselves arrange for the acquisition of land and organize the plan of development. But even then, merchants recognize the value of a professional developer and ask his or her help in financing, construction, and the ultimate day-to-day management of newly developed centers.

FINANCING SHOPPING CENTERS AND STORES

Like most other forms of real estate financing, a basic requirement is that the property itself be pledged by a mortgage as security for the loan. Because shopping centers and stores have developed greater dependence on the lease income to attract suitable financing, it is not unusual for the lender to ask for additional collateral in the form of a claim upon the rental income should default on the loan occur. The claim can take several different forms:

Pledge of the Lease. Some lenders may require that a percentage of the lease income be pledged (and delivered each month) as additional

367

assurance of loan payment. Should the store owner fail to meet the obligation, the tenant would be required to make payment directly to the lender. This requirement may be considered unduly severe and potentially detrimental to the task of obtaining tenants. Consequently, the requirement is often made as a conditional assignment of rental income. Should a delinquency occur, the lender is permitted to notify a tenant that future rental payments are to be made directly to him.

Minimum Rental Requirements.   Because percentage leases are common in stores and shopping centers, lenders often take the precaution of requiring minimum rental rates that will help protect repayment of the mortgage loan. The rates must be realistic and in keeping with the prevailing market; otherwise they can be a severe handicap in obtaining quality leases.

Speculative Store Buildings

Unlike office buildings which are usually partially leased before construction and apartments which are almost never preleased, store buildings are most always leased before construction. There is an exception: many small "strip-type" store buildings are erected on speculation without the benefit of preleasing. These are buildings catering to the local market area and can be found along frontage roads by freeways and at major street intersections. Construction is usually single-story shell, meaning only walls and roof are put in place. The floor, ceiling, heating, air-conditioning and interior finishing are added after the space has been leased. By constructing a fairly long building, the owner can divide it into suitable units that will meet the size requirements of an individual tenant.

Startup Costs

In any type of newly developed property the initial costs involved with the construction, leasing, and finishing out of the units are often underestimated. Carrying charges for interest, taxes, and insurance continue from the inception of the work. Since shopping centers often involve larger areas of land than are initially developed, there is a potential for increased carrying charges from the escalation in value associated with the adjoining land. This could easily raise tax assessments on the unused land before it is ever developed. The selling expenses involved in advertising and leasing units are at least, in part, "up front" money; that is, paid as the expenses are incurred, not delayed until closing as with a sales commission.

A relatively new requirement that can add substantially to the initial costs is a study of the environmental impact of the project. Depending somewhat on how the project is financed, there are federal, state, and local government agencies that may be involved with ultimate approval. Requirements are not always uniform and delays are the norm. Shopping centers are particularly vulnerable to environmental requirements because of the large number of cars that may be drawn into a concentrated area. Don't forget, the delay time can add, even multiply, the startup costs for any new project. When calculations are made to determine financing requirements, these additional costs must be considered.

EXAMPLE OF A
SHOPPING CENTER LOAN

A pro forma operating statement for a shopping center loan provides the lender with a projection of income and expenses. Based on these figures, the lender can determine the net operating income that should be available for repayment of the mortgage loan. Coverage ratios can be established that offer a measure of safety for the lender.

A typical shopping center deal would vary considerably across the country, depending upon land values and construction costs in a particular area. However, the proportions are similar, and the figures confirm this similarity. Assuming land cost at $3.00 per square foot and using the three-to-one ratio on parking space, the rentable shop space would then cost $12.00 per square foot in land contributed. For a reasonably simple structure, the building costs would come to about $35.00 per square foot, which includes paving and lighting the parking lot. The total investment, using these figures, would add up to $47.00 per square foot. At this investment level, base operating costs should not exceed $2.25 per square foot per year. Rentals for space such as this would average $9.00 per square foot per year. Table 36–1 shows how the investment works out using a simplified procedure for greater clarity.

Based on the figures in Table 36–1, the investment would show a 12.9 percent cash return on the equity investment. However, many unforeseen contingencies could upset this return, such as lower occupancy than expected, failure to collect all rentals due, and runaway operating costs. In the example cited, the cash return cannot be considered as the only profit since the principal payments on the loan are also part of the profit, and it does not constitute taxable income since depreciation allowed offers an offsetting deduction. The investor must look to the margin of cash over and above the operating costs and the debt service, in order to estimate the margin of financial safety that can be counted on in any given investment.

TABLE 36–1

Projection for Shopping Center Investment

(Figures are hypothetical using a 50,000 square foot building located on 200,000 square feet of land. Total cost: $2,350,000.)

Capital Investment		
Equity Investment (20%)	$ 470,000	
80% mortgage loan	1,880,000	
Total Investment		$2,350,000
Annual Operating Calculations		
Gross Scheduled Income ($9.00 per sq. ft. × 50,000 sq. ft.)	$450,000	
Less: 5% vacancy and credit loss	$22,500	
Gross Operating Income		$427,500
Less: Expenses		
All operating costs @ 2.25 per sq. ft.		112,500
Net Operating Income		$315,000
Less: Debt service		
13% for 25-year term		
Constant—.1353 × 1,880,000		254,364
Cash flow before taxes		$60,636

MARKET ANALYSIS FOR A SHOPPING CENTER

The market analysis for a successful shopping center must look to the market that is reasonably available for the goods and services offered by the merchant tenants. The question here is not one of finding tenants, as it is in an apartment or office building analysis. The question is: "Will the tenants have a market for their wares?" Market analysts know statistical buying patterns—how much various kinds of people spend on food, on clothes, on eating out, on entertainment, and on all the other things they buy. What is needed are figures on the population in the market area (especially income levels), the area's growth pattern, and freeway and street patterns. With these figures, an estimate can be made of the potential sales volume for each class of store, which in turn determines the gross income that may be achieved from the leases.

The following discussion considers how the trade area is determined, the population of the market, and its income and spending patterns.

Trade Area

Trade areas are *not* determined by drawing a circle around an existing or proposed location and then counting the people within that boundary. A careful examination must be made of the forces that can direct people to the specific location in question. These forces may be identified as traffic patterns, proximity of other competitive facilities, and limiting geographical features.

Traffic patterns

Regional shopping centers are a creation of the freeway system; to a lesser degree, all other shopping centers also develop from traffic patterns. The ease with which a shopper can enter a store or service facility has long controlled both store location and the resulting land value. (Note the growth of smaller communities whose service stations and fast food stores are concentrated on the right-hand side of the entering highway.) To assess the trade area available for a particular location, it is first necessary to examine all streets, highways, and freeways that carry traffic to or through the subject location. Then, study the areas that access routes lead *from*.

What is the land use of the areas along the access routes? If one of the major highways leads from a large steel fabricating plant employing mostly male workers who live on the far side of town, the market potential from that area would be minimal. If another boulevard leads directly from undeveloped land that has been purchased primarily by home builders, the market potential is good, but not immediate. If a major highway or freeway leads from several small communities with limited shopping facilities, that population could be considered market potential. If the subject location sits along a thoroughfare that simply connects several densely populated areas or business districts, the high volume of passing traffic is a substantial market "plus." Of course, a major resource for any shopping center is an established and growing series of residential subdivisions surrounding the proposed location. However, the proximity of a good subdivision is of no benefit to the shopping center if there is limited access between them. Utility line easements or rights-of-way, streams, and political boundaries can separate entire subdivisions, encouraging traffic patterns to develop in directions other than what would appear to be normal.

City planning commissions and highway departments develop master plans for street and freeway development; these are important guides to future population trends. Zoning restrictions for surrounding areas must be charted to provide an indication of how growth patterns might develop. Undeveloped land within a 10-minute drive of the subject location should not be overlooked. A major shopping center itself encourages development of more houses in the area.

Competing facilities

The trade area for a shopping center is restricted by existing competition. Furthermore, the nature of that competition is a factor in determining the types of goods and services that may be offered for sale. People will travel greater distances to purchase major "hard goods" than they will travel to purchase necessities, conveniences, and services. A nearby major regional center usually restricts a new development to a "neighborhood convenience center"–type of outlet. The important considerations are to (1) weigh the market that is served by existing facilities and (2) define the subject location's trade area outside the competitive sphere. A new center always has an initial impact from curiosity seekers, but the trade flow soon returns to that of greatest convenience for shoppers. Attracting traffic from a competing facility is always possible through promotions and special inducements for shoppers—but there is no monopoly on sales promotion ideas, and the traffic can flow both ways. The prudent analyst bases market size on proven statistical values, rather than on transient promotional techniques.

Limiting geographic features

The concern for geographical limitations is not for obvious features like a shoreline or mountain range; it is for the lesser features, such as an unbridged stream. Population trends often follow the line of lowest cost development, and this can mean avoiding expensive stream crossings, rough terrain, and areas of potential hazard such as flooding or sliding land. These limitations are, of course, reflected in street and highway patterns. However, it is an area that a shopping center analyst should consider as a means of increasing the trade area; that is, would an off-site improvement, such as a bridge or connective street, justify the cost. Most communities welcome private support in the construction of new streets or bridges; if a new trade area can be opened, the cost may be justified.

Population of the Market

Once the limits of the trade area have been defined, it is easy to determine the population within that area. The U.S. Population Census statistics (taken every decade), combined with local area planning commission figures, provide a good starting point. The number of electric power meters and water taps give a solid indication of the number of families in a given area. Furthermore, the rate of increase or decrease is determinable from the number of new meters installed during a given period, less the number removed. The population of each neighborhood or subdivision in the trade area should be calculated, along with the estimated growth trend for each.

Income and Spending Patterns

Every decade the U.S. Population Census produces a set of figures on average income levels for each census district. And private market research organizations are constantly attempting to determine income levels in local neighborhoods. These figures are estimates at best, but they do provide a basis for analyzing the buying power of a given market or trade area.

How income is spent varies with the area in question. There are obvious differences in buying habits between rural communities and manufacturing centers, between commercial areas and service industry areas, between older people and younger ones, between upper-income and lower-income families, between two areas dominated by different nationalities, and many more. The Bureau of Labor Statistics (an arm of the U.S. Department of Labor) produces statistics on living costs in the different regions of the country, which provide a guide to how much is spent for basic necessities. Local research is needed to reveal the complete pattern of local spending.

The gross income of the entire trade area can be allocated among all the major categories of purchase. For example, food may take 12 percent of the income from the trade area; apparel, general merchandise, and appliances, 8 percent; drugs, 2 percent; and so on down the list of goods and services that are offered by the subject shopping center. The total buying power of the trade area in each category must then be reduced to that amount which can reasonably be attained by the subject center. Of the total amount represented by food purchases (12 percent of the gross income of the area), perhaps the subject center can attract only 65 percent. For general merchandise sold through department stores, competition is generally greater; the subject location's market share could drop to, say, 40 percent of the trade area's total spending for this category.

With the market share calculated in dollar amounts for each category of goods and services, the shopping center investor can more readily compute the expected rentals from percentage leases. Furthermore, a carefully calculated market share for each category indicates the potential sales volume for each prospective tenant—an important figure for a merchant considering a new or additional outlet.

SPECIAL PROBLEMS ASSOCIATED WITH SHOPPING CENTERS

Physical Plan

There are many ways to build a shopping center, and no single plan insures success. The huge regional centers show great imagination in design, layout, decor, and various attractions offered to the shoppers. Many have become recreational centers as well as shopping centers. Entertainment is often provided in the public malls in the form of musicians, demonstrations, art shows, and other types of exhibits. Modern centers exude something of a carnival atmosphere at times in their all-out efforts to attract shoppers and overshadow the competition from smaller centers. Inevitably, middle-level centers are finding it more difficult to compete with the many extra attractions offered by the largest centers. However, the small convenience centers in good locations hold onto a local trade and are generally sound investments.

The physical plan should be carefully examined to make certain that floor plans are of proper size with access readily available, that there is adequate heating and air conditioning, and that sufficient space has been provided for the handling of incoming merchandise and outgoing waste materials. These are mainly architectural and engineering concerns, but if costly mistakes can be prevented, the investor's money will be better secured. Considering the complexities involved, it is always a safer investment to employ experienced builders.

Tenants

Tenants should have the financial strength to undertake the lease obligations plus the ability to serve the public in a successful manner. Customer problems involving any single store can cast a poor reflection on the entire shopping center. Also a good diversity of stores is helpful in luring shoppers back again.

As previously indicated in this section, the quality of the tenants in a preleased center is a major factor in securing a mortgage loan. Sometimes there is an overemphasis on the desirability of the national chain-type stores as lucrative tenants. Recent statistical data indicate that localized chains and independent stores are very effective sales producers and that more often than not they turn over a larger volume of sales per square foot of floor space than do national operations. Sales volume is the key to larger rental income on percentage leases. A shopping center's continuing success rests to a considerable extent on the ability of the merchants to achieve profitable sales volumes.

Lease Terms

The investment required to furnish a large store requires a long-term lease, which has advantages and disadvantages for the owner. The long term gives the lender good assurance of repayment and makes for better loan terms. The disadvantage lies in the fixed return on an investment over a number of years while costs of all kinds continue to increase. Insurance costs also tend to increase and are related to risks that tenants may introduce. Consequently, long-term leases will normally carry escalation clauses that provide for any increase in taxes and insurance to be passed on to the tenant. In addition, it is common to allow increases in maintenance and operating costs to be added to the rental charges.

Small stores or shops, such as beauty parlors, florists, and boutiques, generally contract a three-to five-year lease which is subject to rental increases periodically in anticipation of rising costs. Small shops seldom agree to percentage leases as they lack the necessary sales volume and the more complicated bookkeeping procedures required.

There are some lease provisions of special concern to a lender, particularly those that could bring about a premature cancellation of the lease. Following are some examples.

Exclusive Sales Covenants. All merchants love exclusive sales agreements. But for the shopping center owner-investor, these agreements are potential pitfalls. A major tenant, such as a supermarket or department store, may demand to be the *only* supermarket or department store in the shopping center. The owner may have to make this concession, but it may present problems downstream for two reasons: (1) the center may expand so that additional stores are needed to satisfy demand and (2) the type of merchandise sold within a store tends to change as trade practices shift to meet competition. Motor oil is not a customary item in a grocery store, yet many supermarkets sell it. The variations in service and food offered under the name of "restaurant" are almost unlimited. Any covenant limiting the freedom of the shopping center to offer specific products or services must be clearly worded, as conflicts can easily occur.

Lease Tie-Ins. A lease that is tied to the continued occupancy of another merchant can lead potentially to the loss of two tenants. A small merchant may count on the heavy traffic generated by a large department store outlet. But if the large store develops internal problems unrelated to the center and withdraws to be replaced by another store, the small merchant under a tie-in would have the right to cancel his lease, compounding the center's problems.

Below-Cost Leases. In order to attract a major tenant to a new center, the owner is sometimes tempted to offer a less-than-cost lease arrangement under the expectation of recovering the cost from the small tenants that will follow. Major tenants are fully aware of their drawing power in the market, and they use it as an effective negotiating point. (The merchandising power of an organization like Sears, Roebuck is such that it seldom leases space anymore, choosing instead to buy land within a center to construct its own building.) However, any agreement by a shopping center owner to grant less-than-cost rental rates results in an extra burden for the rest of the tenants. The competitive disadvantage to the other tenants may preclude their successful operation and shorten the economic life of the entire project.

Parking

Because they are the offspring of freeways and highways, shopping centers require more parking space than any other form of property investment. A rule of thumb has it that for every square foot of rental shop space, there must be three square feet of parking area. The requirement varies a bit with the type of store—supermarkets have the greatest parking requirements, and service facilities the least.

The gradual increase in the number of small cars has changed parking lot design. Architects once assigned about 320 square feet to each car space, but today some have reduced this to 280 square feet. Some centers also provide remote parking lots for employees.

Management

In addition to the management requirements common to all forms of income property, shopping center owners must cooperate with tenants to promote the shopping center. Almost all percentage leases in shopping centers make the landlord a partner in the success of the tenant. Some managements participate passively, granting advertising allowances and special concessions for the tenants' promotional activities. Others take the lead in organizing and directing continuous advertising and promotional programs. The large centers often provide entertainment or interesting displays in the public mall areas and feature the center's attractions in mass advertising programs.

The most common method of cooperation between landlord and tenants is some form of merchants' association. A requirement to join and contribute dues or assessments can be a part of lease requirements. In this manner, decisions on sales promotions are shared by all those who can benefit from them.

37

Warehouses and Leasehold Properties

WAREHOUSES

Since the early 1960s, warehouses have increased in number, in the ways they are used, and in popularity as a real estate investment. The older classification of a warehouse as one form of industrial property is no longer applicable. Warehouses have developed into service centers and retail outlets. "Mini-warehouses" have multiplied. Investor interest stems from several advantages: warehouses can be built on lower cost land in outlying areas, they require minimal maintenance, and they require less management than the "people-oriented" operations of apartments and office buildings. The following section considers the three major classes of warehouses: (1) industrial-type storage, (2) office-warehouses, and (3) mini-warehouses.

Industrial-Type Storage Warehouses

Companies have traditionally used warehouses for part-time emergency or seasonal storage of goods and have preferred to rent warehouse space rather than build their own. Warehouse owners lease entire buildings or parts of buildings, or charge for storage based on the goods stored and the space and time used. Some warehouse companies operate public storage warehouses and provide transportation of goods to and from the warehouse facility. This is a form of business property and not a subject of consideration in this section. It is the industrial warehouse, built for leasing to others, that can be classed as an investment property.

The special requirements of concern to the warehouse investor can be covered under accessibility, construction features, and management.

Accessibility.   A warehouse does not require obvious visibility to the general public. It can be located on a back street or other out-of-the-way area, so long as large trucks can maneuver into a loading position. The availability of railroad siding promotes the usefulness of an industrial warehouse. Warehouses provide an excellent interchange point between rail and truck transportation. (Dockside warehouses and the storage facilities at municipally owned airports are seldom available for private investment.) The street pattern into the warehouse must be considered, as some remote locations cannot accommodate large highway trucks.

Construction Features.   Industrial warehouses can be built with floors either at ground level or at truckloading height, although the latter is preferred. Warehouse floors must sustain heavy loads and should be constructed with 6" concrete and reinforcing bars (compared with 4" unreinforced concrete in a single-story shopping center).

Ceilings must accommodate high racking of stored goods and should be at least 14' high. Ceiling panels are very seldom used in a warehouse, and the "height" is the clearance beneath the roof supports. The roof and walls should be as close to fireproof as practical, and in most areas the installation of a fire protection sprinkler system is an economical measure. Adequate fire protection can reduce the insurance cost for both the building and its contents and should allow a slightly higher rental structure.

In selecting a warehouse site, an investor must not only check the street sizes and patterns, but also research the water lines to make sure they will support a fire protection system. For the most part, warehouses are not air conditioned; when they are, adequate insulation is a necessity.

Industrial warehouses require little office space. Usually a shedlike structure inside the building—used for recordkeeping and security controls, and sometimes heated or air conditioned—will suffice.

Management.   From the investor's point of view, an industrial warehouse leased to a stable tenant requires very little management. The building is constructed for minimal maintenance, the tenant requires few services, and the management consists mostly of keeping adequate accounting records of the lease operation.

Office-Warehouse

The expanding requirements of service industries, manufacturing plants in high-technology industry, and industrial supply outlets with storage requirements have spawned a new type of service-oriented sales center. These rows of single-story buildings with common wall dividers are 85 percent to 90 percent warehouse space, and 10 percent to 15 percent office facility. Limited parking for employees and customers is usually available in front of the units while truck loading accommodations are at the rear entryways.

Construction Features. The buildings are generally lightweight, in that floors are not designed for heavy loads (usually being 4″ concrete with a reinforcing mesh wire). Walls are block, brick, or tilt-wall concrete. Roofs are lightweight, with 12′ to 14′ clearance. Modules used in construction vary from 1,500 square feet to 3,000 square feet and can be leased singly or in multiples.

Office areas are generally well finished, with tile floors or carpeting. Heating and air conditioning units are furnished, but their operation is left to the tenants. The office area may be used for administrative work, clerical activity, or as a sales outlet with display racks and sales counters.

The exterior appearance is usually similar to an office park or modern industrial park, with modest landscaping and paved parking areas. Access need not be from highly visible freeways or thoroughfares, but many are so located because of the emphasis on sales outlets for possible tenants.

Rental Rates and Management. Office-warehouses are leased for rates that are generally higher than for industrial warehouses because of the office-warehouse's more accessible—and thus more costly—land. They offer a *combination* of office and warehouse space at somewhere in between the separate cost of each.

While office-warehouse space is usually offered for multitenant occupancy, the management responsibility does not approach the level required for either an office building or an apartment. Very few services are furnished to tenants. Interior maintenance, utilities, heating, and air conditioning are all responsibilities of the tenant. The management may have the chore of trash disposal, and does maintain the exterior walls and roof. Parking lot and landscaping maintenance also fall to the management.

Mini-Warehouses

Another recent development in warehousing is the mini-warehouse. The demand for such space comes from the increasing number of apartment dwellers and others who have limited storage facilities and a growing amount of personal goods. Older apartment houses often furnish a small enclosure of space, usually in the basement, for the tenant to store out-of-season or surplus possessions. Modern apartments have done away with this feature, but not the need for the space. Thus, long rows of mini-warehouses have been built in most major cities.

Construction Features.   Mini-warehouses are usually long rows of single-story buildings with common walls separating the individual units, which are from 50 square feet to more than 400 square feet each. The construction is of fireproof block or brick, with a single large door to the front. There may or may not be a paved floor. Utilities may be limited to a single light, with no heating and no air conditioning. Usage is usually strictly limited to the storage of goods—no personal use may be made of the lease as a place to work or to offer anything for sale. (Where such rules have not been enforced, there have been cases where individuals converted mini-warehouse space into living quarters.)

Rental Structure.   The big attraction for an investor is the high return provided from a relatively low-cost form of investment. The mini-warehouse requires little management other than policing the area. Costs and rents vary considerably, but one good rule of thumb has it that construction cost is approximately one-half of that for an apartment, while the rental rate per square foot is about the same as an apartment.

Location.   Because the mini-warehouse caters to the general public, it is best located in an area that is easily accessible and generally visible from main thoroughfares. Since most customers come from apartments, it should be located near several apartment complexes.

Other Applications.   The concept of the mini-warehouse has much wider application than just as storage space for apartment dwellers. It is said that the idea originated with an owner of enclosed boat stalls near a country lake. More and more, the owner found that his tenants were using the boat stalls not for boats and marine equipment, but for surplus furniture, clothes, and other personal equipment. The next step was to build "boat stalls" in the city! After all, the need was obvious. Many sports require special equipment which can be stored in protected cubicles while not in use. In some areas of the country, small tracts of farm land can be rented by city folks for "home gardening"—but special equipment needs to be stored. Families with vacation cabins in remote areas need protected space to secure furniture and other personal goods while they are away from the cabin. This story is a classic example of the free enterprise system—find a need and then try to be the first to satisfy it.

LEASEHOLD FINANCNG

As land in urban areas and other high-density communities becomes more valuable and the taxes on *sales* increase, there has been a growth in the use of land *leases* for development projects. In such areas as Hawaii and Orange County, California, leasing of land for the construction of commercial buildings and even houses has long been an accepted practice. This section considers the problems involved with financing buildings constructed on land that is leased—not owned—by the builder.

The lease between a landowner and a builder or developer is generally known as a *ground lease*. The landowner's interest is referred to as the *underlying fee*, and the lessee's (developer's) interest is the *leasehold*. Since a leasehold interest does not include the right to dispose of the land, a question arises: "Can a developer borrow money to finance building on land held under lease?" The answer is yes providing certain conditions are included in the mortgage instrument. These conditions will be explained in the following discussion.

Subordination

The leasehold interest under a ground lease has value in itself and can serve as security for a loan. Such a loan is called a *leasehold mortgage* and is subject to the loss of security in the event of a default of any kind under the lease agreement. The landowner under default has the right to repossess the land and any attachments thereto. A leasehold mortgage of this kind is an *unsubordinated* or a *nonsubordinated* pledge, which means that the landowner has not subordinated his ownership of the land. The definition of *subordinate* according to Funk and Wagnalls, is to "make inferior, or secondary, one's interest to that of another."

An unsubordinated leasehold mortgage is not an attractive loan for most lenders, but several provisions can be included in the lease agreement to make it more acceptable. Since default on the lease agreement presents the greater risk for the lender, a provision can be included in the agreement that gives the *lender* the right to receive prompt notice from the owner of a default by the lessee. The lender is then allowed a reasonable time to step into the lessee's position, cure the default, and pursue such other remedies as may be provided in the mortgage. A second important provision protecting both the lessee and the lender is a specific right to assign the leasehold. Any limitation on the assignability of a leasehold affects its marketability and, thus, its value. The right to assign the leasehold interest becomes particularly important to the lender in the event of foreclosure. What is best for both lender and lessee is the right to assign (sell) the leasehold without retaining liability under the lease.

Under a *subordinated* ground lease, the landowner agrees to make his ownership interest inferior, or secondary, to that of the lender's mortgage. The result is that the leasehold interest becomes a fee interest insofar as the designated mortgage is concerned, and the lender's position of security becomes that of a first mortgage. So, in case of default on the mortgage loan that results in foreclosure, the landowner forfeits his interest in the land to the lender. To protect the landowner, the mortgage should require prompt notice to the *landowner* of any default in mortgage terms. The *landowner* would then be allowed a reasonable period of time to step into the lessee's position and correct the default.

A subordinated long-term ground lease provides the lessee with a financeable interest of similar strength to that of the landowner. The lender is granted a security tantamount to a first mortgage by the fee owner's subordination agreement.

Condemnation

Condemnation action by any government agency can impair a property's usefulness and, thus, its value. If a property is pledged under a mortgage, a loss in value damages the security for the loan. This problem becomes more difficult when the security for the loan is a ground lease. The lender is concerned with the provisions of the ground lease regarding the proper party to receive a condemnation award and the proper division of a lump sum award. If the taking of land under condemnation—for widening a street, for example— reduces a lessee's parking area below a practical minimum, he should be able to cancel the lease. In the event of total condemnation, the lender would wish to be granted the tenant's portion of the award. Partial condemnation should call for a rental reduction. A ground lease should provide for an arbitration of differences in the event of condemnation. The rights of the lender in condemnation of a ground lease should be spelled out as a provision of the mortgage.

Advantages and Disadvantages of Leaseholds

Financing of unsubordinated leaseholds has always been difficult; it still commands high interest rates, short terms for loans, and loan-to-value ratios in the 60 percent to 70 percent range. But a recent change of attitude by landowners—increasing their willingness to accept subordination of their fee interest to the mortgage lender—has substantially increased the use of leasehold financing as a method of land development. The advantages for the *landowner* derive from the retention of ownership of the land. The rental for the land is usually calculated at the full capitalized value for the property. Escalation in land value is retained by the owner and can be cited as justification for rental increases. In return for a subordination agreement, the landowner commonly receives a participation interest in future profits from the building project. An outright sale can result in substantial capital gains taxes, whereas a long-term lease can provide the landowner with a continuing income that spreads the tax burden. And, upon termination of the lease, the improvements revert to the landowner.

For a *developer*, a leasehold can be attractive, particularly if the ground lease is subordinated. A large capital outlay is not required to purchase land that cannot in any case be depreciated for tax purposes. Rental payments for the land are tax deductible. A lease gives the developer a long-term use of the land and the potential profits from its development and rental. With a subordinated ground lease, the lessee-developer has a substantial financial lever. The land itself has in effect been loaned to the developer and can thus be pledged as security for a construction loan, so little additional equity cash is needed. Many franchise outlets including large motel chains, have been built on this basic financing concept.

Of course, the major disadvantage occurs when the lease term expires and the improvements revert to the landowner. In practice, expired leases are often renewed for additional terms, or the property is sold outright to the lessee. The reason is that during the term of a long-term lease, ownership of the land can become divided. And as ownership divides, the ability of the landowners to agree on property management among themselves often deteriorates.

Leasing as a Method of Financing

Normally, financing for real estate investment is seen as a means of acquiring ownership. If one considers only the ownership rights of use and possession, the leasing of property does qualify as a form of ownership. If the investor does not have sufficient cash or credit to purchase property or prefers another form of investment for the cash he has, the leasing of potential income property can provide him with a source of income. And lease payments, being tax deductible, sometimes provide a less expensive form of financing an income property than outright purchase with payments on a loan.

Farms and ranches are sometimes leased by nonresident owners to local people who produce the crops. Rentals can be fixed as monthly or annual payments, or the farmer can pay the landowner a percentage share of the crop. The percentages vary with the crop and the local area. Such a lease is a method of financing an income-producing property.

A *sale-and-leaseback* arrangement is a method to recover invested cash while retaining occupancy of the building. In this transaction, the owner-occupant sells the property to an investor and then leases it back for a long term.

CONDOMINIUMS ON LEASED LAND

Some states do not permit the creation of a condominium upon a leasehold estate; nor is it possible for the owner of a fee simple interest to submit *only* the improvements as a condominium while retaining the land for separate lease to the unit owners. In other states, however, leasehold condominiums are permitted, and there can be advantages to the developer in selling the improvements while retaining ownership of the land.

If the developer retains the land while selling the improvements, there is no taxable gain on the land. Instead of a gain received in one or two years, most likely taxed as ordinary income, the developer would receive rents over an extended period of time. If the land is later sold, subject to the leases on the improvements, the gain would be a capital gain since it would be a case of liquidating property held for the production of rental income.

The IRS has recognized the sale of condominiums coupled with a 75-year lease of the land as just that—a sale of improvements and a lease of the land. No part of the purchase price of the units was treated as advance rentals.* It is possible for a developer to charge something *less* than fair market value for the units, while charging more than market for rent on the land. The inflated rent increases the value of the land, which when sold at a higher price would be taxed at capital gain rates rather

---

*Rev. Rul. 70–607, 1970–2 CB 9.

than as ordinary income, as would the case be had the profit been realized from the sale of the units.

It should be noted that a land lease arrangement may impede a unit owners' association from qualifying for tax-exempt status. The question is whether or not the requirement of common ownership of the underlying land by the unit owners is interpreted to mean common ownership of a fee simple interest.

38

Business-Related Properties

For our purposes, *business-related properties* means land and buildings used to house a business operation which creates income. The difference between business-related properties as used here and *income property* as identified in earlier chapters is that business property income is derived from services rendered that are not so dependent on the property. For example, the success of a restaurant in a motel depends more on the quality of the food and service than on the quality of the building.

Is this type of property a "business" or is it "real estate"? In practice it becomes something of both. Professional real estate brokers have long been aware that a transaction involving a hotel, motel, service warehouse, free-standing restaurant, a specialized recreational facility, or many other such business properties requires as much knowledge of the business operation as of the real estate involved. Business brokers, those specializing in buying and selling going businesses, sometimes offer these specialized business-related properties. One note of caution: if the investment in such property does include rights to land and buildings, it is best to seek professional advice from one knowledgeable of the real estate transaction. Most of all, deal with brokers who are both experienced in the business operation being considered and who have practical knowledge of real estate in the local area. It is difficult to separate the need for both types of expertise in this kind of property investment.

Business Evaluation

With business-related property, the value of the land and building becomes secondary to the worth of the business that is being carried on. For example, a very profitable motel will achieve a value substantially in excess of the cost of replacement—the value of the income stream supercedes the value of the building. Thus, the evaluation of business-related property focuses initially on the profitability of the business operation. It might be added, a business operation that is *not* showing good profitability tends to focus the evaluation on the land, buildings, and *potential or future* profitability that can be achieved.

The very profitable business-related properties are of primary interest to large operators—the established businesses seeking to expand through acquisitions. For the small investor, better opportunities may be found in the less well-managed operations or those in which the owners must liquidate for reasons perhaps unrelated to the business' operation. The trick is to accurately evaluate the business potential so as not to fall into the same trap that may have caused the low profitability for the seller. For such an evaluation, there is nothing better than practical experience in the business under consideration. Next to that, there are some guidelines that may serve as a checklist for the experienced or a study guide for the newcomer. The guidelines are an effort to determine the types of services that are offered by the business and relate these to the local market area. Then, with this information, to develop a practical statement (pro forma) of potential costs and income showing the ratios between the two. If the ratios show reasonably good profitability, further consideration of the investment is justified. The major points for comparison are as follows:

Types of services offered

The kinds of services offered are most important when determining if the business can be sold. For a restaurant, consider the kind of food offered—fast food, Mexican, steaks, seafood, continental cuisine. For a motel, attention should be centered on the number and size of rooms. Does the motel have public facilities to support business meetings and seminars? Does it have adequate food and beverage facilities? A recreational facility may offer swimming, skiing, hiking, games, boating, sports (such as tennis), and most likely a combination of many.

Style of services

While styles vary considerably, it is the quality of service in a general sense which is important here. Does the business offer "luxury" accommodations? Or should it be categorized as "standard commercial" or "minimum utility"?

Price of services

Price is directly related to style—but is it correctly related in the business under consideration? A minimum utility quality of service may be priced at a luxury level, or nearly so, and could very well be the cause of low profitability. Overpricing the market is not a sure road to riches.

Available market

One of the essential keys to future profitability is the available market for the service that is offered. Does the population in the local area represent an income level, an age level, an ethnic quality, that makes frequent use of the services to be offered? What competition is there in the area or near by? Does the competition offer the same quality of services? How successful are these businesses? Does the service respond to seasonal swings in activity that can make overhead difficult to sustain during low periods? Does the local area support any special events or activities such as major sports, fiestas or rodeos, convention attractions, major schools or government activity that create markets?

Operating ratios

With this information assembled, the evaluator of a business property should be better prepared with practical figures for potential sales volumes. Care must be taken in the projection of gross sales figures because they can be easily overestimated. The help of experienced operators can be most important in this projection. The cost figures are more readily determined from the business records or a review of the local costs for materials, supplies, and labor. The difficulty in the cost projection is in using realistic figures that can be realized in later operations. Once a sensible projection of potential gross income and potential operating costs has been made, the future income and the value of the business property become more apparent.

SENSITIVITY ANALYSIS

For the larger, and perhaps more complex, business operations, there is another kind of analysis that helps to predict future profitability. This analysis projects future cash flows for several different levels of operations and several cost levels. It is called a *sensitivity analysis*. The idea is that any projected is subject to errors because of the uncertainties associated with future income and costs. For this analysis gross income is projected at, say, six different levels, rising from poor to fairly good. Then different costs are projected against each of the income levels selected. Earlier analyses of this kind selected those costs that had the greatest potential for error, using projections from a stable cost level and rising at 5 percent, 10 percent, and 15 percent increments. Today, the tendency is to escalate almost all costs in order to assess where the most dangerous problems might arise to create future losses.

RELATION BETWEEN MARKET VALUE AND EARNINGS

As noted earlier in this chapter, a highly profitable business operation can result in a property value considerably higher than the cost of replacement of the property. This may also be true of an "income property" such as an apartment. However, other income properties do not represent the flexibility found in business-related properties: income properties are generally limited to the leasing of their space while business properties offer a wider range of opportunities for increasing cash flows. (There is a major exception: an apartment property suitable for conversion to condominiums might offer a value much greater than the rental income allows).

There is a caveat in business properties in trying to relate present profitability to property value: How much of the success is dependent on the special expertise of the owner? This ingredient of value is probably of greatest importance in restaurant properties. When the owner sells out, does the clientele follow the seller to a new location?

Another question that is found in business-related properties is the possibility of a much smaller market than may be found with other forms of property investment. This smaller market stems from the fact that many investors recognize the need for special expertise in the management of business properties and shy away from them. Also, *sellers* are reluctant to deal with inexperienced persons in the sale of business properties. This is even more so when the seller is asked to assist in the financing of the sale. For a seller to carry a portion of the financing in the sale of a motel, for example, he or she wants to be sure the buyer has reasonable qualifications in the business of running a motel. But there is another side to this question. A highly respected motel operator may be able to command a better price than others in the acquisition of an additional property. The seller prefers the assurance that the sale will be final and not create problems for him or her at a later date.

EFFECT OF INFLATION ON PRICE/EARNINGS RATIOS

Since about the mid-'70s, inflation has been universally accepted as a major factor in investment analysis. Investors have begun to accept inflation as an element of value that can be projected into the analysis of future cash flows. As a result, some investors are ignoring the relation between market value and earnings, in favor of realizing an "ultimate" return when the property is sold at the end of the holding period. Thus, the value of earnings is capitalized at very low rates of return—like 2 percent or 3 percent or even at zero—thereby providing a substantial increase in the sales value of the property. When the investor adds back the anticipated gain upon final disposition, at an inflated value, the investment provides a reasonable return over the full holding period.

Keep in mind that the *rate of capitalization* is defined as "that rate necessary to attract capital." And remember that the rapid growth in property values provides a viable addition to earnings, which increases the return on the equity investment—and this also attracts capital. So the effect of inflation, insofar as real property values are concerned, has been to *lower* the capitalization rates on earnings necessary to attract capital.

Index